THE SHILOAH CENTER FOR MIDDLE EASTERN AND AFRICAN STUDIES
STUDIES IN ISLAMIC CULTURE AND HISTORY

Religion, My Own

The Shiloah Center for Middle Eastern and African Studies
Tel Aviv University

The Shiloah Center is, with the Department of Middle Eastern and African History, a part of the School of History at Tel Aviv University. Its main purpose is to contribute, by research and documentation, to the dissemination of knowledge and understanding of the modern history and current affairs of the Middle East and Africa. Emphasis is laid on fields where Israeli scholarship is in a position to make a special contribution and on subjects relevant to the needs of society and the teaching requirements of the University.

Studies in Islamic Culture and History

The books published in this series deal with Islamic civilization in the broadest sense, including such fields as religion, law, philosophy, literature, art and various historical aspects. The series is published in collaboration with the Department of Middle Eastern and African History.

Arye Oded **ISLAM IN UGANDA**

Aharon Layish **WOMEN AND ISLAMIC LAW IN A NON-MUSLIM STATE**

Haim Shaked **LIFE OF THE SUDANESE MAHDI**

Michael Winter **SOCIETY AND RELIGION IN EARLY OTTOMAN EGYPT**

Religion, My Own

The Literary Works of Najīb Maḥfūẓ

Mattityahu Peled

Transaction Books
New Brunswick (U.S.A.) and London (U.K.)

Published in Collaboration with the Shiloah Center

Library of Congress Catalog Number: 82-17582
ISBN: 0-87855-135-2 (cloth)
Printed in the United States of America

Library of Congress Cataloging in Publication Data

Peled, Matityahu.
Religion, my own.

(Studies in Islamic culture and history)
Bibliography: p. 249
1. Maḥfūẓ, Najīb, 1912- —Criticism and interpretation. I. Title. II. Series.
PJ7846.A46Z74 1983 892'.736 82-17582
ISBN 0-87855-135-2

To the memory of

Prof. Gustave von Grunebaum

Contents

Preface

By dedicating this book to the memory of Gustave von Grunebaum I fulfill a duty deeply felt. Thanks to the support and encouragement given me by this great scholar I could come to UCLA to complete my doctoral studies and write my dissertation on the literary works of Najīb Maḥfūẓ. Having been fully aware of the important developments in Arabic literature during the period following the Second World War, von Grunebaum willingly allocated part of the impressive resources at his disposal to encourage the study of this late phase of Arabic literary history. I was of course grateful for his support and encouragement but most of all I feel greatly indebted to him for undertaking to personally advise me in the capacity of my Ph.D. advisor. This book is in fact an adaptation of my Ph.D. dissertation and I am glad to take this opportunity to acknowledge my debt to the wise, broad-minded and patient instruction I was so fortunate to receive from Gustave von Grunebaum.

Quite unintentionally this book is coming out at a time when the great contributions of Dr. von Grunebaum to the study of Islam and Arabic literature are being fiercely criticised. First Abdallah Laroui and then Edward Said singled him out as the most authoritative figure among modern Orientalists whose calling is subjected to a determined attack. The contention is that Orientalism has never been anything but a pseudo-academic coating on the imperialistic ambitions and overbearing complacency of the West in relation to the Orient. Not directly accusing von Grunebaum of having been in the service of Western imperialism he is nevertheless depicted as a Western scholar whose prejudices and complacency led him to draw a picture of Islam which is slanted, misleading and basically unfair.

The difficulty of dealing with this criticism is that it falls short of specifically disproving the findings of many Orientalists. As regards von Grunebaum, his vast knowledge of Islam, past and present, and of Islamic -- particularly Arabic -- literature, and his rigid methods of research and analysis make it absolutely impossible to devaluate his contributions without undertaking the colossal task of countering him from a position similarly butressed with knowledge and insight.

Undoubtedly, many Orientalists are not only vulnerable on this score but are probably guilty of the charges pressed by the critics of Orientalism. But von Grunebaum is certainly not one of them. Though proud of the great achievements of Western civilization he was clearly conscious of its darker aspects and never allowed complacency to infiltrate his perception of the West. As for Islam he maintained that it could not embrace Western values and remain what it has come to be since its inception. Why should such an assumption cause so much resentment among modern Muslims or Arabs has not been made clear in any of the studies undertaken with a view of disproving it. If the values of Islam are described sometimes by von Grunebaum in terms unflattering to Western educated Arabs or non-Arab Muslims, the reason is probably that von Grunebaum felt that the difference between the two cultures were indeed deep. And being a product of Western culture he evaluated Oriental values in terms of the West. Similar attempts to evaluate Western values in Oriental terms usually produce the reverse results.

The present study, as the reader will find out, owes much to von Grunebaum's research in Islam and Arabic literature. Yet far from wishing to throw unedifying light on Islamic values this book aims to describe the literary achievements of Najīb Maḥfūẓ, who is clearly a Muslim in outlook and feeling, as directly related to his unquestioning acceptance of Islamic values both as a way of life and a cherished heritage. Fully aware of the nature of present day challenges faced by Islam Najīb Maḥfūẓ is demonstrating in his writing an unwavering trust in the capacity of Islamic societies to work out their solutions to these challenges by drawing on Islam's inexhaustible vitality.

During the period this study was conducted the relations between Egypt and Israel did not allow direct communication with Mr. Maḥfūẓ. But Dr. von Grunebaum, who always enjoyed the respect and friendship of many in the Islamic countries, constituted, through personal contact, a link between me and the writer whose works so interested me. Only in the fall of 1978 did I have the first opportunity to meet Mr. Maḥfūẓ at his home in Cairo. Exciting and interesting as this encounter was it led to no new revelations as far as his literary works were concerned. It was quite evident that von Grunebaum, through his studies and as a personal link, made possible the evaluation of the thoroughly Islamic literary production of Najīb Maḥfūẓ. I should perhaps add that seeing great literature produced in the Arabic language, imbued with Islamic *weltanschauung*, came to von Grunebaum not only as a pleasing experience but also as proof of his own conclusion regarding the immense vitality of Islamic culture.

This is not to be understood as if he felt that his sometimes gloomy predictions had lost their validity. But he seems to have realized that what Laroui calls "Islam as behavior or morality" is an area of invetsigation quite unlike others such as "Islam as history" or "Islam as faith" or, for that matter, "Islam as culture."

I am glad that the Shiloah Center has accepted this book into its Islamic Culture Series, where it really belongs. I wish to thank on this occasion Mrs. Edna Liftman for handling the clearly intricate procedures of book production and Mrs. Lydia Gareh for undertaking the final typing of this book.

Introduction

The Egyptian novelist Najīb Maḥfūẓ has been acclaimed by many Arab critics as the greatest living Arabic writer. He was born on December 11, 1912, in the Jamāliyya quarter of Cairo,[1] the location of many of his later novels and short stories.

Very little is known of Maḥfūẓ's private life, and this is characteristic of a culture that has for centuries shown a marked disinterest in the personal traits of its most admired sons, preferring to depersonalize them and even to revere them as types or models attesting to God's unlimited grace.[2] Consequently no detailed study of the writer's psychological development can be attempted at this stage, nor any examination of the influence of his own experience on the situations or characters in his works. All a researcher can go by are the oft-repeated biographical facts which hardly add any new information.

These known biographical facts are few enough. Maḥfūẓ seems to have had a rather happy and healthy childhood.[3] Of his high school days nothing is known which is noteworthy. In 1930 he became a student at the University of Cairo, graduating from the Department of Philosophy in 1934. Even before his graduation he began publishing articles on the history of Greek philosophy in the short-lived monthly magazine *al-maʿrifa,* owned and edited by ʿAbd al-ʿAzīz al-Islāmbūlī. These articles are not distinguished by any intellectual insight or breadth of knowledge.[4] But they certainly show a fluent Arabic style and lucidity of expression. In those years he also published articles in *al-Majalla al-Jadīda*, owned and edited by the noted Copt publicist and thinker, Salāma Mūsā, who acted as a senior friend and adviser to Najīb Maḥfūẓ in the most formative year of his intellectual development.

Although his flair for the written Arabic language was remarkable, Najīb Maḥfūẓ experienced great difficulties in mastering foreign languages. By his own testimony he still has difficulties reading French, and the only foreign language which he reads easily is English.[5] It was in an attempt to master the English language that he translated into Arabic a book on *Ancient Egypt*, which he published in 1932.[6]

While studying philosophy Najīb Maḥfūẓ was attracted to literature and in an attempt to reconcile these two interests he considered writing a Master's thesis in Aesthetics, "the philosophy study closest to literature."[7] Driven by his interest in the arts he even enrolled at the Institute of Arabic Music and learned to play the *qānūn*.[8] But this undecided state of mind was resolved when he decided to give up the study of philosophy and follow his literary impulse.

It is one of the symptoms of the period that such a significant decision in no way affected the author's actual career as a government official. Living by the pen was too risky a venture for a young college graduate, and in 1934, the year of his graduation, he joined the administration of the University of Cairo. In 1939 he was transferred to the Ministry of Endowment Estates, where he worked until 1955. In that year, already a writer of note, he was transferred to the Administration of Arts (*maṣlaḥat al-funūn*) where he was concerned with book publication and film production. His last appointment which he held until his retirement, was that of counselor to the Minister of Culture for Cinematic Affairs. He retired from government service in 1971,[9] concluding 37 years of service as a government official. Looking forward to his retirement Najīb Maḥfūẓ said that this would enable him to do what he had desired all his life -- to dedicate himself to his literary work.

Considering the wealth of his literary production, many volumes to date, it seems that his official duties have not been much of an obstacle to Maḥfūẓ's literary activities. But a note of dissatisfaction with his own works, or with the situation of a lifetime, seems to be discernable when he says: "people call it [my work] literature, but I call it 'literature of government officials'."[10] It would be reasonable to guess that primarily because of financial considerations he spent his lifetime doing what he apparently would have preferred not to do, namely work for the government. As late as his golden jubilee, which was widely celebrated in Egypt, he had to complain to an interviewer:[11] "Two things always give me a great deal of trouble — my financial situation and my health."

The first of these two anxieties was removed with his last high ranking appointment in the Government. But the other, unfortunately, has been a more difficult problem and in 1954, after he married, he discovered that he was diabetic.[12] Disappointing as this must have been to him, his married life has been happily blessed with two daughters, whom Najīb Maḥfūẓ is proud to show in public.[13] His wife, however, is for some reason confined to obscurity. The very fact of their marriage was kept secret from the public for several years, and the identity of Mrs. Najīb Maḥfūẓ is still undisclosed. The reason the author gave for not announcing the marriage is not only characteristic of the man but indicative of his cultural milieu, which maintains the sanctity of the *harīm*. He said that he preferred his private life not to be the concern of the public.[14]

According to a leading Egyptian critic,[15] the uniqueness of Najīb Maḥfūẓ lies in two features of his literary work. One is his complete dedication to pure literature, the second is the ever-changing style and form of his writing. Few Egyptian writers restrict themselves so meticulously to literary work, to the exclusion of any journalistic, polemical or contemplative writings. The writer in Egypt, by virtue of his skill, is more or less expected to participate in all these ancillary literary activities. Thus, Najīb Maḥfūẓ's careful abstention is conspicuous. But the other feature, that of constant change in the form of his writings, is of greater significance in terms of his literary contribution. Beginning with romantic historical novels he later turned to realistic writing, concerning himself with the immediate present and his immediate vicinity. It is through this writing that he has become well-known and admired in Arabic-speaking lands. In his next phase he turned to what he called "new realistic writing." This is "a kind of realistic writing that has none of the distinctive marks of traditional realism, which aims at portraying a complete picture of life. New-realism leaves behind elaborate detailing and characterization. This is a development both of form and content." [16] The motive for writing in this way, as defined by Najīb Maḥfūẓ himself, is to give vent to "specific thoughts and emotions which turn to reality only to use it as a means of self-expression; to give expression to ideational content through the use of a completely realistic phenomenon." [17]

The growth of each one of these phases of the writer's development, and the nature of the changes here alluded to, will be examined in detail in this study. It should, however, be pointed out that in the last few years there has been a noticeable new development in Najīb Maḥfūẓ's writing.[18] It is too early to define its nature or to attempt an analysis of its meaning. The change is characterized by the use of short stories and one-act plays, structured around a dialogue between symbolic or sometimes mysterious figures which, in turn, revolve around questions just as symbolic or mysterious. It is difficult at the moment to determine to what extent this is really new or different from previous Mahfuzian writings. [19] Najīb Maḥfūẓ himself thinks of it as a "new kind" of short story writing, and sets the date for this new phase at June 5, 1967.[20] He stresses the dialogue element in this new kind of writing so much that he prefers to call these short works simply dialogues, *ḥiwāriyyāt.* [21] He believes that the circumstances in Egypt since 1967 "call for a continuous discussion, which makes the dialogue and its display before the public both an artistic and a social necessity." [22] Nevertheless, he feels ill at ease in this role of playwright. "In the novel I am addressing the individual reader, whereas on the stage I am addressing a crowd." [23]

This shying away from direct communication with the mass of people is one of the earliest traits in Najīb Maḥfūẓ the writer. In an interview dedicated to his theatrical pieces,[24] he mentioned one other difficulty he could not face, namely writing in the colloquial language the stage required. He claimed that he simply could not penetrate "the secrets and philosophy" of spoken Egyptian Arabic. There is nothing new or surprising in his opposition to the use of colloquial language for literary writing, a sentiment once pronounced much more bluntly, when he called the spoken language a disease.[25] The impartial observer, however, may wonder whether this fuss about the spoken language may not be a thinly veiled excuse on the part of Najīb Maḥfūẓ for avoiding direct communication with the masses. That Najīb Maḥfūẓ has no difficulty using the colloquial may readily be assumed because this is the language he has spoken all his life. Occasionally it even steals into his published interviews. Apart from that, he has for many years been writing scripts for Egyptian films. In fact, since 1945 he has prepared scripts for no fewer than 30 films,[26] all of them in the colloquial language. Of these ten films are based on his novels, which means that he had to "translate" his own "literary" language into the spoken idiom.

The interesting and very sensitive question of the place and function of the colloquial Arabic languages cannot be discussed here. But it is a fact that in his literary works Najīb Maḥfūẓ is a strict literarist. It has often been asked why he so completely bans the spoken language of the people from his literature.[27] Although he has never really expounded his point of view on this issue, in line with his reluctance to express himself publicly on anything but literature,* a quick chronological review of his works may suggest some reasons for this attitude. His earliest writings were concerned with areas which seem at first sight rather unrelated to each other. His early short stories [28] are concerned with social criticism of a fairly fierce nature. His early novels — the first three — are historical romances concerned with Egypt of the Pharaos. These novels had no place for the colloquial language, describing a society which spoke a language long forgotten. The short stories, written by a novice, were in a language which by its very nature gave the writer a greater control over his work. Control, of course, is a quality needed by writer as well as reader in order to make the work of literature both presentable and palatable.

> Since the latent if not the manifest content of fiction is often concerned with the imaginary gratification of unsanctioned desires and the confrontation of terrible fears, we demand certain safeguards before giving the fantasies of fiction access to the unconscious. At best there is some danger. [29]

For a writer working under circumstances of great social polarity and a nearly fanatic resentment against any inroads on inherited values, and in a political tradition which has but a vague notion of individual liberties, any social criticism may be hazardous. Older and more experienced writers than Najīb Maḥfūẓ had to run the gauntlet of rebuke and harsh criticism by an orthodoxy blindly followed by the masses and staunchly supported by a royal court. Under such circumstances the use in literary works of a colloquial dialect, rich with

* Since 1973 Najīb Maḥfūẓ has engaged in public debates in Egypt over the issue of war and peace. Cf. Najib Maḥfuẓ, *Ataḥaddath ilaykum*, Beirut, 1977.

"secrets and philosophy" all its own, might have proved too explosive and therefore too dangerous. The literary language, with its almost arid lucidity and well-worn clichés, out of reach as it is for most of the masses, would certainly be a safer instrument for writing stories which are bound to arouse anxiety. For it must be realized that even the naive historical novels, for all the remoteness of the period they describe, constitute peculiarly explosive material under the circumstances.[30] In such circumstances literature is in great need of a language which, while suggesting the gratification of unsanctioned desires, can still be soothing and reassuring by the very banal resonance created by the works conveying the anxiety-provoking story. Sometimes the function of language used in fiction is thought of as that of soothing the consciousness of the reader by disguising unpalatable matters, while at the same time, through non-discursive communication, conveying to the unconscious those concealed matters with extraordinary vividness.[31] At times this may be achieved through the reassuring, prestigious "upper class" language whose use, both active and passive, is naturally restricted. Under similar circumstances the use of the spontaneous, lively colloquial language may turn the whole work into something quite unacceptable. The writer may not be able to properly control the images,innuendos and subtle implications, and the reader may be frightened into complete rejection of the story. In any case, a young writer desiring to plunge so boldly into some of the most controversial of topics may well be advised to hold on to the safest possible means of self-expression. Needless to say such a reasoning is itself not wholly conscious, and cultural habits and traditions by themselves can be relied on to lead the tyro on the well-trodden path. It is nevertheless a point worth making that 40 years later as far as Najīb Maḥfūẓ is concerned, not much has changed in this respect.

Social criticism in a Muslim milieu is always a very involved matter, for it must be expressed in the form of a demand to restore proven but neglected virtues of old. In this sense, it is true to say that Islamic culture is basically traditionalist. The high watermark of its achievements is considered to lie in the past. Consequently the reformer would maintain that "the examples to be followed belong to the ever more remote past." The world is considered to be in a process of constant deterioration "and it will continue to deteriorate until it comes to its appointed end." [32] Innovation is therefore, by its very nature, a thing to be shunned since all that is good can come only from the golden ages of the past. "The reformer therefore either adduces a prophetic or Koranic witness for his proposal or advocates the return to the golden age of primitive Islam."[33] This concept of social criticism according to which the present is condemned not for failing to live up to an abstract ideal to be fulfilled but for digressing from a path laid down in the past, underlies all the indigenous reform movements in Egypt in the present century. Whether we think of the dynamist — or Mahdist elements [34] of the more militant movements of reform or the liberal thinkers who saw their heyday in Egypt in the 1920's and 1930's, this much was common to all of them, that reform meant the reestablishment or reassertion of the exemplary way of life of "the first ones." Evidently, in modern times this can be done only with the aid of an apologetic reinterpretation of scripture and the traditions, which is an intellectually agonizing process of far-reaching consequences.[35] It is an essentially defensive measure aimed at preserving the self-esteem of Islam as a culture in face of the onslaught of a foreign culture surpassing it in some very tangible respects. But at the same time this defensive attitude creates an insurmountable obstacle for whatever reform is needed to overcome the difficulties faced by

Islam.

Therefore, when we speak of social criticism in literature written by a Muslim, we should not expect the hero to be the iconoclast peculiar to Western literature who rejects all that is sacred out of a desire either to establish new values or to allow no values at all. In either case, in Muslim society, such a rebel places himself outside the pale within which reform is being sought. He becomes a negative force to be rejected with all the other evils society has produced.

Najīb Maḥfūẓ was one of the pioneers of literature with social content in Egypt, which makes his first experiments in this field doubly interesting. Generally speaking, social criticism has become a theme of literary works in Egypt only since World War II,[36] but for Najīb Maḥfūẓ social problems were from the very beginning of his literary career in the late 1930's, the main area of interest. The criteria by which he judged social issues are therefore easy to discern and there is no doubt that he operated within the mainstream of the critical concepts of his culture. The values he cherishes, the diviations he criticises, the misdeeds he condemns — all form an integral part of the social philosophy of Islam.

This does not mean that his social criticism is insipid. Far from it. Some of his criticism is quite penetrating and often unpleasantly sharp. Merely looking backward to some imaginary past for inspiration rather than forward to an utopian future, does not necessarily blunt criticism. But it does affect the nature of the rebellion and it lends unmistakable colouring to the heroic rebel. The consciousness that we cannot be better than those who have gone before us, and that all we can aspire to is to follow their example, creates a radicalism in the hero-rebel which can by no means be viewed as "radical innocence."[37] This term, as applied to a certain type of hero of American literature, provides a striking example of what, in final analysis, the Mahfuzian hero cannot be. This is not to say that the truly Mahfuzian hero is never a radical or that he lacks innocence. But the innocence of the American literary hero or, for that matter, of the hero of most contemporary Western literature, is radical, we are told, "because it is inherent in his character" and "because it is extreme, impulsive, anarchic, troubled with vision." The innocence of the Egyptian hero, as depicted by Najīb Maḥfūẓ, is of an entirely different kind. It is cultivated, trained to become extreme and anarchic. This may sound self-contradictory, but we are faced with an innocence which is contrived, not spontaneous. The American innocence "is a property of the mythic American Self, perhaps of every anarchic Self." It has in it the quality "to remind us of the ignoble savage...a faithful copy of an absolutely undifferentiated human consciousness, corresponding to a psyche that has hardly left the animal level." All these terms create images which are adorable, and have a history of being adored in Western culture, of which "today American is simply the most accomplished exponent"; a culture or a civlization, whose "ever-broadening general trend...may be characterized as the *extraversion of man*." [38] Egyptian Islamic culture in its present phase of development is so radically different that none of these Western notions can evoke in it even the faintest echo. The mythic Islamic-Egyptian Self is so different and its cultural trend is so different that "a radical innocence" of the American type can only be abhorred as totally unacceptable. It is viewed as a harmful deviation which cannot be countenanced. The only point of similarity between the two cultures is that the hero-rebel in both literatures has eventually to pay dearly for his affront. But this should be attributed to the transcending power of the instinct of all societies for self-preservation. Yet the difference is fundamental. The feeling of alienation in the modern Western hero comes from a frustration at seeing the greatest achievements of his civilization solving so little.

The Behemoth of state and nation seems to be insatiably hungry for ever more victims. The scientific and technological breakthroughs seem to be unable to offer the happiness everyone hoped for. And all the while the individual seems to be pushed into ever greater insignificance. The outcome, therefore, may very well be expressed, as Camus puts it, in the cry "I rebel -- therefore we exist." But the feeling of alienation of the Egyptian hero stems from an entirely different sort of frustration. His is the frustration of one seeing all these magnificent achievements of state and nation and science and technology by-passing his own civilization, leaving it in the lurch, so to speak. There were days when the blame for these failures was put at the door of the West itself. But Najīb Maḥfūẓ belongs to a generation which would not exonerate its own society from at least some responsibility for its shortcomings. Hence the urge for rebellion, to break loose from the chains which make progress unattainable. This is an admirable development, no doubt. But in order to be meaningful, the achievements so eagerly sought after must somehow be defined in traditional cultural terms before, or while, the rebellion takes place. The vision of the happier life to be achieved by these exertions must be adumbrated. And this can be done only in terms of past models if the entire cultural heritage is not to be discarded. Herein lies the internal conflict; a conflict within the society and within each individual in that society. The consequences may often be paralyzing as is demonstrated by many personal experiences of distinguished men.[39] The dilemma of turning a self-contractory introverted culture into an expanding extraverted culture is more bewildering than the inexperienced are capable of appreciating. Some may try to define a solution and then, faced with the force of "dashing waves," give up. Others may end up rejecting in despair their own culture, and yet others may end up hating the foreign models. But a solution is bound to exist, hidden perhaps somewhere in the future, and the most important task for the present is therefore to remain in one piece until it is reached. This is at least the way responsible people would see the problem. And Najīb Maḥfūẓ is undoubtedly a responsible thinker. He understands the predicament of his society and its culture, and he realizes that there are no shortcuts out of it. He also believes very firmly that, in final analysis, the solution to his society's problems depends on its own exertions. He believes that the strength of his society, hidden in the past and in inherited values, will overcome its maladies. In one of his collections of short stories,[40] there is a story called *Ziyāra* (A Visit) telling how a very sick and lonely woman overcame her helplessness, after a visit to her bedside by an old holy man, who revived her faith in God. This is a story of Islamic rebellion, inspired by a rekindled faith in eternal values.

It need hardly be stressed that during Najīb Maḥfūẓ's life-time Egypt has undergone considerable changes, political and otherwise. These changes must have had a marked impact on the thinking of many people, particularly in relation to the problems created by Egypt's cultural encounters. Some people claim to have found all the solutions clearly outlined by the new regime, which needs only to be faithfully followed to the end. Others, with whom Najīb Maḥfūẓ should be counted, encourage no such expectations and offer no easy guide to the understanding of the nature of these changes. Literary works are probably not designed to make the study of such matters easier, but it may be doubted whether any other medium can reflect them more faithfully. Some writers may suggest ways of reading and interpreting their works in written prefaces or in talks, that is to say, by actively participating in public debates on related issues. But Najīb Maḥfūẓ writes nothing except his literature. Nevertheless, for a person of his active mind and lively imagination, the events and exciting developments undergone by Egyptian society in the last 40 years must have been traumatic. For this reason a detailed biography, or an autobiography, would be invaluable for an understanding of his works and his times. It is not at all surprising that the question of his autobiography keeps coming up, just as it is perhaps understandable that he is so reluctant to write one. Asked whether he would not consider writing his autobiography in spite of the fact that he might have to touch on sensitive topics he wrote:[41]

> The idea of writing an autobiography does occur to me occasionally. At times I think of it as a strictly autobiographical novel. But the adherence to the truth required in such work I find a serious problem and a crazy adventure. Especially since I have lived through a long period of transformation in which all our values have been rocked, and falsehood become prevalent, and every individual has been split in two: one part is social and televisionary while the other part breathes a different life in the dark.
>
> No my dear, I think and therefore, I do not exist.[42]

This is a surprising manifestation of a Kafkian logic in a context so far removed from the world of Kafkaesque images.[43]

The scheme of this study is fairly simple, for it follows more or less the chronological development of Najīb Maḥfūẓ's work. Part One examines his historical novels, Part Two his realistic period, and Part Three deals with his "neo-realistic" period. Since each of the first two periods has a fairly definable beginning and an end, an Epilogue has been added to them as a summary of their ideational content. As for the third period, it is still questionable whether it really came to an end on June 5, 1967. It may very well be that the formal change in the writings of Najīb Maḥfūẓ, noticeable in the years following that date, is merely a phase in the development of this third period, which is rich with experiments in form. In any case,

I do not feel that an epilogue can be written to this third period as yet.

NOTES

1 This and other details of the writer's childhood are based on ʿAbbās Khidr, "*Ṭufūlat al-udabāʾ*" (The Childhood of Writers), *al-Risāla al-Jadīda*, No. 54, September, 1958, pp. 6 *seq*. Place names are spelled according to the conventional rules of translireration and not phonetically. Thus Jamāliyya and not Gamāliyya. Most of the available biographical data relating to Najīb Maḥfūẓ is given in Sasson Somekh, *The Changing Rhytm*, Leiden, 1973, particularly Ch. 2.

2 On the trend of depersonalizing the individual in Islamic literature see G.C. von Grunebaum, *Medieval Islam*, Chicago, 1962, pp. 221 *seq*.

3 Ghālī Shukrī, *al-Muntamī*, Cairo, 1964, p. 26, reports that Najīb Maḥfūẓ was afflicted by epilepsy at the age of ten. However, Dr. Adham Rajab, a close personal friend of the writer for many years, speaks of him as an outstanding soccer player in his youth and a very merry personality. *Al-Hilāl*, February 1970, pp. 93 *seq*.

4 An article entitled "The Philosophy of Socrates," published in October 1931, is three pages long. An article on "Plato and his Philosophy," in the November 1931 issue, is six pages long. Each article reviews the biography of the philosopher, his intellectual development, the chief controversies in which he was involved and his main contributions to science and philosophy.

5 Fu'ād Dawwāra, "*Maʿa Najīb Maḥfūẓ fī ʿidihi al-dhahabī*," (With Najīb Maḥfūẓ on his Golden Jubilee), *al-Kātib*, No. 22, January 1963, p. 11.

6 Fāṭima Mūsā identifies the writer as James Baikie. See "*Najīb Maḥfūẓ wataṭawwur fann al-riwāya fī miṣr*," *al-Kātib*, No. 86, May 1968, p. 72.

7 Dawwāra, *ibid.*, p. 7.

8 Dawwāra, *ibid.*, p. 9. The *qānūn* is a stringed musical instrument.

9 Having retired, he later turned down an offer of a government post. See *Ṣabāḥ al-Khayr*, August 31, 1972.

10 *Adab muwaẓẓafīn.* See interview by ʿAbd al-Tawwāb ʿAbd al-Ḥayy in *al-Muṣawwār*, January 31, 1969. This term was also used by Najīb Maḥfūẓ publicly in a talks with Yūsuf al-Sharūnī, published in *Majallat al-Idhāʿa*, December 21, 1957.

11 Dawwāra, *ibid.*, p. 23.

12 Reported by Muḥammad Tabāraka, *Akhir Sāʿa*, December 12, 1962.

13 In the special edition of *al-Hilāl* dedicated to him (February 1970) there are several pictures of himself and his two daughters.

14 Tabāraka, *ibid.* The *ḥarīm* is not the harem as understood in the West. *Ḥarīm* means sanctuary and is applied to all female members of the family as well as to the wife. The concealment of his wife's identity gave rise to rumours that she was non-Egyptian. But this is denied by Najīb Maḥfūẓ.

15 Yūsuf al-Sharūnī, *Dirāsāt fī riwāya wa-al-qiṣṣa al-qaṣīra*, Cairo, 1967, cf., *ibid.*, the article "*al-Taṭawwur al-riwāʾī ʿind Najīb Maḥfūẓ,*" written in 1962.

16 Al-Sharūnī, *ibid.*, p. 22.

17 Quoted by al-Sharūnī, *ibid.*

18 The product of this new phase has been published in some fourteen volumes of short stories and novels, and calls for a special study.

19 Maḥmūd Amīn al-ʿAlam, in a long article entitled "A New Phase in the World of Najīb Maḥfūẓ" successfully conveys his own impression that all this is really new and significantly different. But he is hard put to demonstrate exactly the reasons for his impression. Cf. *al-Hilāl*, February 1970. The same difficulty will probably be

experienced by any one who attempts at this stage to analyze Najīb Maḥfūẓ's latest works as a dictinct body of literary production.

20 ʿAbd al-Tawwāb ʿAbd al-Ḥayy, *ibid.*

21 Muḥammad Barakāt, *"Ḥawla masraḥ Najīb Maḥfūẓ,"* (On the Theatrical Works of Najīb Maḥfūẓ), *al-Hilāl*, February 1970, p.202.

22 *Ibid.*, p. 200. In 1972, he felt the situation had cleared up. This he expected to reflect in future writing. *Ṣabāḥ al-Khayr, ibid.*

23 *Ibid.*, p. 203. The tributlations the playwright is subjected to, beginning with the "order" for a play, the caprices of the star-actors and the whims of the director, are the subject of one of these late works of Najīb Maḥfūẓ, entitled *"Mashrūʿ li al-munāqasha"* (A topic for Discussion), printed in *Taḥt al-Miẓalla* This very subject was also treated in a similar vein in *"Zayna,"* printed in *Dunyā Allāh*, published in 1963.

24 *Ibid.*

25 Dawwāra, *ibid.*, p. 20: "I consider the colloquial language a disease and this is a fact. This is a disease caused by lack of learning."

26 Hāshim al-Naḥḥās, *"Dawr Najīb Maḥfūẓ fī al-sinamā al-miṣriyya,"* (The Role of Najīb Maḥfūẓ in the Egyptian Cinema), *al-Hilāl*, February 1970, pp. 184 *seq*. This article is a comprehensive review of Najīb Maḥfūẓ's activities in the cinema industry. It is apparent that even in the 18 films for which he wrote scripts based on other people's novels the locations and characters bear great resemblance to those of his own novels. The study of his scenarios might very well contribute to a better understanding of his literary works. This is demonstrated by al-Naḥḥās, *Najīb Maḥfūẓ ʿalā al-shāsha*, Cairo, 1975, which updates the data in the article.

27 The Egyptian writer Yūsuf al-Sibāʿī, himself an outspoken advocate of the use of the colloquial in literary works, tells of his old uncle, Ṭaha al-Sibāʿī Bāshā who, after reading and enjoying Najīb Maḥfūẓ's novel *Zuqāq al-midaqq*, commented that it might have been a most perfect novel had its characters only spoken in the colloquial dialect. Yūsuf al-Sibāʿī's own stand is made clear when he says: "I am writing mainly for the masses, not for the privileged few, skilled in the pure and eloquent language, and these masses have a much greater need for literary nourishment they can understand and writing they can relish." See Introduction to al-Sibāʿī's novel *al-Saqqāʾ mat* (The Water-Carrier Died).

28 Collected in *Hams al-junūn* (Whisper of Madness), (1938).

29 Simon J. Lesser, *Fiction and the Unconscious*, New York, 1957 p. 135.

30 This will be further discussed in Part One of this study.

31 Lesser, *ibid.*, p. 175.

32 Quoted from von Grunebaum, *Islam*, London, 1961, p. 6.

33 *Ibid.*

34 H.A.R. Bibb, *Modern Trends in Islam*, Chicago, 1945, p. 116, uses the term "Mahdist" to characterize the fanatic activities of the reformist movement in Islam. W.C. Smith, *Islam in Modern History*, Princeton, 1957, p. 89 prefers the term "dynamism" to characterize their attitude.

35 See J.M.S. Baljon, *Modern Muslim Koran Interpretation*, Leiden, 1960.

36 R. Makarius, *Anthologie de la litterature arabe contemporaine: Le roman et la nouvelle*, Paris, 1964,pp. 43 *seq.*, defines the period of social criticism in Egyptian literature as the second period of revival of modern Arabic literature. Most writers who wrote in the period between the wars showed little awareness of social problems.

37 Ihab Hassan, *Radical Innocence*, Princeton, 1961, pp. 6 *seq.*

38 *Ibid.*, p. 15, where this is quoted from Erich Kahler.

39 Characteristic is the following statement regarding Aḥmad Amīn (d. 1954), a noted intellectual leader in Egypt and a man of bold reformist ideas: "In the intellectual sphere he was a modernizer, but in day-to-day matters he was bound by tradition." A.M.A. Mazyad, *Aḥmad Amīn*, Leiden, 1963, p. 19. This dichotomy in his life resulted in a rather sad ending, as he wrote in his autobiography: "When I was young, I started planning my future in my imagination, according to the highest ideals I could think of for my character, my behavior, my ways of reform. But these ideals collided with reality...I tried to stand fast in the middle of the waves that dashed upon me but I was not able to hold myself...On account of this, I was a better man in my youth than I am in my old age, and more of an optimist...I had great hopes of reforming many things and accomplishing important deeds. However, I saw most of these hopes evaporate because I was incapable of translating my thoughts into action." Quoted *ibid.*, p. 33.

40 *Kummārat al-qiṭṭ al-aswad.*

41 *Al-Hilāl*, February, 1970, p. 48.

42 *Anā ufakkir idhan fa-anā ghayr mawjūd. Al-Hilāl*, February, 1970, p.

43 The phrasing of Najīb Maḥfūẓ's concluding sentence brings to mind the one used by Erich Heller, *The Disinherited Mind*, Cleveland, 1965, p. 202. There it is offered as a transformation of the Cartesian *Cogito ergo sum*, demonstrating the distortion of truth forced by the logic of Kafka's writings. Heller conceives of it as an unknown "It" which does all the thinking that matters, a cursed intelligence whose being

denies the existence of man. The formula becomes "It thinks, and therefore, I am not," which can also be expressed, if we restore intelligence to its human locus, "I think, and therefore I am not." Cf. Ḥasan, *ibid.*, p. 33. The contention subsumed in this analogy (which has probably been created inadvertently by Najīb Maḥfūẓ) that a sincere Egyptian intellectual faces a Kafkaesque abyss seems to be implicit in Najīb Maḥfūẓ's reply.

Part One
THE ARCADIAN

Chapter One
Invoking the Spirit

Egyptian literary critics seem to be hard put to define Najīb Maḥfūẓ's role as a historiographer (*mu'arrikh*) of contemporary Egypt. Except for the three historical novels,[1] most of his works revolve around events and situations of contemporary Egyptian history, more specifically of the period since the second half of World War I. It appears, however, that some Egyptian readers fail to see in this writing anything more than a straightforward record of events, situations and personalities. Thus, on the occasion of the writer's 50th anniversary, a well-known literary critic asked him directly: "I have heard a great critic describe you in a debate as more of a historiographer than an artist because your works are devoid of any definite viewpoint from which you present the story, events and people; and he pointed particularly to the /Cairo/ trilogy.[2] What do you think of this description"?[3]

The question reveals a definite concept concerning the recording of history which is deeply rooted in the idea of historiography in Islamic culture. It has been pointed out[4] that traditionally

> Historiography did not set out to tell the saga of the evolution of society, nor did it wish to judge and interpret. Rather it meant to collect the accounts of the witnesses, marshalling them with the greatest possible completeness and with no concern for their contradictions. The reader was left to draw his own conclusions. The historian merely furnished the material.

It is for this reason that Najīb Maḥfūẓ's reply is of particular significance:[5]

"And does the historiographer present history without a point of view?" he asked. "Where is he to be found, this historiographer of yours?" Najīb Maḥfūẓ goes on to explain that this is not the real difference between the historiographer and the artist. For the historiographer studies history as "a general phenomenon," and brings forward those events which help to explain the phenomenon, whereas for the artist, who "gives expression to life through the particular relations" between ordinary people, historical events are nothing more than "secondary factors" affecting these people. He further emphasizes that there can be no historiographer without "a point of view," whereas "it is possible for an artist to be without a point of view" and to restrict himself to giving a direct expression to the various experiences of life without there being behind this expression "any definite philosophy."

It is clear that the old Arabic term "*mu'arrikh*" for Najīb Maḥfūẓ no longer has the traditional meaning of historiographer, but that of the modern Western "historian." As for artistic writings Najīb Maḥfūz is here vehemently rejecting the demand made on him to become *engagé* in a very specific sense. On the other hand, he most certainly does not consider himself to be one of those writers who give expression to experience without having a philosophy of their own. He specifically rejects the criticism levelled in the question against his trilogy, and says:

> As regards the /Cairo/ trilogy, I believe there is in it an accentuated point of view, which you can see in a definite line of development of the events therein, which can be summarized in two words, and that is the struggle between great and burdensome traditions, on the one hand, and freedom in its various political and intellectual forms, on the other...

I shall later have an opportunity to discuss the Cairo trilogy in greater detail: at this junction it is important to point out that the story in this great work does stretch from 1917 to 1944 and to a considerable extent reflects the intellectual history of Egypt over this extended span of time.

An important segment of this history is brought out through the personal history of Kamāl, the son of Aḥmad ʿAbd al-Jawād, whose intellectual development is traced systematically from boyhood on. The second book of the trilogy, however, ends in 1927, while the third book opens eight years later in 1935. Kamāl's intellectual development over these missing years, between the ages of 20 and 28, is left rather vague. In order to see the significance of this omission it should be realized that this is approximately the period when Najīb Maḥfūẓ himself was undergoing his high school and college education. He graduated from high school at the age of 19, in 1930, and from college at the age of 23 in 1934. Kamāl is therefore Najīb Maḥfūẓ's senior by four years, and the "omitted" period covers his post high school education.[6]

It is not intended here to reconstruct Maḥfūẓ's intellectual makeup at the time he graduated from college, but we can obtain an idea of his turn of mind from the fact that two years later he wrote his first historical novel and that he continued to write historical novels for the next two years, discontinuing only after completing the third.[7] And as Maḥfūẓ himself has stated, when he started writing these historical novels he had planned to write 40 of them, out of a desire to tell the whole story of ancient Egypt "in novel form, in the same way that Walter Scott had done with regard to the history of his country."[8] This tremendous passion to relate the ancient history of Egypt in a modern, Western, literary form must have been cultivated precisely during those years in the biography of Kamāl which Najīb Maḥfūẓ preferred to leave out of his story.

The Cairo trilogy was written in the years 1945-1952, and what we are witnessing could, therefore, is an attempt by Najīb Maḥfūẓ to draw a curtain over what may perhaps have been the most decisive years in the development of his artistic talent. It is proposed now to take a deeper look into Najīb Maḥfūẓ's historical novels. After this an attempt will be made to understand the peculiar change which came over him when the third novel was completed, by which "suddenly the desire for this romantic historical writing died in me." [9]

The years during which Najīb Maḥfuẓ attended high school and college were years of a very lively search for a national identity. The Egyptian intellectual was faced with the dilemma of choosing between the alternate possibilities of identification: that of the Egyptian-Arab-Muslim, or that of the Egyptian-Arab-Pharaonic. Whereas the first alternative was not necessarily religious, for the hard core traditional Muslims were still averse to the very notion of modern Nationalism, the second was definitely secular, and as such was much more attractive to people of a Western, modern and liberal turn of mind. For about a decade after 1926, the issue was important enough to stir some of the deepest emotions in Egyptian public and intellectual life.[10] It is therefore not at all surprising to find Najīb Maḥfūẓ as a young man of a very inquisitive and impressionable mind, engulfed in the debate and electing to take a definite stand in it. His choice fell on the Pharaonists, who could boast of such luminaries as Ṭaha Ḥusayn, Luṭfī al-Sayyid, Tawfīq al-Ḥakīm, and others. Of particular importance for Najib Maḥfuẓ were his close personal relations with Salāma Mūsā, a believer in the Pharaonic concept, who also encouraged him to publish his first novels, and printed the first one in his own monthly magazine *al-Majalla al-Jadīda*.[11]

An intellectual current of such importance could not fail to produce literary works praising the glorious past of Egypt and thus lend its support to the Pharaonic trend in the growing awareness of national identity. To be sure, the historical novel was not an unknown form of literary writing when this trend began to reveal itself in literary works; it was a genre of writing that had already been considerably popularized in Arabic by Jirjī-Zaydān and others.[12] Altogether, the very idea of taking pride in the glorious past in order to enhance national sentiment in the modern sense was already much in vogue at that time in Arabic literature and poetry.[13] The Pharaonic trend, therefore, made no particular contribution to the development of new forms in modern Egyptian literature. Its main contribution has been ideological in so far as it has maintained that ancient Egypt had a civilization which preceded Islam and Christianity by thousands of years, and that modern Egypt could again secure its rightful place in the world by reviving the spirit of that ancient civilization.

The most striking literary expression of this idea was offered by the French-educated Egyptian writer, Tawfīq al-Ḥakīm, in his novel *ʿAwdat al-rūḥ* (The Return of the Spirit) published in 1933.[14] Although it was not in itself a historical novel, it brought out the most essential element of the Pharaonic concept, by calling for the return of that spirit which had lifted the Egyptians of the past to summits still seen and admired in the magnificent remains of their culture.[15]

Evidently the reactions were not all favorable. That the ardent Muslims could hardly accept the idea of a Muslim people taking its inspiration from a pre-Islamic era requires no elaboration. But people of a definitely modern bent also had strong reservations regarding the sincerity and justification of al-Ḥakīm's call. The Egyptian writer, Yaḥyā Ḥaqqī, expressed them in an article published in 1934.[16] He failed to understand the claim that Egypt could not live except through the magic of "a Pharaonic talisman," -- "for," he said, "the glory of the Pharaos is just as remote a dream as it is beautiful." He concluded that the proper name for the novel by al-Ḥakīm should be: "The Rising of the Spirit"[17] (*Ṭulūʻ al-rūh*) rather than "The Return of the Spirit."

Thus, for a young man and aspiring writer in Egypt of the middle 1930's, it was an adventure fraught with some danger to join his pen in support of the Pharaonites. But having the courage of his convictions and greatly encouraged by a man he admired and probably by the facility offered him for publication as well, Maḥfūẓ decided to take to the field.

After the discussion of the three historical novels an attempt will be made to evaluate the ideological motivation behind them. To what extent was Najīb Maḥfūẓ's urge to write these novels with the ancient Pharaonic history as their background prompted solely by a Pharaonic ideological approach? The importance of this question will, it is hoped, be readily admitted once it is remembered that the historical setting may often be chosen, not necessarily for the purpose of influencing a "manner of viewing history," but rather with the purpose of evading the limitations imposed on the writer by the circumstances of the present.[18] It will be well to bear this in mind in the following detailed examination of these novels.

The Egyptian critic, Fāṭima Mūsā, has rightly pointed out[19] that Najīb Maḥfūẓ's first novel, *ʻAbath al-aqdār* (The Mockery of Fate) clearly reveals the dual source of his inspiration, "nay, of that of his whole generation," for the marks of *ʻAwdat al-rūḥ* in it are obvious, while the influence of Walter Scott is frankly admitted by Najīb Maḥfūẓ himself. His great interest in the life of the early Egyptians became manifest when he translated from English and published in 1931 or 1932, a small scholarly book on ancient Egypt.[20] The novel, however, was the first published product of Najīb Maḥfūẓ creative talent and it is not at all surprising therefore to find that he has retained a very special place for this novel in his heart, as though it were his first-born daughter.[21] But in a more sober moment he has declared that although he may have felt that he had done something really great the day the novel was published, he now considers it to be a mere "child's play."[22]

The story of this novel takes place in the reign of Khūfū, the second King of the Fourth Dynasty and the builder of the great pyramids of Gīza, probably in the years 2596-2573 B.C.[23] It is based on *Hordedef's Tale*, one of the famous tales of ancient Egypt.[24]

The reasons for choosing this period and this event as the setting for a historical Egyptian novel may not seem hard to guess. It was the age which had produced the most impressive pyramids, and in which a change of dynasties had taken place accompanied by a fundamental religious and cultural development. The Fifth Dynasty was probably a priestly usurpation, and there is no doubt "that under it the Heliopolitan priesthood began to wield an unprecedented influence," followed naturally by numerous other changes and innovations.[25] A moment such as this, in the history of a nation, when the peak of political power, symbolized by the construction of the pyramids, is soon followed by dramatic changes of dynasty and cult, would naturally be very attractive to an historical novelist in search of a theme. Yet it must be admitted that the drama of this historical moment was completely overlooked by Najīb Maḥfūẓ. If the "classical historical novel"[26] is expected to depict the drama of historical change, then *ʿAbath al-aqdar* can hardly qualify as such.

In our novel Khūfū, who rules Egypt from Memphis, loses no time before he sets out to seize and kill a baby, born in Ōm, to the young woman Rūd-dīdīt. The author has no use for the supernatural conception of the child as told in the old Egyptian tale, and in the novel the child is the natural offspring of the old priest of Raʿ.

However, the father knows that his son is destined to rule the land, having been told so by the god Raʿ himself and the information reaches the King's ears. The King had decided to lead his forces to Ōm in person because to him it was "a gigantic battle between Khūfū and the fates." In so doing, the King is knowingly acting against the dictates of the accumulated wisdom of Egypt. For his trusted *wazīr*, Khumīnī, the priest of Ptāḥ, the god of Memphis, had admonished him that according to the famous instructions of Qaqimma,[27] "precaution is of no avail against fate."[28] Thus the drama is set: the rest of the story is designed merely to illustrate the helplessness of man against fate. The King's excursion to Ōm results in a baby being killed in its mother's arms by the heir-apparent Raʿkhaʿūf,[29] and the party returns to Memphis satisfied that the threat to the dynasty had been removed.

The newly born child, however was not the victim; named by his father Raʿ-dadaf,[30] he was secretly sent out of Ōm with his mother, accompanied by a maidservant Zāyā, a childless young woman. In the night this young servant, under the impression that their lives were in jeopardy, snatched the baby from its sleeping mother and ran away to Memphis. There she married Bishārū, the inspector of works, and thus a home was established in which Raʿ-dadaf could grow up in relative prosperity. Having received the best education as a boy, Raʿ-dadaf then joins the military academy, where he prepares himself for a military career.

King Khūfū's chief interest is to keep the peace of the land.[31] Still, state affairs oblige the King to sanction a military operation against the nomads of the Sinai Peninsula, and the leadership of this operation is entrusted to Ra'-dadaf, who has by this time risen to a position of trust and authority in the court. The war is conducted very successfully and its general returns home as a great victor. He then makes bold and asks the King's permission to marry his daughter.

Permission is, of course, granted.

At the same time another important event takes place. Among the prisoners he brings home, Raʿ-dadaf discovers his real mother, who in due course tells him the story of his birth. His step-father happens by chance to hear the story, and he feels it is his duty to report the news to the King. However, before he had an opportunity to do so, Raʿ-dadaf manages to foil an attempt on the King's life by his son, the very same person who had killed the baby in Ōm in the belief that he was defending his hereditary rights. By the time Bishārū is admitted into the King's presence to inform him of the imminent danger, the King is already a much wiser man. He realizes that no man can resist fate, and consequently he appoints Raʿ-dadaf to be his successor.

It would appear from this that the author carefully steered clear of two out of the three dramatic issues alluded to in the ancient tale of Hordedef. The religious issue he simply ignored by making Raʿ-dadaf a loyal, unquestioning follower of Ptaḥ, the god of Memphis, thus turning the fact of his birth in Ōm as the son of a priest of the god Raʿ, into an irrelevant detail. The political issue he evaded by calling Rūd-dīdīt's child Raʿ-dadaf, and by making him join the royal family, ascending to the throne as the third King of the Fourth Dynasty, although in the ancient tale, all three children of Rūd-dīdīt bear the names of the kings of the Fifth Dynasty. Only the third issue of that tale captured the author's imagination, namely the conflict between a man's will and his fate. In treating it the author clearly followed the spirit of the ancient tale by making fate victorious. But he did this in a way which almost deprived the conflict of any dramatic tension. From the very beginning we know that the King was wrong in believing that he could win against fate, because the whole historical experience of Egypt bore evidence that nothing avails against fate. Furthermore, the triumph of fate over the King does not come at the end of a heroic struggle. Fate seems to gain its victory in a most unspectacular way, merely by placing its chosen child at the service of its challenger and by making him render to the King the most loyal and unselfish service. The hero does not seek victory, and his success comes through no conscious exertion of his own. The drama almost becomes a comedy, for the human heroes of the story look more like blind dwarfs, utterly helpless against the dictates of fate.

The novel is truly something of a puzzle. There is hardly anything in it to justify a voyage to a 4,500 years old past which, when seen at close quarters, is not as glorious as it seemed from afar. Yet the novel is not devoid of value and interest. It would appear that the historical setting is nothing but a disguise, contrived in order to create a "never and nowhere" situation sufficiently recognizable to the contemporary Egyptian reader to enable the writer to say something meaningful to him. Therefore, both "the psychology of the characters and the manners depicted are entirely those of the writer's own day." What Lukācs said of 17th century European historical novels[32] can with full justification be said of *ʿAbath al-aqdar*: that what is lacking in it "is precisely the specifically historical, that is derivation of the individuality of the characters from the historical peculiarity of their age."

This is not to imply any deficiency on the part of Najīb Maḥfūẓ. One can sense a carefully designed scheme. By choosing the setting of ancient Egypt the writer could render some service to the political ideology which apparently fascinated him at the time. The quality of this service, aesthetically considered, was rather mediocre. A few phrases and scenes can be found which truly reflect the influence of Tawfīq al-Ḥakīm.[33] Nevertheless, very significantly, al-Ḥakīm's great leader of that epoch, *al-Maʿbūd* (The Worshipped one), under whose inspiration marvels were supposed to have been worked, turns out to be, in the person of Khūfū, rather pale and uninspiring. But for the writer, a far more important result of the "historical" setting was the freedom gained to say things which he truly wanted to say, unfettered by limitations imposed by circumstances of the present. With this assumption in mind, we can now try to adumbrate what the novel actually sets out to tell.

Obviously we need not expect much from the "internal fiction," to use Northrop Frye's expression. What we have to concentrate on is the "external fiction which is a relation between the writer and the writer's society." [34] In this case, "as soon as the poet's personality appears on the horizon, a relation with the reader is established which cuts across the story, and which may increase until there is no story at all apart from what the poet is conveying to his reader." [35]

It is a story of a people who have a great cultural and spiritual heritage. Most of them live in a city, under the autocratic rule of a King, and are subject to the power of inscrutable fate. They enjoy the goodness bestowed on them by circumstances, and the order guaranteed them by the wisdom of their rulers. They are deeply religious and they are patient and obedient. Fate is inscrutable, but not cruel; it is awesome but benign. Life is therefore good and happy and reliable. With wisdom, moderation, and devotion to inherited values, the inherent balance of social life is bound to work in everyone's favor. Their life is not free from conflicts and violence, but even these have a place within the general balanced order of life.

Within this general framework, there is understandably no place for dynastic upheavals or religious strife. Miracles are part of daily life, mystery is everywhere to be encountered, but the highest wisdom is to interpret everything in accordance with the precepts handed down over the generations. The interest in the Fourth Dynasty is not to be sought therefore in the dramatic changes which it ushered in, but in the orderly happiness it secured. Man is liable to commit follies even though he may be a king. But fate is not revengeful, and within limits crimes are duly rectified. King Khūfū, in a moment of foolishness, challenged fate and killed an innocent baby. He was not a worse king for that. But fate, in its infinite wisdom, so worked things out that eventually the king's son was killed while attempting to commit regicide, and essentially balance was restored.

A concept such as this, of an organized and orderly social life, under the supervision of an essentially benevolent fate, could, with good reason, be depicted as the one which prevailed at the time of the Fourth Dynasty. With this dynasty the search of the Old Kingdom for security and order reached its climax.[36] Furthermore, its philosophical religious system, often epitomized as "The Memphite Theology,"[37] not only considered Ptāḥ, the god of Memphis, as the "heart and tongue" of gods, but saw all things as first existing in the thought of the god and believed that the utterance of the thought in the form of a divine fiat brought forth the world. This may well be the reason for Najīb Maḥfūẓ's reluctance to treat the conflict which resulted in Raʿ's ascendancy in the Fifth Dynasty. The kind of society and government which we find in *ʿAbath al-aqdār* had to collapse with the change in dynasties, and this was definitely not the story Najīb Maḥfūẓ set out to tell.

Raʿ-dadaf's role is certainly very central to the story. On the day of his birth his old father dies, and the next day he is snatched away from his mother's arms. Then, when years later Raʿ-dadaf becomes the king, we have almost the complete mythological story of Horus, the son born to Osiris, after the latter's death at the hands of his brother Seth, who aspired to rule alone in Egypt. And Horus, too, comes to his legitimate heritage in the face of Seth's opposition.[38]

But in the story of the child's escape, something which to many might have been most natural has been clearly avoided by the writer. The child is not put in a box and left to float on the Nile but is taken into the desert. When he arrives at Memphis he is a parentless child, who has come from the desert. Moses, too, it will be recalled, returned to Egypt after a period of exile in the desert, but his life was first saved by the Nile. In *ʿAbath al-aqdār* the Nile has no place whereas the desert is always present.[39] The desert for Najīb Maḥfūẓ seems to be the awe inspiring, mysterious place where fate resides and occasionally reveals itself. Raʿ-dadaf's own life made its full cycle between the day he was taken away from his mother in the desert and the day he found her again in the desert.

It has been remarked that none of the characters in the novel consciously influence his own fate. Raʿ-dadaf is no exception. He lives his life completely unaware of this origin and his destiny. His only distinction is the facility with which he provokes love and admiration everywhere, like an Egyptian Billy Budd, whose purity and charm are inexplicably connected with the absence of parents in his life. In the light of Najīb Maḥfūẓ's later writings this feature of his hero is of particular interest. What makes the boy's success so secure seems to be the perfect symmetry between his own individuality and the "collective norm."[40] It looks as though the writer is trying to show that a person who grows up in society, free from the imposition of parental presence, would naturally be recognized as Fate's most favored child. The implication is that perfect individuation cannot take place with over-bearing parental presence constantly inhibiting the child's free development in his formative years. This impression is strengthened toward the end of the novel when Raʿ-dadaf's mother is discovered and brought home. For the first time in his life our hero is faced with worries, with fears regarding his life and his future, caused by the presence of his natural mother. She is the one who reveals to him the circumstances of his birth, and places on his shoulders the heavy load of a past in which he had no part. And so he says to his mother: "Only yesterday was I ʿdadaf Bishāru, yet today I am a new person whose past abounds with misfortunes, who was born this moment to a murdered father and a wretched mother...my birth was a calamity." But a mother has not only to reveal the past and its anxieties but also to offer advice: "forget your sorrows and think of escaping." He can hardly comprehend the advice, but she explains it to him most meticulously: "for I do not wish to lose you again, having found you only after years of agony." He would not consider running away, for he feels that he has done no wrong. But as a mother, she also insists: "Have pity on my heart, which is torn by fear." Luckily for our hero his mother has returned too late to cause any real harm, and as fate would have it, when the real identity of Raʿ-dadaf becomes known to the king he is already prepared to submit to his own fate.

There is no need to go any deeper into the novel. It clearly had a message to deliver. How well the message was received at the time of its publication is an entirely different problem, which need not concern us. This was Mahfüz's first novel and it was heavily coated with Pharaonist ideology, probably more than the average reader then cared to swallow. But time moves inexorably forward, as Najīb Maḥfūẓ realizes so well, and today this novel is read and cherished by many, some of whom are still searching for its message. In a review written years later, we read: "*ʿAbath al-aqdār*... describes a tyranical king, and ridicules his power and tyranny.It ends with the king abdicating his power in favor of one of the common men of the people."[41] Another critic, quoted with approval in the same review, stresses that the novel shows "the necessity of turning political power over to the people."

Such appraisals seem to go beyond what may reasonably be read into the novel. But perhaps they do prove that the ideal society described in the novel, and the image of a perfect harmony between the individual and society, appeal strongly to present day readers in Egypt.

NOTES

1 *ʿAbath al-aqdār* (1938), *Rādūbīs* (1943), *Kifāḥ ṭayba* (1944). The dates here and following are those of the first editions. References will be made to the editions indicated in the bibliographical list on p.

2 *Bayn al-qaṣrayn* (1956), *Qaṣr al-shawq* (1957), *al-Sukkariyya* (1957); to be distinguished from the "Pharaonic" trilogy.

3 Fu'ād Dawwāra, "With Najīb Maḥfūẓ on his Golden Jubilee," *al-Kātib*, No. 22, January 1963, p. 17.

4 G. von Grunebaum, *Medieval Islam*, Chicago, 1962, p. 281.

5 Dawwāra, *ibid.*, p. 18.

6 For additional points of comparison between the author's biography and that of Kamāl, see Ghālī Shukrī, *al-Muntamī*, Cairo 1964, pp. 26 *seq.* Answering a question by Ghālī Shukrī, Najīb Maḥfūẓ said: Kamāl reflects my own intellectual crisis which was, I believe, a crisis of a whole generation." Cf. *Ḥiwār*, No. 3, March-April 1968, p. 67.

7 The periods in which Najīb Maḥfūẓ had actually written his novels are given by Ghālī Shukrī, *op. cit.*, p. 346.

8 Dawwāra, *op. cit.*, p. 17. The purpose of this impressive program is worth noting. Unlike his great predecessor Jirjī Zaydān, Najīb Maḥfūẓ was not interested in the story of Muslim civilization, but in that of Egypt only. On earlier attempts of historical novel writing in Arabic, cf. Krackovski, "Der Historische Roman in der neuerer arabischen literatur," *Die Welt*

des Islam, No. 12, 1930, pp. 51-87.

9 Dawwāra, *ibid.*

10 Cf. Nadav Safran, *Egypt in Search of a Political Community*, Cambridge, 1961, pp. 143-47.

11 Dawwāra, *ibid.*, p. 12.

12 Cf. ʿAbd al-Muḥsin Ṭaha Badr, *Taṭawwur al-riwāya al-ʿarabiyya al-hadītha fī miṣr, 1870-1938*, Cairo, 1963, pp. 93-115.

13 Cf. Anīs al-Khūrī al-Maqdisī, *al-Ittijahāt al-adabiyya fī al-al-ʿālam al-ʿarabī al-ḥadīth*, Beirut, 1960, pp. 176-98.

14 For an English translation of the most pertinent passages in this respect cf. Safran, *Egypt in Search of a Political Community*, Cambridge 1961, pp. 146-7. Be it noted that the message of the spirit is delivered by a Frenchman talking to an Englishman.

15 For an illuminating demonstration of the impression made by this novel on young readers of the time, see George Vaucher, *Gamal Abdel Nasser et son équipe*, Paris, 1959, pp. 56-57.

16 *Fajr al-qiṣṣa al-miṣriyyā*, Cairo, n.d., pp. 133 *seq.*

17 *Op. cit.* p. 135.

18 The "costume historical novel" is largely a result of such an "escapist" impulse. The quotation is from Erich Auerbach, *Mimesis*, Princeton, 1965, p. 443. All this is further discussed in the Epilogue to Part One.

19 *"Najīb Maḥfuẓ wa taṭawwur fann al-riwāya fī miṣr,"* *al-Kātib*, No. 86, May 1968, pp. 70-71.

20 *Ibid.*, p. 72. The book is that of Baikie. Cf. Introduction, n.6.

21. Stated by him in an interview. See *al-Muṣawwar*, January 31, 1968.

22 The pun is unmistakable in Arabic: "*ʿAbath aṭfāl mush ʿabath aqdār.*" Dawwāra, *ibid.*, p. 22.

23 Alan Gardiner, *Egypt of the Pharaohs*, Oxford University Press, 1969, pp. 79, 434.

24 For the story in full see Flinders Petrie (ed.), *Egyptian Tales*, First Series, IVth to XIIth Dynasty, London 1926, pp. 22-45. Very succinctly the story relates the birth of triplets who grew to become the founders of the Fifth Dynasty. They were born to Rūd-dīdīt, from the seed of the god Re, in the city of Om. That Khūfū meant to kill the babies is definitely stated, but evidently he failed, for his dynasty was replaced by the followers of Re.

25 Gardiner, *op. cit.*, p. 84.

26 The term is that of Georg Lukacs, in *The Historical Novel*, London 1962. See particularly pp. 63 *seq.* Lukacs considers it the role of the historical novel to bring out the sense of the historical necessity of change by showing the complex interaction of concrete historical circumstances in this process of transformation with the actual human beings who have grown up in these circumstances.

27 On the Precepts of Qāqimma, composed in the reign of Senefru,the first King of the Fourth Dynasty, see Wallis Budge, *The Gods of the Egyptians*, London 1904, V. I, pp. 122 *seq.* Samples of the instructions of this sage are given by Adolf Erman, *The Egyptians*, New York 1966, pp. 66-67.

28 Budge actually cites the admonition of Qaqimma: "Not (are) known the things which maketh God," *op. cit.*, p. 123. Erman, *op. cit.*, p. 67 has "one knoweth not what may chance, what God doth when he punisheth."

29 The old Egyptian name is Raʿkhaʿf -- cf. Gardiner, *op. cit.*, p. 81.

30 The historical name is Raʿ djedef, who was the third king of the Fourth Dynasty. See Gardiner, *op. cit.*, p. 82.

31 "Khufu...was a greater builder than fighter, and it seems doubtful if any military expeditions were undertaken during his reign... Khufu built for his tomb the Great Pyramid at Gīzah, and his name

will be remembered for ever as the builder of this mighty monument." Budge, *A Short History*, pp. 40-41.

32 Lukacs, *op. cit.*, p. 19.

33 These are shown at some length by Fāṭima Mūsā, *ibid.*, p. 71; cf. *'Abath al-aqdār*, pp. 10-12.

34 Northrop Frye, *Anatomy of Criticism*, New York, 1969, p. 52.

35 *Ibid.*

36 See John A. Wildon, *The Culture of Ancient Egypt*, Chicago, 1968, Ch. 3.

37 *Op. cit.*, p. 59. See also J. H. Breasted, *Development of Religion and Thought in Ancient Egypt*, London, 1912, pp. 46-48.

38 See Erman, *op. cit.*, p. 140.

39 The opposition of Nile and desert is a constant feature in Najīb Maḥfūẓ's later writing. See infra Ch. 8.

40 Cf. C. G. Jung, *Psychological Types*, Pantheon, 1964, "Individuation," p. 561.

41 Dawwāra, *"al-Wijdān al-qawmī fī adab najīb maḥfūẓ," al-Hilāl*, February 1970, p. 103.

Chapter Two
Snares and Nets

Five months after concluding *ʿAbath al-aqdār*, Najīb Maḥfūẓ began to write *Rādūbīs*.[1] The events related in this novel take place towards the end of the Sixth Dynasty, approximately in the year 2150 B.C. The hero of the story is Pharaoh himself, the ill-fated Merenraʿ,[2] of whom it is known that he was killed after a short reign of one year, and that his death was avenged by his sister Nitōcris (Nītūqrīs in the novel), who succeeded him to the throne.[3] The Sixth Dynasty was the last of the Old Kingdom by present reckoning,[4] and its collapse was due to several factors, all of which were economically detrimental to its fortunes.[5] One of these factors was the concessions made to the temples of certain economic privileges which deprived the state's treasury of considerable income.

The conflict between the young and vigorous Pharaoh and the established clergy is one of the two main axes around which the novel revolves. As has been remarked by a shrewd observer, all of Najīb Maḥfūẓ's stories revolve around two main themes which run parallel to each other; politics and women.[6] The love story in this novel is based on the following information related by Herodotus.[7]

> Rhodopis...was a Thracian by birth, and was a slave of Iadmon...Aesop, was one of her fellow-slaves...Rhodopis really arrived in Egypt under the conduct of Xantheus the Samian; she was brought there to exercise her trade, but was redeemed for a vast sum by Charuxus...brother of Sappho the poetess.

> After thus obtaining her freedom, she remained in Egypt, and as she was very beautiful, amassed great wealth, for a person of her condition; not, however, enough to enable her to erect such a work as this pyramid...[8]

Sappho, of course, refers to her as Doricha,[9] which was her real name. Rhodopis, which means the rosy-cheeked, was merely an epithet. She was confounded with Nitocros "owing ... to her also having been called "the rosy-cheeked" like the Egyptian Queen, who is described by Eusebius (from Manetho) as "flaxen haired with rosy cheeks."[10]

So much for Rādūbīs' identity. But we know something else connected with her:

> Aelian's story of Psammetichus being the king into whose lap the eagle dropped the sandal of Rhodopis, and of her marriage with him...shows that he mistook the princess Neitakri of the 29th Dynasty, the wife of Psammetichus III, for the ancient Nitocris (Neitakri)...Strabo, from whom Aelian borrows it, does not mention the name of the king, but says that the pyramid was erected to the memory of 'Doricha, as she is called by Sappho, whom others name Rhodope'...Diodorus...says 'some think the pyramid was erected as a tomb for Rhodopis by certain monarchs who had loved her'...[11]

Obviously the material here offered the novelist is rich and enticing. In the story Najīb Maḥfūẓ constructed out of it, the young king Merenraʿ, only recently ascended to the throne, shares the monarchy with Nītūqrīs, his wife and sister. He is soon engulfed in a fierce conflict with the clergy owing to his desire to revoke their privileges and satisfy the needs of his treasury. While he is sitting by the pool in the palace garden an eagle drops a golden sandal in the king's lap. Ṭāhū, the commander of the royal guard, immediately recognizes the sandal as belonging to Rādūbīs, with whom he is very much in love. The king is visibly delighted and decides to seek her acquaintance.

The love affair which develops between the king and Rādūbīs and the king's struggle with the clergy, combine to bring about his downfall. On the face of it the combination is very simple. The clergy for all their power are not at all immune to the king's wrath. But his infatuation with the well-known singer and the vast sums of money he is spending on her, cause resentment among the people. Thus, the clergy have a powerful argument which gains them the people's sympathy.

It is reported that in 1957 the author disclosed that in this novel he had alluded in fact to the love affair of the then young King Fārūq with a certain dancing girl.[12] Thereafter, this became the main point of the novel in the eyes of several Egyptian critics.[13] In the final analysis, however, it is hard to see Najīb Maḥfūẓ as a revolutionary writer or to read any of his novels as a call to revolution. *Rādūbīs* is certainly a deeper novel than *ʿAbath al-aqdār*. The plot is much more intricate and does not lend itself to an over-simplified interpretation in the light of a supposedly obvious theme. What lends it depth is the fact that the world of Najīb Maḥfūẓ is permeated with mystery and subject to the dictates of inscrutable fate. Thus, in *Rādūbīs* we are basically in the same world as in *ʿAbath al-aqdār*. Already in the first chapter, we see Rādūbīs confronted by a frightfully ugly old woman "who claims to know that which is hidden." Later, when Rādūbīs returns to her palace on the island of Bīja [14] and goes down to her pool to relax, a "formidable eagle" swoops down, steals one of her sandals, and disappears. That night, before she learns where the eagle has taken her sandal,

> her heart was beating hard, her soul was burning in a mysterious flame, and her imagination strayed in strange valleys... could it be that what is in her is a touch of magic brought upon her by that cursed sorceress? O yes, what has befallen her

> is clearly magic, and if it be not a sorceress' magic, then clearly it is the magic of the fates who dominate all destinies.

So Fate is at work again, and surely it is a mark of distinction for any human being to notice it. For few are endowed with the power to discern the special attention given them by Fate. We may wonder what it was that made Rādūbīs so perceptive? The answer is not far to seek. The one qualification for communicating with Fate -- that of being a native Egyptian -- is not what we should expect, knowing the historical antecedents of Rādūbīs, but we soon discover that the writer had Egyptianized the Greek Rādūbīs. In the novel her hair is black, not blond and her eyes have typically Egyptian beauty for they are deep black and large (*daʿjāwain*). After Pharaoh's first visit to her castle she reviews her life:

> She was a beautiful peasant girl. And there was a sweet voiced sailor [who]...invited her to his boat and she followed him... Suddenly the sailor disappeared from her life...A mature man with a long beard and a weak heart gathered her. She had a good life and on his death she became rich... People were attracted to her...and thus she became Rādūbīs.

When the king comes to Rādūbīs he discovers that she is not a mere singing girl, but a person worthy of his true and only love. He also finds that she is no Cinderella waiting anxiously to be "incoro-rated" into the royal household.[15] He accepts these facts and thus allows the little peasant girl to be on a par with Pharaoh.

Up to this point there is nothing in the story to give the reader cause to resent this relationship between Pharaoh and Rādūbīs. But the stage is set for the coming tragedy, in which the king is murdered and Rādūbīs takes her own life. It is important, however, to know precisely why this must be so, because the fall of a tragic hero is not related to his own personal guilt or innocence. He has to fall, because this is the only way in which he can be isolated from his society, and if there is any guilt in him it is only "in the sense that he is a member of a guilty society."[16] What should concern us here about this romance is to understand in what sense its incongruity with the surrounding society had become so acute that death becomes inevitable.

We know that the conflict between the king and the clergy began before he became aware of Rādūbīs's existence, and the conspiracy against the king was well under way when the Nile festivals were held. In the "White Palace" of Bīja,[17] the matter was amply discussed by the cream of Egyptian society. Feelings were very much in favor of the king's scheme, and the consensus of opinion was that the clergy -- *Kahana* --[18] "have come to own a third of the cultivated land, and their influence had extended into the regions and spread over the people, and there are, no doubt, better uses for this money than spending it on the temples." It was also realized that since the king had allowed his guard to be substantially reduced the clergy dared to challenge his authority openly. All this is historically true. The story continues to relate that while this great political issue was being fought in the highest councils of state, the affair with Rādūbīs was taking place.

The king was no doubt too young and too inexperienced for the struggle he had undertaken. But the cause of his defeat lies elsewhere. He planned to raise an army and suppress the resistance of the clergy. His stratagems were not less subtle than those of his enemies. But he was betrayed by a man he had trusted most -- Ṭāhū, the commander of his guard, who could not forget his own love for Rādūbīs. The romance was therefore at the root of the king's defeat but in a much subtler way than suggested.

The first manifestation of victory over the king was the people's demonstration in favor of the clergy, and their assault on the king's palace. But as Ṭāhū knew full well the direct cause of the king's defeat was his own betrayal. The people can always be manipulated by the winner as they were now by the clergy, but they cannot be the arbiters in such a struggle.

This brings us to the core of the drama of the hero's inevitable fall. When the mob assaulted the palace the king ordered his troops to withdraw, and he remained alone opposite the gate. As they crashed through the gate the mob were taken aback at the sight of Pharaoh standing there alone wearing on his head Egypt's double crown.

> The feet of those who were at the head became nailed to the ground. They spread their arms to stop the flooding current gushing behind them, and shouted at the crowd:
>
> - Take it easy...Take it easy.
>
> A faint hope entered the chief chamberlain's heart when he saw bewilderment overcome the leaders of the rebels, paralyzing their limbs and turning their look into a perplexed gaze. His fainting heart expected a miracle to take the place of his dark fears. But there were among the rebels artful men, apprehensive of that for which he hoped, and they feared lest their success should turn into a defeat and their cause be lost forever. So a hand was stretched to a bow, and an arrow placed at its center, and it was aimed at Pharaoh, and let go...

This description, in the chapter entitled "The People's Arrow," is so explicit as to make us suspect that we should read the title as an ironic comment.

The king's decision to expose himself alone to the mob was the only way he could accept of fighting for his cause to the very end. Before doing so he took leave of his parents, whose statues were standing in the hall, saying that he had embarrassed them by his way of life, but that they would certainly not be embarrassed by the way he was going to die. He believed that his death would be honorable. He then went to see his wife-and-sister and asked her forgiveness. He could not explain his behavior in the past few months, and said:

> ...a strange madness possessed me. I cannot, even at this very moment, say that I am sorry. Oh, what a grief that the mind can only acquaint us with our folly and triviality, but it seems to me that it is not capable of redressing them.

The proud king, once so arrogant and confident, has come to realize that he was driven by something stronger than himself. He calls it madness. This was not a recent discovery, for on the first night he had met Rādūbīs he said to her: "Rādūbīs! Sometimes I can read my destiny. From now on madness will be my motto."

What is the nature of this madness? Certainly not his falling in love with the young Egyptian woman who is beautiful and clever, and has truly dedicated herself to Pharaoh after undergoing a special abolution in the temple of the goddess Sūtīs.[19] Nor does the king's madness consist in his desire to curb the power of the clergy. When this madness first came over him, it was manifested in terms of his concept of himself in society. He was too frank, too honest, too direct for society. This trait of his personality was noticeable before he ever set eye on Rādūbīs. In fact, when he came to see Rādūbīs for the first time, her maid, without knowing who he was, noticed that he showed signs of madness. We notice these signs even earlier, in his rejection of such values as the inherited wisdom of the dynasty, self-restraint, and forbearance. He was confident that he knew what he wanted and what he should do. To Rādūbīs he said that it was not his habit to resist an impulse, and to his wife-and-sister he admitted that a man is often a target of tyrannical passions and may at times fall victim to them. Both in his private affairs and in affairs of state, his impatience, his abrupt reactions, his frank and direct approach, his unbending will, brought him into conflict with society irrespective of the actual political issue. Even the king's advisers, his staunch supporters in the conflict with the clergy, began, as the situation became more complicated, to think that the king was subject to some magic spell, for which Rādūbīs was blamed. This was of course a convenient way of abandoning the king. The chief Chamberlain found it too hard to cope with the growing resentment of the clergy. The chief of the Royal Guard had less compunction for he had already betrayed the king in his own heart. They could therefore agree, in one of the more subtle scenes in the novel, that their troubles were due to the fact that the king was under Rādūbīs' spell.

Thus the circle closed around the "mad" king. He had become alienated in a society which, irrespective of its internal conflicts, found it impossible to make its peace with an overbearing, inflexible, idealistic individual. Najīb Maḥfūẓ, as we will have occasion to see, always refers to such behavior on the part of an individual as "madness." But it is extremely important to notice the fine distinction made by him between madness, as first understood by the afflicted person, at the beginning of the road, and madness as seen by him towards the end, when society has consolidated its resistance to him. At the beginning, madness is considered a heavenly blessing, accepted gladly, almost as a voluntary transformation and motivated by high hopes. Then towards the end, it becomes an obsession, indeed a spell, driving its helpless victim to his doom. As for society, its attitude towards the hero's madness undergoes a parallel change, from tolerance to active resentment. This dual process is interlocked. The more obvious the manifestations of madness, the greater the resentment shown by society, until the final confrontation takes place.

This theme is illustrated very clearly in a short story, entitled *Hams al-junūn* (Whisper of Madness), published in a collection of short stories under the same title.[20] Although some critics justly feel that some of his short stories served Najīb Maḥfūẓ as brief outlines for his novels,[21] this particular story is no sketch for any novel yet written by Najīb Maḥfūẓ, but rather a study of a phenomenon which was to continue to engage his interest for many years. This is the case of a person who has lost his world, lost his communication with society, except for what may be termed mere technical communication, until suddenly he awakens to life but in a peculiar state of mind. He will not abide by conventions any longer or remain indifferent to social injustice or submit to social inhibitions, but will surge forward, protesting, correcting the wrong, forcing people to yield to whatever action he deems it proper to take. He soon finds himself in great trouble, but not before society has shown a measure of forbearance, which he mistakes for acquiescence.

At the opening of the story we meet our anonymous hero in a hospital, referred to by the very significant term *khānka* which is also a *Ṣūfī* convent or monastery. We are told that he knows where he is and that he "remembers -- even now -- his life's past, just as some people do." The word for sane people used here is *ʿuqalāʾ*. The image is very clear: we are faced **with** a sane madman in a *Ṣūfī* convent, that is, with one of the *ʿuqalāʾ al-majānīn*. A story of one of them, Luqmān, may help us to appreciate the significance of the image.[22]

> In the beginning Luqmān was a man learned in the law and pious, but afterwards he ceased to perform the duties of religion. When he was asked how this change had come to pass, he replied: "The more I served God, the more service was required of me. In my despair I cried, 'O God! kings set free a slave when he grows old. Thou art the Almighty King. Set me free, for I have grown old in thy service.' I heard a voice that said: Luqmān! I set thee free'."

And "the sign of this freedom was that his reason was taken away from him," which meant that God had emancipated him from his commandments. Obviously, this emancipation need not be construed in a way that would deprive the emancipated of his own inherent virtues. It may be that what happens in such a case is that the "own-world," or *Eigenwelt*, to use the terminology of the existential analysts,[23] is emphasized to the exclusion of the "with-world," or *Mitwelt*. This may very well be what happened to the hero of *Hams al-junūn* before he was taken to the *khānka*.

This brings us back to king Merenraʿ and his tragic end. He, too, somehow lost the reality of being-in-the world, owing probably to the fact that he saw no authority, moral or otherwise, higher than himself, and consequently he allowed himself, so to speak, what God had allowed Luqmān. But instead of locking himself up in a *khānka* he continued to rule the land, trying to bring about changes not unlike those attempted by the hero of *Hams al-junūn*. This was something society was not prepared to permit, and as a result it isolated him and then destroyed him.

Najīb Maḥfūẓ's first two novels thus seem to create two lasting archetypes in his literary world. The one, the hero of *ʿAbath al-aqdār*, is an individual who is so perfectly in harmony with the social structure, that he rises to the peak of society. The other, the hero of *Rādūbīs*, is the individual who is so out of harmony with society that he had to die. By placing each of them on the throne, the one as a reward for what he is, the other only to emphasize the drama of his downfall, the writer turns these two archetypes into two symbols of value.

NOTES

1 In September 1936. See Ghālī Shukrī, *op. cit.*, p. 347.

2 Merenrēʿ in later books on Egyptology.

3 Gardiner, *op cit.*, p. 107.

4 *Ibid.*, p. 107.

5 See Wilson, *op. cit.*, pp. 98 *seq.*.

6 Ibrāhīm ʿAmir, "*Najīb Maḥfūẓ siyāsiyan*," *al-Hilāl*, February 1970, p. 27.

7 *The History of Herodutus*, ed. George Rawlison, New York, 1859, V. 2 pp. 178-181. Cf. also M.S. Khaffāja and A. Badawī, *Herūdūt yataḥaddath ʿan miṣr*, Cairo, 1966., pp. 262 *seq*., where the name is spelled Rūdūpīs.

8 Herodotus begins the story by refuting the report that Rhodopis had built the "Fourth pyramid" of Gizah. Regarding this report, see Wilson, *op. cit.*, pp. 97-98.

9 *The Love Songs of Sappho*, trans. Paul Roche, Mentor, 1966, p. 120.

10 Herodotus, *op. cit.*, p. 179, n. 2.

11 *Ibid.* Cf. also Herodotus, *The Ancient Empires of the East*, ed. A. H. Sayce, London, 1893, book 2, p. 198, n. 9, where the whole tangle is briefly explained.

12 Cf. J. Jomier, "Trois Romans de M. Naguib Mahfuz," *Mideo*, No. 4, 1957, p. 31, n.1.

13 Fāṭima Mūsā, *op. cit.*, p. 73, thinks that the novel was a warning to Fārūq that the people might rise against him. Fu'ād Dawwāra, *Ibid.*, reads the novel as a call to the people to revolt against Fārūq.

14 Pronounced Biggeh, in the vicinity of the first cataract.

15 Frye, *ibid.*, p. 44, where the Cinderella archetype is discussed.

16 Frye, *op. cit.*, p. 41. It will have been noticed that the treatment of this problem follows Frye's analysis of tragedy in the central or high mimetic sense.

17 The usual reference to Rādūbīs's castle.

18 The very term used here, and throughout the novel in reference to the clergy, is rather disrespectful. Cf. Khālid Muḥammad Khālid, *Min huna nabda'*, where the term *kahana* is used purposedly in order to discredit the clergy.

19 Najīb Maḥfūẓ writes "the god Sūtīs," but obviously he meant the

goddess Sothis who was the principal counterpart of Khnemu, the first member of the great triad of Ābu, or Elephantine, and was worshipped there with him. See Budge, *The Gods of Egypt*, V. 2, Ch. 4.

20 *Hams al-junūn* (1938). For a summary of this short story, see Akef Abadir and Roger Allen, " Nagib Mahfuz, His World of Litarature," *The Arab World*, September-October, 1970, p. 8. The comparison made there with Camus' Sisyphus seems rather forces.

21 Ghālī Shukrī, *op. cit.*, p. 291. Cf. also Dawwāra, *ibid.*, p. 14, where the information is given that the collection of *Hams al-junūn* includes 30 out of 80 short stories published in various magazines.

22 See R. Nicholson, *Studies in Islamic Mysticism*, Cambridge, 1967, pp. 6-7. The concept of *ʿUqalāʾ al-majānīn* is elaborated in a book by Ḥasan b. Muḥammad al- Naysābūrī (d.1015), part of which was translated by Paul Loosen in his *Die Weisen Narren Des Nisābūrī* (1912). The English rendering of this expression is "intelligent madman," cf. "*buhlūl*" in *Encyclopedia of Islam*, first edition. The basic idea emerging from Nisābūrī's book is that madness is a state of being different. It may be arrived at either spontaneously or by choice, when it is contrived, for a variety of reasons enumerated by the author. To most people, however, a madman is one who deviates from the customary, and behaves in a manner of which they disapprove. "And therefore the nations called [God's] messengers madmen." Cf. *ʿUqalāʾ al-majānīn*, ed. Wajīh Fāris al-Kīlānī, Cairo, 1924, p. 8, where the Qur'ānic verse is cited telling that Noah was called a madman by his people (Qur'ān, 54:9). Cf. also the Biblical verse, Hoshea, 9, 7: "the prophet is a fool, the spiritual man is mad." It seems that the issue raised here by Najīb Maḥfūẓ, not perhaps

as clearly as in later works, is that of the existential problem of truth as an object and truth as a relationship. Cf. Rollo May, "Contributions of Existential Psychotherapy," in *Existence*, ed. Rollo May, Ernest Angel, Henri F. Ellenberger, New York, 1958, pp. 25 *seq*.

23 *Ibid.*, pp. 61 *seq*.

Chapter Three

The View from Nebo

The third and last historical novel of Najīb Maḥfūẓ was written between September 1937 and April 1938. The events it describes take place under the last two sovereigns of the 17th Dynasty, and under that of the founder of the 18th. This was a very tense and dramatic period in which the Pharaohs of Thebes fought off the invading Hyksos and finally expelled them from Egypt. The novel is therefore properly named *Kifāḥ ṭayba* (The Battle of Thebes). The choice of this period for a novel clearly indicates a desire to study the reaction to adversity of the idyllic society portrayed in the previous two novels.

At the opening of the novel, around 1600 B.C., the Hyksos had already been ruling Lower Egypt for over a century, and the Pharaohs of Thebes ruled Upper Egypt and Nubia under the suzerainty of the Hyksos kings.[1] The opening scene is based on the late Egyptian story of King Apōphis and S kenenreʿ, found in a papyrus of the 13th Century B.C.[2] According to this story King Apōphis, in his capital city of Avaris, decided to demand that Pharaoh Sekenenreʿ should abandon the Hippopotamus Canal reputed to have been kept by the Thebans for ritual purposes.[3] The reason for Apōphis's demand was that "it suffereth not sleep to come to me."[4]

In the novel we are told of two additional demands made by the Hyksos King, namely, to build a temple in Thebes for the god Sēth, worshipped by the Hyksos,[5] and to refrain from wearing the "white crown of Egypt," which was the crown of Upper Egypt.[6] All three demands are immediately rejected by Sekenenreʿ,[7] after duly consulting members of his family and his councillors. All of which is fairly reasonable. The additional two demands bring up issues which are well rooted in the history of the period and they make the war which ensued more plausible to the modern reader. The king's bold reaction, though hardly compatible with the papyrus story, can be accepted owing to the fact that the war started probably under Sekenenreʿ, whose mummified corpse, twisted as though in mortal agony, shows terrible wounds on head and neck.[8] There is no proof that he died in battle with the Hyksos, but that supposition has been made before.

The first stage of the war as described in the novel was catastrophic to the Egyptians. The king was killed on the battlefield, the royal family fled to Nubia, and the Hyksos occupied the whole of Egypt. All this is highly doubtful historically, for the furthest point the Hyksos ever reached was probably the town of Gebelen, near Thebes, where the name of a Hyksos king has been found on a temple wall.[9] The general consensus, however, is that the Hyksos never reached further than a point about midway between Memphis and Thebes. By preferring this development, the writer got himself into obvious difficulties, since he had to invent some way of liberating the whole of Egypt from the Hyksos. The plan he invented was that after a decade in exile the Egyptian royal family smuggled great numbers of trusted Thebans to Nubia, who were then organized into an army strong enough to invade Egypt and defeat the Hyksos. Apart from the great difficulties involved in such a plan, the story of the war itself becomes rather tedious, for it is a long way from Nubia to the Delta.

It should be remarked that Egyptian critics are fully aware of the problem created by this plot. Fāṭima Mūsā, for instance, says[10] that in this novel the writer shows no interest in examining closely the historical framework, "his object being patriotic and contemporary."

She unhesitatingly identifies the Hyksos with the British who were ruling Egypt at the time the novel was written. Such an interpretation can indeed be supported by certain expressions in the novel which have an explicit contemporary sound. For example: "and so it had been ordained that the whole of our people should suffer these agonies together," or: "I have vowed before God and before my people that I shall liberate the whole of Egypt." Such expressions might have lost some of their poignancy had the war of Egypt's liberation started in Thebes rather than at the Nubian border, that is the present-day Sudanese border. But still, what a price to pay for merely adding a few sentences which in themselves contribute only marginally to the main story!

Nabīl Rāghib [11] shows that the writer was so intent on emphasizing the virtues of the Egyptian people that the characters he describes in the novel remain stiff -- *namaṭīya* -- throughout. They turn into symbols of whatever virtues Najīb Maḥfūẓ wished to stress in the Egyptian people. Love of liberty is certainly one of these virtues, but there are others, such as patience, faithfulness, honesty, respect for tradition, obedience to precepts which convey the accumulated wisdom of a people or a culture. In this context Nabīl Rāghib makes an interesting observation: [12]

> Najīb Maḥfūẓ has given us the shining aspect of the picture without...showing the human aspect as a whole...The source of the [author's] idealism here was his hankering after the grandeur of the past which is exemplified by the Pharaohs, while the reality in which this novel was written was so depressing.

The question raised by such an analysis is whether the symbols and images created by the writer in this novel are indeed romantic or idealistic in nature? Is it their purpose to actually offer an escape from a dark present by dreaming of a supposedly bright past? It has already been suggested that Najīb Maḥfūẓ's writing lends itself to superficial analogy — largely because of the unmistakable impression that he means to convey a message of some immediate import. Yet, too hasty analogies are apt to be misleading (which is not the worst penalty) and miss the deeper meaning of his writing (which is the greater loss). Nabīl Rāghib certainly helps to understand the novel by drawing attention to the symbolic nature of its characters and by suggesting that they reflect a vision which is somehow related to the present. But we still have to understand the symbols and their relevance. This will clearly be difficult so long as the plot remains unexplained.

Kenneth Burke makes the following comment, which may prove helpful to our analysis:[13]

> The work of every writer contains a set of implicit equations. He uses 'associational clusters'. And you may, by examining his work, find 'what goes with what' in these clusters -- what kind of acts and images and personalities and situations go with his notions of heroism, villainy, consolation, despair etc...There is no need to 'supply' motives. The interrelationship /of all these equations/ themselves are motives. For they are his situation; and situation is but another word for motive. The motivation out of which he writes is synonymous with the structural way in which he puts events and values together when he writes.

The main event in *Kifāh ṭayba* is the long march of the Egyptian army from the southern border to the Delta of the Nile. This is preceded by the first battle in which the Egyptian army is defeated. The war itself lasted 12 years, 10 of which, after the Egyptian defeat, were spent in preparations for their next assault. In this long period, the Egyptians had three kings: Sikenenraʿ, who was killed in the first battle; Kāmīs -- the historical Kamose -- who organized the army in Nubia and liberated Egypt up to Umbūs — or Ombos — just south of Thebes,[14] where he was killed on the battle-field; and his successor, Aḥmas — the historical ʿAḥmose I, "whom later ages consequently honored as the founder of the Eighteenth Dynasty"[15] — who continued to lead the Egyptian army until the Hyksos were completely out of Egypt. This description, which, except for the Nubian phase, is truly historical, seemed to Najīb Maḥfūẓ too disjointed, apparently, as if lacking the coherence needed to supply a proper symbolic significance. Then, as if to correct this fault, he creates the image of the old and "sacred mother" Tūtīshīrī — the historical Tetisheri.[16] She is described as Sikananraʿ's mother, which is probably true historically, but as a person we do not really learn anything about her. She is mentioned no less than 40 times, but just as a deity would be mentioned. She figures in the story to the very end over a period of 12 years until, overwhelmed by the excitement of victory, she has a premonition that at her age "the fulfilment of hope hastens the end." But her death is not reported.

It is quite clear that this semi-goddess does not represent the immediate natural mother. The real mother fares ill with Najīb Maḥfūẓ up to this point. We saw already in *ʿAbath al-aqdār* the mother whose greatest contribution to her son's success was her absence from his life.

In *Kifāḥ ṭayba* we meet again the natural mother, in the person of Ibana, the widow of Sikanaraʿ's devoted general Bībī, and mother of the future Pharaoh's namesake Aḥmas. This was a historical family. Baba -- Bībī -- did indeed serve under Sekenenreʿ, though he did not fall in the same battle as described in the novel, but continued to serve under the succeeding Pharaoh until he was eventually replaced by his son ʿAḥmose, son of Abana -- Ibānā.[17] This lady must have been a remarkable woman if her son was known by association with her name rather than with that of his father, who evidently lacked no reputation of his own. It is interesting, therefore, to see her in the novel.

When the royal family flees from Ṭayba, and Bībī falls in battle with his troops, Ibānā leaves her palace and, like most of the Egyptian nobility, mingles with the common people to avoid being noticed by the victorious Hyksos. Several years later, the young heir apparent Aḥmas, who enters Ṭayba disguised as a merchant, happens to see Ibānā, not knowing who she is, in a court of law, where she is brought to trial for refusing to join the harem of an officer of the Hyksos army. Aḥmas manages to release her paying the fine ordered by the judge, and thus becomes a very close friend of the woman and her son, his future comrade-in-arms. Later, when the Egyptian troops lay siege to Ṭayba, the Hyksos scandalize them by tying the women of Ṭayba naked to the walls of the city in order to prevent the Egyptian assault. The king Ahmas cannot bring himself to order the assault, but while he is standing there hesitating, Aḥmas the son of Ibānā comes urging him to launch the attack. "My heart tells me that my mother Ibānā is among those wretched women. And if my feelings are right I do not doubt that she is praying to God now to make your love for Ṭayba greater than your compassion for her." Once the attack begins Ibānā's son, who is commanding the fleet, will not be gratified until he learns that his ships have come close to the walls of Ṭayba and are participating in shooting arrows onto them. Inside the city, after a fierce battle, the dead women are brought together to be identified and buried. When the King goes to pay them his respects, he hears the commander Aḥmas crying with a trembling voice: "Mother"!

Thus Ibānā is killed by Aḥmas. The historical fact that both Pharaoh and his lieutenant had the same name is used here by Najīb Maḥfūẓ to make Aḥmas the son of Ibānā the *alter ego* of Aḥmas the Pharaoh. The fictional function of the former seems to be merely to turn the story of the killing of Ibānā into the drama of sacrificing the mother whose honor was violated.[18] However this was not the only death in which the King had a personal interest. Two deaths occurring in or near Ṭayba, preceded Ibānā's death, and were directly connected with her fortunes. The first was the death of the Hyksos officer Rakh, who had attempted to drag Ibānā by force into his wagon and take her to his harem. Although he failed in this attempt the author nevertheless felt that the Hyksos who meant to violate her honor must be made to pay with his life. And so, within a few days, as Aḥmas is sailing on the Nile, we see Rakh challenging him to a fight. In this fight Rakh is killed.

The second feat is that of the Hyksos dignitary who ruled Upper Egypt from Ṭayba. This ruler installs himself in the palace formerly belonging to Bībī and Ibānā and makes his home there. He also keeps in his service Bībī's old gardner, Shārif. Obviously this name is symbolic, and is unmistakably meant to bring in the concept of *sharaf* (honor).[19] This term, as used at present in Egypt, has almost the same meaning as the term *ʿirḍ* in classical times.[20] We are faced therefore with a situation which is clearly meant to symbolize the status *dhull*, which "*ipso facto* taints the *ʿirḍ* ,"[21] and constitutes the highest manifestation of a humiliating impotence in face of an enemy. Here the status of *dhull* is manifest in two respects. First, the home of the Egyptian nobleman is being humiliated by the fact of its becoming the dwelling place of the enemy, while its owners are seeking protection elsewhere.[22] Secondly, it transpires that the Hyksos ruler, named Khinzir,[23] is the very man who dealt the deathly blow to Sikananraʿ, Aḥmas's grandfather. Here again is a direct challenge to honor, since in such a case the requirement of *ʿirḍ* or *sharaf*, is that the next of kin fulfill the duty of *thaʾr*, that is, of taking blood revenge. And indeed, as Aḥmas approached Ṭayba at the head of his army, he cannot overlook this duty, and he challenges Khinzir to a fight.

However, even though the two men who symbolized the humiliation of Egypt are dead, the shameful stain has not yet been removed. The object of this humiliation has to be purified as well and nothing purifies more than death. So Ibānā, who symbolizes the humiliation of Egypt, must also die. The circumstances of her death are so contrived as to make it also fall within the concept of *sharaf* and its obligations. Exposed naked from the city walls her people are thrice put to shame. She has been driven out of her home, she has become a prisoner and her nakedness has been exposed.[24] Only by death can honor now be redeemed.

The hero of this novel is Aḥmas who, like all heroes in romance, should be something of a revolutionary, something of a nihilist and, eventually he should expand into a psychological archetype.[25] Yet, up to now only his conformist, or conservative traits have been outlined. But earlier in the story Ṭayba has become an arena of conflicting emotions. While he was discovering the humiliation of his people, confronted with the duties of revenge which he understood so well, he also fell in love with Amanarīdis, the daughter of Abūfīs -- Apōphis. This love story has in it some of the elements met with in *Rādūbīs*. Aḥmas's own wife-and-sister is a replica of Maranraʿ's wife-and-sister, both of whom represent family tradition, political continuity and the social values of their societies. Amanarīdis and Rādūbīs, on the other hand, constitute some sort of challenge to all this, both in their personalities which are much more vital and in the very dilemma with which they confront their royal lovers. Yet in spite of this similarity there is a fundamental difference between the two love stories. Rādūbīs was Egyptian, a subject of Pharaoh, and the dilemma created by her relations with him was entirely indigenous. The Hyksos princess, however, is fully and frankly a foreign challenge to Egyptian values, a factor previously missing in the in the novels of Najīb Maḥfūẓ, though not in his short stories.

That *Kifāḥ ṭayba* is not free from the problem of cultural confrontation can be sensed in the first meeting between Abūfīs' emissary and King Sakananraʿ. But in the relations between Aḥmas and Amanarīdis this problem becomes personalized, endowing it with a subjective intensity. She is fair of complexion, her hair golden, her eyes blue, the racial distinctions of the foreigner stressed at the beginning of the novel. The Egyptians are dark, "as if derived from the marrow of their land," the Hyksos are white "as if the sun had never expurgated them." The Hyksos are depicted as shepherds,[26] with long and dirty beards, whereas the Egyptians are peasants[27] and clean shaven.

It should be pointed out that these racial distinctions need not be taken to reflect the physiognomical differences between native Egyptians and Western non-Egyptians. When Najīb Maḥfūẓ emphasizes these distinctions he has in mind people of Asiatic origin, generally referred to as Turks, who are always depicted as foreign, harsh and haughty. In the short-story collection, *Hams al-junūn*, we find the story *Yaqẓat al-mūmīyā'* (The Awakening of the Mummy) where the confrontation is made between an ancient mummified nobleman who has come back to life, and a present-day (1938) Egyptian Pasha in whose grounds the grave of the mummy has been uncovered. The Pasha is of Turkish descent, his eyes are blue and he despises the Egyptian peasant. The mummy who happens to come to life while the Pasha and his associates are inspecting the newly found grave, is none other than "Hūr, one of the grandees of the Eighteenth Dynasty," indeed the same person whom we meet frequently in *Kifāḥ ṭayba* as one of Aḥmas's lieutenants. This ancient Egyptian nobleman has the same features as those of a poor peasant whom the Pasha humiliated only a short while earlier, and when he turns his eyes to the Pasha he recognizes him immediately as one of his own slaves. He begins to belabor him there and then for all the wrongs the Pasha's race had done to Egypt, he reminds the Pasha that his white skin is the mark of slavery, and then, quite in line with the spirit of the story in *Kifāh ṭayba*, he goes on to express his astonishment that *dhull* and *ʿizza*[28] have changed places in Egypt. He continues in this vein, until the Pasha dies of fear.

It seems then, that if there is a transposition of interracial or intercultural confrontation from recent times to the ancient past, it is that of the Egyptian versus the Turk and not that of the Egyptian versus the English. It may, of course, be argued that the Turk stands here exponentially for the English. But this would be impossible to support by evidence derived from the novel itself. The main problem raised by the novel is not so much political independence as it is cultural integrity. This becomes clear in the romance we have just begun to consider.

The first meeting between Aḥmas and the Hyksos princess takes place when her attention is drawn to a dwarf[29] walking on Aḥmas's ship. This dwarf has a remarkable role in the story. Occasionally one is tempted to see him as the "nature spirit" which eludes "the moral antithesis of heroism and villainy," and represents "partly the moral neutrality of the intermediate world of nature and partly a world of mystery which is glimpsed but never seen, and which retreats when approached."[30] If one hesitates to see the dwarf as a "spirit of nature" in this sense it is because the dwarf, for all we know, may have taken sides having in fact run away from the princess, to whom he was given as a present.[31]

The point is that although the novel is written in the form of a romance, its characterization lacks the "dialectic structure, which means that subtlety and complexity are not much favored."[32] When Ahmas first meets Amanarīdis and is overwhelmed by her foreign beauty he remembers his wife Nīfartārī -- the historical Nofreteroi -- and her own beauty, her bronze-brown face and enchanting black eyes, and whispers: "What two incompatible beautiful faces." Incompatible indeed, but not for him. For when Amanarīdis becomes his prisoner after the liberation of Ṭayba, he wishes her to become his wife. What prevents him from taking her to his harem is the fact that she feels humiliated because when she was taken prisoner her nakedness was exposed. She will not permit herself to be further humiliated by joining her enemy's harem.[33] Towards the end of the war, however, when the Hyksos, making their last stand at the capital, offer to evacuate in return fo all their captured brethren, Aḥmas is ready to ask Abūfīs for his daughter's hand. It is up to Amanarīdis to remind his again that her father, having been humiliated by defeat, would never give his daughter to an enemy. However, there is a marked difference now. As long as she considered herself a prisoner she would not even admit her love for Aḥmas. But once she realizes that her father is prepared to leave Egypt, and she can have her liberty, she becomes as distressed as Aḥmas at the conventions which make it impossible for them to marry. Unlike the story of Rādūbīs, the tragedy here does not consist in the hero's death, or in his being rejected by his society, but in his surrender to the dictates of convention and his permitting his beloved to join her people. Thus when the Hyksos leave Egypt a feeling of fulfilment fills the heart of every Egyptian but Aḥmas's.

In order to fully realize the deep significance of the closing scene, it should be remembered that this is supposed to be the story of the great liberator of Egypt, the historical 'Aḥmose the First, founder of the 18th Dynasty. What might have been a very outgoing romance, "a wish-fulfilment dream,"[34] with the quest successfully ended, and the hero in a state of exaltation, turns out to be something different. We have indeed a protagonist -- in the persons of three Pharaohs --[35] we have an antagonist in King Apōphīs. There is no doubt that the hero is analogous to the mythical Messiah, and the enemy to a demonic power. We have the hero disguised in a merchant's garb, and then standing forth in the cloak of the prince. The theme of the "dragon killing" is also there. That the enemy is sterile we are reminded time and again. The hero on the other hand symbolizes fertility, as indicated by the fact that after the liberation of Ṭayba, Aḥmas is informed that a son has been born to him. In short, there are in the novel all the elements which could have culminated in a very heroic *finale*, but in fact, we are led to an anticlimax on reaching the actual end which is written in such a low-key. To be left with a frustrated hero, on the day of his greatest victory is not indeed what might have been expected. Evidently *Kifāḥ ṭayba* is not the heroic story it has been assumed to be by some readers.

Aḥmas' feeling of frustration stems from various factors, chief among them his having to give up his beloved. This was not the case of Maranraʿ who in his madness would have made himself abhorrent to his society. Aḥmas however yielded to the dictates of responsibility. A second source of his frustration is that Amanarīdis remains alive, and together with her people is going to face "another day beyond the unknown desert." By thus going away to create a new life for herself beyond the desert, the hope that the relations between the two people might one day rest on a new foundation is forever lost.

Mention has been made earlier of the old sacred mother Tūtīshīrī and her spiritual supremacy. Altogether, the archetype of the Great Mother, or Goddess, is quite familiar in Egyptian Mythology.[36] In this particular case the concept has some historical foundation as well.[37] But Tūtīshīrī of *Kifāḥ ṭayba* is inflated to a complete archetype image, or a symbol,[38] almost to the point of exaggeration. A twofold question arises from this: what is the need for such an archetypal image in the novel, and why should it be a female image rather than a male one?

The novel does not pretent to have this symbol manifest itself spontaneously, for it is indeed a contrived symbol. Yet it need not be seen as an allegory, which would be "an intentional transcription or transformation of a known thing." [39] It should be considered rather as a "dead" symbol. This image of the Great Mother, consciously contrived, will never be met with again in the writings of Najīb Maḥfūẓ because, it may be assumed, it probably does not evoke in the Egyptian reader what the writer meant it to evoke, namely: an image of the guardian of tradition and a symbol of moral authority.

But the image of Tūtīshīrī could not in any case have been replaced by that of a male symbol in this novel. The problem of symmetry certainly had a great deal to do with it. Amanarīdis is the symbol of the positive and the beautiful in the enemy's culture. She had therefore to be countered by a female figure. Yet, she could hardly be matched by Nīfertārī, Aḥmas's wife, or by Ḥūtbī — Hottepi — his mother. In the world created by Najīb Maḥfūẓ no wife has the power to curb her husband's impulses, and no natural mother has any tangible influence over her son. In the circumstances of the royal family of Ṭayba, Tūtīshīrī was the only possible force to counter that of Amanarīdis. With her tremendous authority, which encompassed all matters of politics, morals, traditional values and religion, she dominated the young Pharaoh completely. What is more important, she set the standard of behavior for the King.

Aḥmas was different from the rest of his family and his people. He looked further and aspired to higher goals. At the same time, he realized that his aspirations were futile because they were beyond what his society could possibly accept. He therefore gave up. He heard the whisper of madness, but resisted its magic force, released Amanarīdis and relinquished his dreams. The next day he ascended a nearby hill overlooking the gates of Hawārīs — Avaris — to watch the departure of the Hyksos. Although a great spectacle for the joyous

Egyptians, for Ahmas it was a heart-breaking sight. He could not restrain his tears as he saw the royal party coming out through the gate. He kept asking himself if she was there thinking of him as he was thinking of her. "He followed the cavalcade with his eyes...and he kept looking at them until they disappeared beyond the horizon and were enveloped by the invisible."

The victorious Pharaoh, the great liberator of Egypt, shed tears at the sight of his enemy's departure into a future in which he can have no share. Instead of a victor we see a man left behind, as one obeying the decree: "thou shalt not go over."

It has been stressed earlier that there is no need to read political relevance into this story and there is no need therefore to impute to the writer any regrets over the prospect of the British evacuating Egypt. The situation of Egypt at the time the novel was written warranted neither hopes nor regrets at the possibility of such an occurrence. The novel should be read in an entirely different context which is the same for all historical novels of Najīb Maḥfūẓ, namely, that of the relationship between the individual and his society.

NOTES

1 Wilson, *op. cit.*, pp. 158 *seq.* Gardiner, *op. cit.*, pp. 165 *seq*

2 The complete text is printed in Erman, *op. cit.*, pp. 165-167.

3 Cf. Budge, *Gods of the Egyptians*, V. 2, p. 559.

4 Erman, p. 166.

5 As to the identity of the god Sēth worshipped by the Hyksos see Gardiner, *op. cit.*, pp. 164-65, where it is stated that he "was certainly more Asiatic in character than the native original." Najīb Maḥfūẓ gives the Egyptian name of this god and not the name Sutekh, used by the Hyksos.

6 The crown of Upper Egypt was white, that of Lower Egypt red. When borne together they formed the Double Crown of United Egypt, and symbolized that unity.

7 The Arabic spelling.

8 Gardiner, p. 164.

9 Gardiner, p. 168.

10 *Op. cit.,* p. 73. The same view is expressed by Dawwāra, *op. cit.,* p. 105.

11 *Qaḍiyat al-shakl al-fannī ʿind najīb maḥfūẓ*, Cairo, n.d., pp. 52-53.

12 *Op. cit.,* p. 53.

13 *The Philosophy of Literary Form,* New York, 1957, p. 18.

14 In the novel it is placed, probably by mistake, north of Thebes.

15 Gardiner, p. 168.

16 *Ibid.,* pp. 172-73.

17 *Ibid.,* p. 168.

18 I.e., by being exposed on the city walls. Regarding the question of honor here involved cf. *infra,* ns. 20, 24.

19 The name Shārif is *nomen agentis* of the radical *sh-r-f*, the *nomen verbi* of which is *sharaf* that is honor.

20 Cf. Bichr Fares, *L'Honneur chez les arabes avant l'Islam,* Paris, 1932, pp. 32-35; and also the article *ʿIrḍ* by B. Lewis in the *Encyclopaedia of Islam,* supplement, 1938.

21 Fares, *op. cit.,* p. 113.

22 *Ibid.,* p. 69.

23 That this name is designed to evoke its homonym *Khinzīr,* which means swine or pig, seems obvious.

24 On the humiliation caused by the exposure of a woman's nakedness and the woman captive in relation to *ʿirḍ* cf. Fares, *op. cit.,* pp. 75-81.

25 This is following Frye, *op. cit.,* p. 304, where the differences between a novel and a romance are discussed.

26 The problem of the Hyksos' identity, and the fallacy of their racial homogenity are discussed by Gardiner, pp. 156-57.

27 The word *fallāḥ* is undoubtedly used here because of its contemporary connotation. Since 1919 progressive minded men in Egypt have consistently tried to purge this word of its traditional derogatory connotation and turn it into a dignifying epithet.

28 *'Izza* or power "was not merely an element of honor but the very germ of honor, at once its infrastructure and its guarantee." Fares, *op. cit.*, p. 114. As for the question of the racial marks of the Turks and their significance for Najīb Maḥfūẓ, cf. Ch. 5 *infra*.

29 Dwarfs were considered in the 15th century B.C. objects of great interest.Cf. Budge, *A Short History*, pp. 44, 48.

30 Frye, *op. cit.*, p. 196.

31 Commenting on the behavior of the dwarf in Spemser's *The Faerie Queen*, Frye says that he "represents, in the dream world of romance, the shrunken and wizened form of practical waking reality," *ibid.*, p.197. Perhaps this would be the correct interpretation of the behavior of the dwarf in this case, too.

32 *Ibid.*, p. 195.

33 Note the similarity of the situation with that of Layla, the daughter of the tribe of Lakīz, in face of the King of Persia, Fares, *op. cit.*, p. 75.

34 Frye, *op. cit.*, pp. 186 *seq*.

35 The following description in Frye, *ibid,*, p. 187, has a direct bearing on our case: "Thus the romance expresses more clearly the passage from struggle through a point of ritual to a recognition scene...A threefold structure is repeated in many features of romance -- in the frequency, for instance, with which

the successful hero is a third son, or the third to undertake the quest, or successful in the third attempt."

36 Erich Neumann, *The Great Mother*, New York, 1955, p. 22 and *passim*.

37 Gardiner, p. 172.

38 Cf. Neumann, *op. cit.*, p. 7: "The symbols are the manifest visibility of the archetype, corresponding to its latent invisibility."

39 Jung, *op. cit.*, Definitions: Symbol, p. 601 *seq*.

Epilogue to Part One

At this point several questions can be asked. As mentioned earlier, after his three historical novels, Najīb Maḥfūẓ's desire to write any more such novels suddenly died,[1] and some 37 novels which he had planned remained unwritten. This he tells us [2] was the second of three halts — *tawaqqufāt* -- in his intellectual development. The first resulted in his forsaking the study of philosophy for the sake of writing literature. The second resulted in abandoning the historical novel. The third happened after the revolution of 1952, "for when the old society vanished all desire vanished in me to criticize it, and I believed then that I was finished as a writer."

This description of each halt indicates the passion which, as the writer believed, motivated the preceding activity. The first was a passion for philosphy, the second for romantic historical writing, and the third passion was for criticizing the "old society."

For the moment we are concerned with the second cessation of activity and the passion preceding it, and in this context it would be well to recall the discussion referred to at the beginning of this study in which Najīb Maḥfūẓ defined the roles of the historian and the artist. The artist, he maintained, is interested in historical events only in so far as they affect the people he is writing about. In themselves they have only secondary significance for him. Yet when we look back on his historical novels the impression is clear that the roles of people and events are quite the reverse of this. Characterization is rather flat, and individuality is frequently absorbed into the symbolic image. On the other hand, historical events dominate the novels with the force of divine decree; besides making man look insignificant they deprive him of all influence over the course of his own life.

The conscious and purposeful use of history by the novelist always causes the critic an obvious uneasiness.When the novelist himself turns into a critic this uneasiness often develops into an apologia. The relationship of people and events seems to be at the heart of the difficulty. Discussing "The character of the period," [3] Tolstoy made the following remark:

> An historian and an artist describing an historical epoch have two quite different tasks before them...
>
> For the historian considering the achievement of a certain aim, there are heroes; for the artist treating of man's relation to all sides of life, there cannot and should not be heroes, but there should be men...
>
> In the description of the events themselves the difference is still sharper and more essential.
>
> The historian has to deal with the results of an event, the artist with the fact of the event.

Little wonder that these hard and fast definitions have not settled the arguments which continued to rage about the role and even the legitimacy of the historical novel. The question how far the historical truth is at all relevant to the historical novel seems to be as unresolved as ever. Alexander Dumas is known to have said: "History is merely the nail on which I hang my portraits." [4] Yet a modern critic would probably classify him, with other "writers /who/ are not hampered...by the facts of history," as "historical romancers," and "artists of the boudoir, not the battlefield."[5] For such a critic, a good historical novelist would be one who "brings history to people who might otherwise not be exposed to it." He should certainly be "a story-teller if he is to reach that audience," but at the same time "he ought to be acutely conscious of his role as purveyor of knowledge, as well as information, because it is in this respect that he joins hands with the historian in performing a vital function in our society."[6] Lion Feuchtwanger, on the other hand, considers Dumas as the most famous representative of that literary genre which is "part literary art, and part vulgar scribbling,"[7] adding that he has nothing whatsoever against this sort of story-telling, although "critics and snobs nowadays look down upon this art."[8] What worries him is that this sort of writing, which he himself reads at times "not without pleasure," contains some poison for the masses. Because "most people...shrink from the effort of seriously reflecting about the course of historical events," the conception "of the vulgar historical novel therefore aids and abets the spiritual laziness of the masses and confirms them in their tendency towards escapism."[9]

This seems to be a sort of criticism which can equally be levelled against any other literary genre. In any case, the "poison" is not indispensable to an historical novel irrespective of how truthfully it supplies the reader with historical information. As has been noted by another observer, an historical novel "may be in a way true to history without being true to fact."[10] On the other hand escapism, regardless of how we evaluate it, cannot of itself relegate an historical novel to the category of the vulgar or the popular. As Feuchtwanger himself, in his discussion of the "Serious Historical Novel," admits -- the play *Götz von Berlichingen* was created out of Goethe's desire to

> escape from the misery of the contemporary political situation. An entire epoch is present, with emperor, mercenaries, ecclesiastical princes, gypsies, rebellious peasants...All of this is invented, even if artistically so.[11]

We may therefore question whether a writer's faithfulness to historical fact, so central a factor in almost any discussion of the historical novel, is a serviceable criterion for judging any particular historical work of fiction.

Peter Green, in his *Aspects of the Historical Novel* has made an inclusive attempt to classify all historical novels, "with some exception, into three broad categories, which may for convenience be labelled Propaganda, Education, and Escapism." [12] This classification is based, to be sure, not on an aesthetic consideration but on the problem of historical truth, "and while the first and third pervert or ignore historical truth, the second abuses the medium of the novel." [13] The distinction appears to be well conceived. Propaganda type historical novels will generally have a political or religious *leitmotiv*. Educational novels aim to supply the reader with factual information, and those novels in the category of escapism are intended mainly to provide entertainment, "and pander to certain psychological needs by encouraging popular myths." [14] Green is obviously right in stressing that this category *can* produce creative work of the first rank. While admitting that it can also lead to commercialism of the very worst sort, he cites Walter Scott as the writer who put this type of historical romance on an altogether more serious footing.[15] However, he points out that the historical novel today is undergoing an unmistakable renaissance, [16] because "it is moving steadily towards a form which subsumes both scrupulous scholarship and psychological insight to re-create the events and the climate of the past." More specifically, if today the historical novel has vindicated itself as a creative medium, it is because we have now acquired "a detached *sense of period*, as well as an ability to see the past in its own terms rather than our own." [17] Not that modern historical novels are completely free from present-day prejudices, but "the overall degree of our prejudice is a good deal less than it was, and we see all round a problem with greater readiness than our ancestors." [18] Green makes no reference at all to Lion Feuchtwanger's historical novels. But Feuchtwanger seems to have had a concept such as Green's in mind when he wrote: [19]

> Readers and critics who wish to laud historical literature frequently say that the author has succeeded in lending life to the period he has portrayed. They obviously regard this as the ultimate purpose of historical literature, and that is a mistake...The creative writers desire only to treat contemporary matters even in those of their creations which have history as their subject. Such writers want only to discuss their relation to their own time, their own personal experience, and how much of the past has continued into the present.

He then goes on to emphasize that [20]

> The reader learns more about the author than about the epoch in which the action of the story plays.

As for the purpose of placing the story in the ancient past, Feuchtwanger says:

> Historical disguise often enables an author to express truths, notably those of a political or daring erotic kind, he would fear or be incapable of stating in a contemporary setting.[21]

We are thus back to a view of the historical novel as escapist literature, whether as Peter Green says, it is undergoing an "unmistakable renaissance" or not.

It is not the purpose of this discussion to lead to final conclusion. What can, however, be gleaned from the foregoing is that when we actually look back into history or dress up the present in ancient garments the sensation of the past thus created serves as "a bridge leading us over the gulf that divides past and present, so annihilating time." [22] As long as the historical novel does this, its function is fulfilled.

The phrase "annihilating time" which probably expresses fairly accurately the subjective reaction of the reader, is otherwise rather unfortunate. It means to say that the fences dividing past and present are felt to have disappeared. But "time is the heart of existence," [23] it is always in the process of becoming, always developing. It is only in our consciousness that time splits into past, present and future. That "great split which preceded the splitting of the atom by several hundred thousand years," as F. A. Polak sees it,[24] has burdened us with the need "to bring the past into the present as part of the total causal nexus in which living organisms act and react," in order then to be able "to act in the longterm future."[25] The relationship between past and future is very peculiar, as Polak shows:[26]

> Images projected into the past represent, of course, a romantic idealization of the past, a condition of unattainable bliss...
> Still, they serve the future, however indirectly. This aching nostalgia for the time of unspoiled beginnings...represents a kind of vision of the future, even though it is by definition unattainable. The dreams out of the past do operate on the future.

As the psychoanalists have found, anxiety arises about something that may happen in the future, therefore our memory operates in a way which mirrors the individual's expectations of the future. What he wishes to happen determines what he remembers of his past. In other words, the past "is the domain of contingency in which we accept events and from which we select events in order to fulfill our potentialities and to gain satisfactions and security in the immediate future."[27]

It has also been observed by psychoanalists that the events in the past which a person carries consciously with him have little connection with the "quantitative events" that actually happened to him in childhood. One single thing that occurred at a given age is remembered and thousands of things are forgotten. The same phenomenon is clearly observable in the historical novel. Very little, if any, historical truth is needed to create the vision which may capture the imagination of the reader. The essential aspect of such a novel is its capacity to nourish the readers illusions of the future. Nevertheless, the historical novel of Western culture is hardly used for the purpose of painting in detail a picture of the future. This is normally the function of a different genre of literature, the Utopian. The relationships between the three elements of time in the historical novel and in the utopian are entirely different. According to Polak, the dreams out of the past operate on the future, and this is the realm of the historical novel. But he also makes the following distinction: "When man projects his vision directly into the future, however, we find the future, operating directly on the present,"[28] and this is the realm of the utopia. Whereas the historical novel is basically a literature of escapism, the utopia is usually a deliberate attempt to face the challenge of the unknown. And although attempts to envisage the future in some way or another are common to many different cultures, the deliberate and sober intellectual effort to project contemporary man into a future time is strictly limited to modern Western culture.

This is why Polak's great study on the image of the future is limited to the experiences of Western man,[29] as is almost any other study of modern utopias. The basic difference between modern Western utopias and non-Western utopias, is that the former are almost invariably placed in the future,[30] whereas the latter are just as invariably placed in the past.[31]

The differences between cultures as reflected in their images of past and future cannot be analyzed here. But something must be said of past and future in Islam, before returning to the novels of Najīb Maḥfūẓ.

Islam's first pronouncements on the present state of man, delivered by the Prophet Muḥammad, were gloomy and pessimistic. The vision of a happy and good life lay completely in the world to come, contingent on man's willingness to follow the teachings of the Prophet. The success of Islam was so rapid however that for almost ten years Muḥammad was able in person to lead the Islamic state, both in its peaceful activities and in its military engagements. This fact had a tremendous impact on future Islamic thought. Although throughout his career Muhammad had emphasized his human nature,

> he had been dead only for a short while when popular fancy, overruling the very wording of the revelation as well as the somewhat feeble protests of the more conscientious theologians, retold the Prophet's life as that of a powerful thaumaturge. [32]

Supernatural eminence has eventually been attributed to the entire Islamic state under the Prophet and this was extended over that of his immediate successors for about 30 years. These 40 years came to be regarded by the Muslims as "the age in which human society had come as near perfection as couldbe hoped for," and the Islamic state of this period eventually became the model of "that perfect order which was Allah's." [33]

As the Islamic empire expanded, the gap between this ideal and the prevailing sorry state of affairs widened. "Social and political life was lived on two planes, on one of which happiness would be spiritually valid but actually unreal, while on the other no validity could ever be aspired to." [34] And thus, as history inexorably progresses, the examples to be followed are left in the ever more remote past. In such a situation any aspiration to a better future can be expressed only in terms of a return to the golden age of Islam. And the way to achieve it can always be shown in the greatest possible detail by merely pointing to the political and social theory which is built into Islamic theology. From this point of view, one may perhaps say that no utopia could ever present a more detailed system than that elaborated by Islamic treatises on the theory and practice of its political system.

This tendency to look on a period in the past as the good and happy days that are gone is certainly not limited to Islam, and the myths of a "Golden Age" are probably shared by every known culture.

Nor are these myths sheer fables. "Many of them had foundation of fact. Some of them were more or less shadowy records of societies which had excellent traits, appealing to the cravings of men for good society."[35] But in Islam we have a unique example of an ideal state actually placed in historical times, with historical personalities who had lived in places still inhabited by their descendants. This unique situation has given rise in recent times to a tremendous amount of literature whose main concern is to elucidate the ways to overcome problems and difficulties of the present by means of reliving and reinterpreting and even rediscovering facts and processes relating to that ideal state of the past.[36] Such literature must of necessity be apologetic because it has somehow to explain the discontinuance of that ideal state which is looked on as a model for the future. It nevertheless enjoys great advantages over other utopian literature, in so far as it is free from the psychological obstacles inherent in any attempt to convince people of the possibility, or the probability, of something which is utterly strange and unknown to their culture. "In the creation of Utopia man imposes his will on the imagination, and the non-existent ideal country loses its mythical force and becomes a device, a construct, a fiction. Spontaneous imagination and traditional belief are replaced by the fictive activity of logical thought."[37] In order to overcome these difficulties, writers have had to resort to various contrivances to create in their readers' minds some willingness to trust the story they were told. Maps are drawn to show the location of the ideal state, symbolic journeys are described, a great deal of detailed information is supplied, sometimes the whole story is told in the past tense, and in the first person, merely to take advantage of a greater readiness to believe a personal narrative.[38] All this is unnecessary for the Muslim describing his Utopia. And there need be no doubt that the emotional appeal of the Muslim utopian literature to its readers surpasses the appeal of Western utopias to theirs. Entire religio-political movements have sprung up in modern times aiming at realizing this Islamic utopia.

One can safely say, therefore, that the Arab historical novel may fulfill two different fictional functions — that of the Western historical novel and that of the Western utopian novel. By merely looking backward the Arab novel does not necessarily become "historical" in the usual sense. Nevertheless, as has been pointed out earlier,[39] modern Arabic literature is rich in historical novels. How much of it can be considered utopian in the sense discussed here is a question which cannot be answered without a more careful examination.[40] But it would be true to say that the prevalence of the utopian element is unmistakable in a good many of these novels. Usually, the utopian tendency can be discerned in the overflowing optimism, in the perfectly balanced happiness sought for and won — against forces of unrest and disorder — by the strict application of known principles of conduct revered in the writer's own society but — alas — neglected in application. People, both men and women, are physically beautiful, the masses live in a state of collective bliss, guarded and protected by a benevolent ruler. It should be pointed out that these utopias are similar to most of the "classical" Western utopias,[41] with the exception that religion in the Arabic utopia is never "reduced to a psychological impulse, a social force which has to be and can be directed in accordance with the ends of man, which in their turn are created by man himself."[42] Since religion in Islam is not only the source and constitutional base of the happy state, but also the guardian of the people's happiness, no Arabic utopia can envisage a state of "religion without dogma"[43] which is so characteristic of Western classical utopia. The whole situation is indeed not far removed from the traditional Islamic vision of felicity — *saʿāda*.[44] Another feature common to the Arabic utopia and the classical Western utopia is the apparent lack of any concept of historical process. How things came to be what they are, and what process will result from — that is, has resulted from — the happy situation described is never revealed.[45]

This characterisation of the Arabic utopia may be applied to each of Najīb Maḥfūẓ' historical novels. And indeed only when we read them appreciatively as utopias, rather than as historical novels, do their shortcomings as fictional literature become more comprehensible. Having examined these novels as literary fiction, something has to be said now of their utopian quality. The first thing to note is the fact that the stories are placed outside the realm of Islamic history. This is not only very daring, considering the time of their writing, but at first sight, it is somewhat incomprehensible. Placing the stories in a period preceding Islam by thousands of years the author might be expected to allude at least to some values of social and individual life which are incompatible with Islam. But we find none that can be so considered. Rather the contrary, the society and state elaborated in the novels are wholly Islamic in nature. The good ruler is depicted in terms which conform completely to the traditional Islamic concept.[46] He is wise and benevolent, he loves his people and consults his advisers, he is patient, he respects tradition, he is resolute and courageous in action, and is well-versed in the books of wisdom.

The society described in the novels is an urban society, and its culture is an urban culture, which again is a typical Muslim outlook.[47] Even the typically ancient Egyptian celebrations and customs, usually connected with the regime of the Nile, as described in one of these novels, have a very contemporary aura, being actually a depiction of the *mawālid*, the popular celebrations, which are largely a continuation of the ancient ones.[48] In fact, Najīb Maḥfūẓ went so far in emphasizing the similarity between the urban civilization of contemporary Egypt and that of the Pharaonic era described by him, that the historical distortions are often hard to swallow. When we read of the military academy, of pensions to retired officials, of prime ministers and chiefs of bureaus, of parades and of social parties, of poor quarters in the city and large mansions in the suburbs, this intention becomes all too obvious.

The question therefore, is what has been gained by this imaginary leap to the Pharaonic epoch, if all we find there is the familiar setting of Islamic civilization, and more particularly, of its Egyptian version. The answer is easier to arrive at if it is realized that the same picture could not have been painted by using a setting within the Islamic era. The ideal Egyptian state cannot possibly be placed within the Islamic era without implicitly approving of a situation where the national, linguistic and even denominational separation between people and ruler, between governed and governor, is a foregone conclusion. Therefore, when a model is sought after, which should be relevant to Egypt of the late 1930's, of a state where all segments of society live in harmony and act in unison, abiding by the same moral precepts, seeking the same national goals, then the Islamic epoch must be ruled out. As for the Islamic state centered in Arabian Medina for the first 40 years of Islam, this can be of no use when the purpose is to create a specifically Egyptian utopia. But fortunately, the ancient history of Egypt is no less concrete than that of early Islam for an Egyptian who can see the Pyramids from the roof of his house, and can examine the mummies of the Pharaohs at will, or visit the remains of Pharaonic palaces and temples. Certainly the fact that an ideal state can be placed outside Islam is not what an ardent orthodox Muslim will delight in, but it is not really sacrilegious. For just as Thomas More does not specify that the inhabitants of his Utopia are Christians and does not thereby place them outside the Christian concept of the ideal state,[49] so a Muslim utopian writer can make his Utopians non-Muslim without thereby placing them outside the fold of Islamic political philosophy. The Muslim historian and political philosopher, Ibn Khaldūn, admitted a century and a half before Thomas More, that a state based on certain rational principles may be a happy one even without having the Islamic law — *sharīʿa* — to guide it.[50]

The fact that Najīb Maḥfūẓ can see his ideal state outside the fold of historic Islam is certainly not to be construed as a critique against the religion of Islam. There seems to be in this, too, a striking parallel to More's basing his Utopia on heathen virtues, thereby making "his satire upon contemporary European abuses more pointed. The virtues of Heathen Utopia show up by contrast the vices of Christian Europe."[51] Like More's Utopia, Maḥfūẓ's ancient kingdoms of Egypt are models of virtue which, if given the benefit of Islamic guidance, should become the closest thing to a heavenly kingdom on earth. Even without the formal Islamic coloring, they are depicted as the best an Islamic state can be expected to be.

In these Utopian novels, the human element is clearly idealized, in an attempt to create what Vaihinger[52] called an abstractive, or neglective fiction, with regard to Egyptian society.

> The factor common to all fictions in this class consists in a neglect of important elements of reality. As a rule the reason for the formation of these fictions is to be sought in the highly intricate character of the facts which make theoretical treatment exceedingly difficult owing to their unusual complexity...
> Since, then, the material is too complicated and confused...thought makes use of an artifice by means of which it provisionally and temporarily neglects a number of characters and selects from them the more important phenomena.

The use of the abstractive fictions "should be accompanied by the consciousness that they do not correspond to reality and they *deliberately substitute a fraction of reality for the complete range of causes and facts*."[53] Vaihinger points out that in the abstractive fiction "we have the postulation of schematic, general types conceived as absolutely bare and deprived of all those characters of reality that might interfere with the procedure." [54] These he considers as a separate subgroup of abstractive fictions, one variety of which is formed by Utopian fictions. Of these he says that "as long as such fictions are taken for what they are and not called hypotheses, [55] they can frequently be of great service to science." [56]

It is noteworthy that Vaihinger felt the need for a distinction between scientific and aesthetic fictions, because the latter include "those ideational forms that deal even more freely with reality." [57] Yet he insists that

> The aesthetic fiction and its theoretical explanation are, in part, clearly related to the scientific fiction. Aesthetic fictions serve the purpose of awakening within us certain uplifting or otherwise important feelings. Like the scientific, they are not an end in themselves but a means for the attainment of higher ends.

The insights of Vaihinger seem important to an understanding of the function fulfilled by Najīb Maḥfūẓ's historical novels. They combine the function of the abstractive fiction of the utopian class, with that of the aesthetic fiction. As one example of the former, Vaihinger cites the story of "Haji Ibn Jokdhān," [58] the case of an artificial isolation of an individual, created for the purpose of showing "the gradual evolution of man's capacities." He also cites, to illustrate the same class of fiction, cases of artificial isolation where "a whole city or community...is thought of as shut off from the rest of the world, e.g. Fichte's isolated commercial community." [59] Najīb Maḥfūẓ's historical novels, too, have to be classified as such an abstractive fiction of a whole society, together with most of the known utopias, to which Vaihinger also refers.[60] This explains the lack of the historical process in the novels which is inherent in any utopia.[61] But again it must be emphasized that this utopian fiction is placed in historical times which are well known and are constantly being investigated and they are devoid of the sacred halo which protects the "hagiographic biographies"[62] of the Prophet and his four divinely directed successors from the scrutiny of ordinary common sense.

Yaḥyā Ḥaqqī[63] criticized the Pharaonic literature partly on the ground that Egypt's ancient history was largely unknown to the readers and partly because it was uninteresting. If this were wholly true then Najīb Maḥfūẓ's task as an utopian writer would have been that much easier. But it can safely be assumed that the history of ancient Egypt is familiar enough to the educated readers; pride in that history can be sensed in the eagerness with which news reports are followed of the archeological finds, and in the wide dissemination of historical writings relating to that period. Under such circumstances, grafting an utopian situation on the historical past is clearly a very complicated task; what can save the utopia as a novel is the historical story. Indeed, what makes the public cherish these novels[64] is their quality as historical novels, which appeals far more to the emotions than to reason.

But paradoxically, by Najīb Maḥfūz's own testimony, it was as historical novels that these works had least value in his own eyes. He never refers to them as utopian novels, but in view of subsequent writing it is easy to see that their main value for his intellectual development was in their fictional-utopian role in the sense defined earlier. Having created his ideal society, as an abstractive fiction, and having examined it once under internal stress, and again under external stress, his fictive model rendered all the service of which it was capable. All his subsequent writings bear witness to its value. What concerns him most, throughout his writings, is the interrelationship, in a given cultural setting, between society and the individual, and this is examined and re-examined under a variety of circumstances and in a variety of literary genres.

Having achieved his aim, his desire for this sort of writing died, as we now know.[65] He certainly had no more interest in romantic writing, whether utopian [66] or historical. As for the utopian writing, we can assume that Najīb Maḥfūẓ realized that the days of the romantic utopia were gone. In the West, the tendency in the late 1930's was noticeably towards an "aversion to images of the future as such, in the sense of positive and constructive visions, whether of a natural or supernatural order." [67] In literature, the era of the anti-utopia has been ushered in as utopian optimism disappears. "Utopia is no longer perfect, it is put in doubt, it is full of the social and moral conflicts...Utopia is nearer our own imperfect world." [68] For a writer who is constantly keeping abreast with contemporary literary developments as Najīb Maḥfūẓ most certainly is, there is hardly any interest in further depicting the fictive, in a romantic style.

But what of his Pharaonic proclivities? In Egypt, it looks as if after the first ardor for self-identification in Pharaonic terms, there is now a search for a synthesis, in which the ancient history will be accepted as a positive element, free of the former negative implications for Egypt's Islamic or Arabic identity.[69] There are of course Egyptians for whom the concept of Pharaonism is still a value which most definitely displaces existing Egyptian values though perhaps in a rather indefinable way.[70] But such an attitude is never to be met with in the writings of Najīb Maḥfūẓ. At present, the entire Pharaonic ideology seems to occupy much less of his interest than it used to. Perhaps the reason is to be found in the hopeless intellectual impasse in which Egyptian intellectuals find themselves with regard to this issue. Examples of this confusion are too numerous to count. [71] But it is certain that motives found in Najīb Maḥfūẓ's historical novels continue to have an appeal to both writers and readers in Egypt, and the problems of the racial and cultural identity of the Egyptian people are very heatedly argued.[72]

As for Najīb Maḥfūẓ, it is probable that once his interest in Pharaonic times was lost, feeling that all he could get from it had been achieved, it was not likely to be reawakened later when it became clear that the argument about the place of the Pharaonic epoch was but a veiled argument over current political issues.[73] Rather than continue to handle contemporary problems through utopian writing or trying to appease current passions by means of historical novels, he turned to a more realistic style of writing, applying himself directly to the present and its problems.

Thereafter, his references to Pharaonic Egypt will be fleeting and casual. Only once does the issue come up for serious treatment, and this in the very first novel he wrote after *Kifāḥ ṭayba*, in 1939. In this novel, *al-Qāhira al-jadīda*[74] (The New Cairo), the main character, Maḥjūb ʿAbd al-Dā'im, takes a girl for a tour of some new archeological finds near the Pyramids. He points to two columns at a temple site and says: "Look at these columns, how they have withstood the ages." She answers: "And what do you suppose might have happened had they been obliterated"? The story proceeds:

> He pointed to an inscription on the column and said:
> - 'If we could only read the hieroglyphs we might learn amazing and surprising things.'
> - 'Really'!
> - 'Most certainly. Aren't you acquainted with Pharaonic history'?
> She shook her head.

In fact, Maḥjūb himself thought very little of the ancient objects. Eventually they entered a small room in a grave structure with beautiful pictures painted on the walls, one of them depicting naked peasants. Standing there alone with the girl he desired, and watching the naked peasants of ancient Egypt, Maḥjūb was overwhelmed by his own passions and tried to embrace her forcefully. This brought the visit to an immediate and very distressing end.

What an anti-climax after the historical novels! The remnants of the past leave two young Egyptian intellectuals totally indifferent to what they symbolize. The most these symbols of past glories can do is provoke an ugly and untimely outburst of passion that can serve no useful purpose.

Egypt's ancient history as such has lost its charms. Little wonder then, that when a few years later, Najīb Maḥfūẓ wrote the history of young Kamāl, the son of Aḥmad Ibn ʿAbd al-Jawād, he felt that he would rather skip the whole chapter of the Pharaonic episode than again live through that confusing, ephemeral experience.[75]

NOTES

1 *Supra*, p. 22

2 Dawwāra, *ibid.*, p. 17.

3 See Leo Tolstoy, *War and Peace*, Norton Critical Edition, New York, 1966, pp. 1366 *seq.*

4 Quoted by Lion Feuchtwanger, *The House of Desdemona*, Detroit, 1963, p. 37.

5 John Tebbel, *Facts and Fiction, Problems of the Historical Novelist*, Lansing, 1962, p. 2.

6 *Ibid.*, pp. 10-11.

7 *Op. cit.* p. 36.

8 *Ibid.*, p. 41

9 *Ibid.*, p. 43.

10 H. Butterfield, *The Historical Novel*, Cambridge, 1924, p. 51.

11 *Op. cit.*, p. 65.

12 Peter Green, "Aspects of the Historical Novel," in *Essays by Divers Hands*, New Series, V. 31, London, 1962, p. 37.

13 *Ibid.*

14 *Ibid.*, p. 38.

15 *Ibid.*, p. 39

16 *Ibid.*, p. 35. The lecture was read in January 1958.

17 *Ibid.*, p. 41.

18 *Ibid.*, p. 50.

19 *Op. cit.*, p. 129.

20 *Ibid.*, p. 131.

21 *Ibid.*, p. 133.

22 Butterfield, *op. cit.*, p. 50.

23 Quoted by Rollo May, *op. cit.*, p. 67.

24 *The Image of the Future*, Leyden, 1961, V. 1, p. 24.

25 Rollo May, *ibid.*, p. 66.

26 *Op. cit.*, pp. 25-26.

27 Rollo May, *op. cit.*, p. 69.

28 *Op. cit.*, p. 26.

29 *Ibid.*, p. 35. The image of the future in Western culture has undergone fundamental changes. The modern image of Western man's future emerges with the Renaissance. Cf. *ibid.*, Ch. 9.

30 A "List of English Utopian Fantasies 1901-1951" appended to Richard Gerber's *Utopian Fantasies*, London, 1955, offers an illuminating proof of this tendency.

31 An elaborate discussion of non-Western utopias has no place in this study. But some idea of their nature can be gained from Arthur E. Mordan, *Nowhere was Somewhere*, New York, 1947, where illustrations are given of instances of utopias in Aztec, Inca, and Chinese culture, all placed in the past.

32 G. E. von Grunebaum, *op. cit.*, p. 92.

33 *Ibid.*, p. 143.

34 *Ibid.*

35 Arthur E. Morgan, *op. cit.*, p. 120.

36 Cf. G. E. von Grunebaum, *Modern Islam,* New York, 1964, pp. 158 *Seq*., where some of this literature is discussed.

37 R. Gerber, *op. cit.,* p. 4.

38 *Ibid.,* Part 3, Chs. 3 and 4. "In a utopia the narrator first jumps forward into the future in order to be able to look back at the present. This process enables the writer to use the 'prophetic past', for he is not content with merely looking forwards and speaking in the future tense or the conditional." *Ibid.,* p. 181.

39 *Supra.,* p. 34.

40 No study of Arabic or Muslim utopias in literature has been written to date.

41 As defined by F. Gerber, *op. cit.,* p. 10 and *passim.*

42 *Ibid.,* p. 9.

43 The phrase is used by Ernst Cassirer, cf. *Twentieth Century Interpretations of Utopia,* ed. W. Nelson, Prentice Hall, 1968, p. 106.

44 Cf. G. E. von Grunebaum, *Islam*, London, 1964, p. 111: "The Muslim's apprehension of the purpose of his earthly life as the outreach for felicity, *saʿāda,* through service, *ʿibāda,* has shaped the fundamental aspirations of his civilization both on the political and on the epistemological levels."

45 Gerber, *op. cit.,* p. 10.

46 See Reuben Levy, *The Social Structure of Islam,* Cambrdige, 1962, p. 285. An extended discussion of the traditional Islamic view of the ruler can be read in E.I.J. Rosenthal, *Political Thought in Islam,* Cambridge, 1962, Ch. 2. Ibn Khaldūn's concept of rulership seems to be very much the basis for Maḥfūẓ's portrayal of the kings in his novels. Cf. *Al-Muqaddimah,* tr. F. Rosenthal, London, 1958, V. I, Ch. 3, sec 24.

47 "The Muslim...was prone to identify urban life and civilized life as definitely as had his classical predecessors." von Grunebaum, *Islam,* p. 155.

48 Cf. J. W. McPherson, *The Moulids of Egypt,* Cairo, 1941, p. 3: "A Moulid is a popular religious feast in honour of some saint, in Egypt usually of Islam...they in many cases are continuations of Feasts held hundreds or even thousands of years before the Prophet..." On p. 228, commenting on the *mawlid* (pl. *mawālid)* of Sīdī Ismā'īl Imbābī, the author says: "Islamil's moulid is fixed by the season of the year, not by the lunar calendar... absorbing and superseding an ancient festifal of Isis, of which the traces exist till this day." The festival described in *Rādūbīs* falls exactly on the date of this *mawlid* known also as *Laylat al-nuqṭa,* cf. Budge, *Gods of Egypt,* V. 2, p. 47. The ceremonial announcement of the innudation described by E. Lane, *Manners and Customs of the Modern Egyptians,* Every man's Library, 1966, pp. 496-97, can be easily recognized as the source of the ceremonial announcement in *Rādūbīs.*

49 R. W. Chambers, "Rational Heathens," *Twentieth Century Interpretations,* pp. 17 *seq.*

50 Cf. Rosenthal, *op. cit.,* Ch. 4. The passage in *al-Muqaddimah, op. cit.* V. I, p. 391: "It should be known that the religious law does not censure royal authority as such..." is of particular relevance.

51 Chamber, *ibid.,* pp. 18-19.

52 H. Vaihinger, *The Philosophy of "As if",* New York, 1925, p. 19.

53 *Ibid.,* p. 20.

54 *Ibid.,* p. 24.

55 "...scientific Fictions are to be distinguished from Hypotheses. The latter are assumptions which are probable, assumptions the

truth of which can be proved by further experience. They are therefore verifiable. Fictions are never verifiable, for they are hypotheses which are known to be false but which are employed because of their utility." *Ibid.*, p. XLII.

56 *Ibid.*, p. 26.

57 *Ibid.*, p. 82.

58 *Ibid.*, p. 192. For a brief summary and discussion of the story *Ḥayy ibn yaqẓān* ("Alive son of Awake") by Ibn Ṭufayl (1105-1185), cf. W. Montgomery Watt, *Islamic Philosophy and Theology*, Edinburgh, 1962, p. 138. Cf. also *Encyclopedia of Islam*, 2nd. ed. *"Ḥayy ibn yaqẓān,"* by A. M. Goichon.

59 *Ibid.*, p. 193.

60 *Ibid.*, p. 26.

61 *Supra.*, p. 128.

62 The phrase in this context is used by von Grunebaum, *Modern Islam, op. cit.* p. 159.

63 *Op. cit.*, p. 135.

64 *ʿAbath al-aqdār* came out in a seventh edition in 1974; *Rādūbīs* and *Kifāḥ ṭayba* came out in their seventh editions in 1971, and 1972 respectively.

65. Answering a question Najīb Maḥfūẓ said: "The inclination towards history disappeared suddenly...But this is only an apparent discontinuation, for the thoughts behind the historical novels have never been discontinued." *Hiwār*, No. 3, March-April, 1963, p. 67. Cf. also p. 68: "I never intended to carry the reader into the past, but I continuously was describing the present," which should be taken to mean: "I was continously concerned with the present."

66 As used here, the term includes both classes of utopias as defined by J.C. Garret, namely those written before the Romantic period and those written during that period. See *Utopias in*

Literature, University of Canterbury, 1968, Ch. 1. What is common to all these is the attempt to create an ideal state "with which contemporary life could be unfavorably compared." *Ibid.*, p. 9.

67 Polak, *op. cit.* 2, p. 14.

68 Gerber, *op. cit.*, p. 120.

69. This is actually the position taken by President Jamāl ʿAbd al-Nāṣir in the unity talks with the Syrian delegation in March-April 1963. Cf. *Maḥāḍir muḥādathāt al-waḥda*, ed. *al-Ahrām* August 1963, pp.191 *seq*. The Egyptian president definitely rejected the Syrian delegation's criticism that the Pharaonic legacy of Egypt stands in the way of an all-Arab unity, and by implication he conceded the right to Syria of a Hittite nuance and of Iraq to an Ashurite nuance in the Arab national image.

70 An outstanding spokesman of this attitude is Ḥusayn Fawzī. Cf. his *Sindbad maṣrī*, Dār al-Maʿārif, 1961, where Arab and Muslim conquerors of Egypt are placed on the same level as non-Arab and non-Muslim conquerors, whose exploits are humiliating to the Egyptian people, pp. 12, 48 and *passim*. Fawzī does not neglect to express his gratitude to the revolutionary regime in Egypt, maintaining that such a book as his would never have been permitted under the old regime. p. 10.

71 See for instance, Luīs ʿAwad's article "*Min kifāḥina al-qawmī*," in his book, *Dirāsāt fī al-naqd wa al-adab*, Beirut, 1963, p. 124, where an argument, recorded in a papyrus, between Alexandrian notables and Claudius Caesar, is hailed as an expression of Egyptian national struggle.

72 In an article published in the weekly *Rūz al-Yūsuf* of July 17, 1967, an attempt is made to set everything in order. The article is a reaction to a new book by Muḥammad al-ʿAzab Mūsā on the Hyksos' defeat in Egypt. The author is taken to task for writing

as if present-day Egypt were a continuation of Pharaonic Egypt, and for claiming that the first revolution of liberation in Egyptian history was that against the Hyksos. The writer is further criticized for claiming in another book that the first revolution against feudalism took place in Egypt 4,000 years ago. The writer is condemned as lacking in historical understanding, and is rebuked for taking pride in Pharaoh's superiority over the Semites, whose skin was white, and who let their beards grow, and who were nomads. "The writer forgets" says the article "that modern Egypt is Semite, because it is Arabic, and its modern people, even though they are not of purely Semite blood, are nevertheless Semites by virtue of their conviction, their situation, their interest, their future and their destiny." Consequently, rather than consider the Hyksos and other Semites as raiders of the desert, they should be considered as one instance of the reciprocal process of immigration of Semitic people. "Therefore, we feel no shame that the Semitic Muslim Arabs conquered Egypt by force and arabized it, and spread in it their religion and accepted it as a trust for the preservation of their legacy and history, and since this is the case, we cannot consider our victory over a Semitic migration as contributing to our national honor."

73. The article referred to in the former note, is actually a discussion on the justification of Egypt's espousing the cause of the Palestinian Arabs against Israel. The writer feels that the Pharaonic pretensions weaken Egypt's political stand on that issue.

74. *Al-Qāhira al-jadīda*, 1945.

75 *Supra.*, p. 25.

Part Two

GOD'S WORLD

Chapter Four
The Neighborhood

Beginning with *al-Qāhira al-Jadīda* Najīb Maḥfūẓ concerned himself directly with the world he lived in.[1] Between 1939 and 1952 he wrote five novels [2] and his great Cairo trilogy, referred to earlier.[3] In April 1952 he finished writing the trilogy, and had a plan for seven additional novels "of the same realistic and critical tendency."[4] But as we know, when the revolution of July 1952 occurred, desire for further writing died in him, and he never came to write those seven novels.

He announced that he was not going to write any more, and later, he added, "and I was sincere in that. It was not a mere pretense as suspected by some people." And indeed between 1952 and 1958 he wrote nothing; after which he found himself writing his *Awlād ḥāritnā* (The Children of My Neighborhood), published in 1959.[5] Then he wrote continuously, and by 1967 he had published six new novels [6] and two collections of short stories.[7] He never ceased writing since then.

This long period of silence left its mark on the writing of Najīb Maḥfūẓ.[8] All he wrote up to and including the trilogy is rightly considered by critics as truly realistic writing, based on a very intimate knowledge of subject-matter and, on the whole, imbued with a solid optimistic outlook. It is not a naive, indiscriminate optimism, but a sober recognition that life in this world of ours, despite its many evils which he never hesitated to challenge, was essentially worth living. All he wrote after 1958, however, is shrouded in gloom, filled with a sense of hopelessness. The writings are consequently bewildering in their effect, causing great discomfort to the perceptive reader. Rajā' al-Naqqāsh [9] remarks, very correctly that the difference between these two periods is evident even from the names of the novels. In the realistic period most of the novels are called after place-names, such as an alley or a quarter, of old Cairo. In the post-realistic period the names given to his books by Najīb Maḥfūẓ "awaken notions that are not restricted to certain places which are the physical environments of the novels." Another helpful distinction made by Rajā' al-Naqqāsh[10] is that in the first period Najīb Maḥfūẓ "resembled more the historian in observing the reality he described, whereas in his new phase...he became more like a poet observing reality." To be sure, all along he was looking at reality; it was his reaction to what he saw that changed. In other words, to use the terminology of Leslie Fiedler, the Archetypal material naturally remained the same, but the Signature, that is "the sum total of individuating factors in a work, the sign of the Persona or Personality, through which an Archetype is rendered," [11] changed radically.

This change is perplexing to many critics, some of whom consider it to be virtually a shirking of the writer's duty toward his society.[12] The writer's "metaphysical" inclinations, as those critics see it,[13] are totally out of line with the urgent needs of the educational processes of the people. But it must be borne in mind that the year 1952 had a far-reaching effect, not only on Najīb Maḥfūẓ but on the entire society of which he was part. He felt that his pre-1952 writings were realistic and critical of the society of that day. At present, it is generally agreed that this is the great merit of his works.

It was six years before he resumed his writing, and he did not do so merely to write again about pre-1952 society. He continued to concern himself with his contemporary society, but he did it in a way which revealed an unmistakable dissatisfaction with what he saw. This writing was not completely nonrealistic as yet, but it certainly did make a more extensive use of symbols and metaphors, whose evocative force is more easily sensed than measured. On reading his post-1952 novels one very often feels that the writer is probably saying more than can be readily understood. Commenting on *al-Liss wa al-kilāb* (The Thief and the Dogs). Anouar Abdel Malek says[14] that this work is fiction

> slashed through the euphoria of the newspapers and their daily proclamations of victory in red-ink headlines. It portrayed the condition of man, who was still downtrodden... It reiterated faith in the spirit of the people alone and its contempt for the careerist 'dogs' of the suffocating government apparatus.

How much faith in the spirit of the people is there in these novels? That precisely is the question which befuddles readers who seek in the novel "to allay the anxieties and guilt feelings our experience arouses." [15] This later writing of Najīb Maḥfūẓ certainly has greater depth, but one wonders whether it has not turned so deep as to become esoteric. Such questions hardly arise in his pre-1952 writings.

In any case, it is clear that, after 1939, we are faced with two distinct periods in the literary life of Najīb Maḥfūẓ. The first period will be discussed in this part of the study. The second period will be dealt with in Part Three.

It is generally accepted that the trilogy is probably the work of Najīb Maḥfūẓ which shows the Neighborhood at its best. Each of its three parts is named after some locale in the neighborhood. *Bayn al-qaṣrayn* (Between the two Castles),[16] *Qasr al-shawq* (Castle of Desire), and *al-Sukkarīya* (The Sugar Bowl). Geographically *Bayn al-Qaṣrayn* is located between *Qaṣr al-Shawq*, somewhat to the North East, and *al-Sukkarīya* to the South, just across the old gate, *Bāb al-Zuwaila*. It would have been amazing if these figurative place-names had not been used by the writer symbolically. But it must be emphasized that this is not a symbolic work. The conscious symbolic element is only in the use of the topographical features of the city, as will be demosntrated later.

The story of the trilogy need not be summarized here because this has already been done by Jaques Jomier in his excellent monograph *La vie d'une famille au Caire d'apres trois romans de M. Najuib Mahfouz*, mentioned earlier. Significantly Jomier presents the story to a non-Arabic reader through a discussion of each of the main characters in the story, because as he later explained,[17] everything that takes place in the novel is described as perceived by the people whose lives it relates.

This remark is very pertinent, for it sums up what may be considered the most important single element that makes contemporary Arabic literature modern. This is brought out clearly by Dr. von Grunebaum:[18]

> In [Arabic] classical literature, even in biography and especially in autobiography, impenetrable discretion veils what seems to us the essential life of the spirit... That which is non-recurring and unique in inner experience is seldom described...Because man, properly understood, is not a free agent, genuine significance accrues to his activity and movements only with regard to his relationship to God in his capacity as believer...*The opening of the inner life as subject and problem of literary endeavor is one of the most significant results* of contact with the West.[19]

In this respect Najīb Maḥfūẓ is distinctly within the modern trend of Arabic literature. We know that he is well acquainted with Western literature, and from the very beginning of his literary career has conceived himself as a modern writer in this sense.[20]

But if one nevertheless feels some uneasiness regarding the manner chosen by Jomier to present the story, this is probably due to our reaction to his view of Najīb Maḥfūẓ as a mere transmitter of Western literary techniques to the Egyptian environment.[21] These techniques and approaches have certainly not been conveyed by one person, or by a single work.[22] An emphasis on the achievements of Najīb Maḥfūẓ in adopting Western literary techniques may overlook two truths. One is that the trilogy does not claim to be a Western work of literature describing in Arabic an Egyptian environment; it stands rather as an Egyptian work of literature reflecting the difficulties of Egypt's dilemma in defining its changing cultural identity. The second is that the influence of Western literature on Najīb Maḥfūẓ is not in the nature of a borrowing of something alien in order to make oneself look better, but rather as a means recognized to be of value in tackling an indigenous problem. Surely, Western influence is there for all to see, if we think of influence as a case "when (a) a solution to a (cultural) problem, (b) a problem or (c) both, are introduced from outside into a system to which problem and/or solution are not germane."[23] Yet, in order to realize the achievement of the writer in this case it would be well to recall how the situation initially looked to H.A.R. Gibb in 1929 when he spoke of the Egyptian "Modernists":[24]

> They know that what they are expressing is not the feeling of the people as a whole, but the views of a small minority who are striving...to convert and educate the people...For their final aim...is not to create an intellectual culture, a culture of decadence and mere words, but a natural culture, a culture of progress.

Feeling perhaps that such an achievement has finally been reached in the trilogy this great work is looked on as epoch-making in modern Egyptian literature.

It is interesting to note that Ṭaha Ḥusayn, one of the "modernists" referred to by Gibb, has stressed that the achievement of Najīb Maḥfūẓ was in some way the success of the University of Cairo.[25] Since Najīb Maḥfūẓ graduated in Philosophy from this University, his entire higher education was secular, although it was acquired wholly in Egypt.[26] He can no longer be classified as English-educated or French-educated, as were his elder colleagues.[27] Whatever he learned of Western culture he learned in Egypt, without being exposed directly to a Western environment. In a way this was probably a blessing if we are to assume that the unnerving, or at least the unbalancing effects of a long stay in the West, evident in the experience of other Egyptians, might have been his lot, too, Egyptian writers are quite frank in their descriptions of the nerve-wracking trials involved in such an experience.[28] The consequence is sometimes irreparable damage, as is demonstrated by Ṭaha Ḥusayn in the story of *Adīb*. The crisis may begin even before the first glimpse of the West.[29] But very soon afterward a strong feeling of alienation is experienced. A unique description of this feeling is the one given by the *Adīb:*

> You expect me to describe to you my life in Paris... However, this cannot be done by the written word... But go to the Pyramids...and enter into the deep recess of the big one, and there you will become weary of life...you will feel choked to death and your body will become soaked in sweat, and you will imagine that you are carrying on yourself the whole weight of this giant structure, and that it will soon kill you. Then go out from the depth of the Pyramid and face the outdoor breeze and know that life in Egypt is the life in the depth of the Pyramid, and that life in Paris is the life after coming out of this depth.[30]

No wonder that the shaikhs of al-Azhar said that "he who goes to France is an infidel or at least a heretic."[31] This explains why Ṭaha Ḥusayn should feel so elated with the results of the education of the University of Cairo, as evinced in Najīb Maḥfūẓ. It enables its graduates to learn all that is worth knowing of the West without exposing them to its seduction.[32]

The problem goes far beyond the limits of the individual experience. When Najīb Maḥfūẓ began working on his trilogy in 1945,[33] Egypt had already known a century and a half of cultural turmoil resulting from the impact of the Western culture. And now, just as World War II was ending, the problem rose to the surface. It was the same problem which Gibb formulated many years earlier: Can a body of Arabic literature be created

> which will express the distinctive contribution of Arabs and Egyptians to modern civilization, not as imitators of alien culture, but as members of an original and vigorous organism, in the same way that Russian literature has expressed the distinctive contribution of the Russian genius? [34]

No such contribution can be made by a single writer, but it can with justice be argued that the kind of literature exemplified by the trilogy is well on the way toward realizing these hopes. If some exception has been taken to the way the trilogy has been presented to the Western reader by Jomier,[35] it is mainly because he fails adequately to bring out the fact that its greatness lies not in the application of Western techniques but in its being a work that marks a distinctive literary contribution of the Egyptian genius.

Jomier very properly warns his readers: "la trilogie n'est pas une vie de saint." [36] The warning is timely, because it has long been the habit of Egyptian writers never to admit that the lives of Egyptian men and women in Egypt can be less than saintly. Not that Egyptians are less liable to sin, but this is usually the result of being involved with Western people, primarily women, and mostly out of Egypt. This is very much the consequence of the "philosophical" outlook which considers the East basically pure and spiritual, and the West basically corrupt and materialistic.[37] The trend is not new and has always found a place in the minds and hearts of Egyptian literati.[38] Often the tendency is to depict the Egyptian as redeeming a European woman — always the symbol of European moral degenration — from the pit of sin.[39] What is unique in this respect about Najīb Maḥfūẓ's writings is the absence of such a dichotomy of values, which has become a recurrent theme in contemporary Egyptian literature. For him life is not divided into pure and soiled, good and bad, noble and mean. Judging by the mood of his writing, Najīb Maḥfūẓ would probably decline to subscribe to any formula, but if there is a dichotomy of any kind in his concept of life it is probably that of a satisfying life as opposed to an impaired or unsatisfying life.

As seen by Najīb Maḥfūẓ the fulness of life is not only something to be desired, it is something real that has been attained by many and is attainable by many more.

Speaking of Aḥmad ʿAbd al-Jawād, thehead of the family whose history is told in the trilogy, Jomer says [40] that he has two personalities, that of the austere and intractable father on the one hand, and that of the *bon vivant* on the other. He admits he was surprised by the discovery that such people exist at all in a Muslim milieu and he tries to understand the phenomenon:

> On cherche à comprendre. Aḥmad ʿAbd al-Gawwād n'est pourtant pas un Tartuffe; il est sincère, sincère lorsqu'il fait punctuellement ses cinq prières quotidiennes, sincère dans sa dureté de mari et de père, et encore plus sincère lorsqu'il est en joyeuse compagnie, le soir. Et petit à petit, le lecteur comprend que ce marchand du XXe siècle représente un type de "l'homme," tel que certains pouvaient se l'imaginer jadis.

Jomier also remarks,[41] quite correctly, that there is a certain parallel between the waning authority of the father over his family and the waning rule of the British in Egypt. Both authorities are oppressive, and their disappearance is a welcome relief. And indeed the decline of the father's authority enables everybody else to relax. Not that his sensuality is ever condemned, for sensuality is never conceived of as negative. But by removing the oppressive pretense, symbolized by the father's dual life, that sensuality and so-called respectability are essentially incompatible, both respectability and sensuality become less mutually exclusive. The futility of the father's attempt to isolate his sensual life from his family life, by insisting on a Hanbalite [42] regime at home, while permitting himself an unrestrained sensual life outside, becomes obvious quite early in the first novel. In fact, this enables the writer to create the numerous occasions, which vary from the funny to the pathetic, in which this duplicity is mercilessly condemned. Jomier's comment inclines to gloss over the deep significance of some of these situations when he says: [43] "Il est neanmoins penible a certain moment de voir le pere et le fils se succeder aupres les mêmes femmes." Because one of the clearest ideas brought out in the trilogy is that out of rigorous conservatism some of the most objectionable situations may develop.

The story *Bayn al-qaṣrayn* tells that the first time the eldest son, Yāsīn, sees his father enjoying himself at night in the mixed society of strangers, just when he himself is secretly visiting a girl belonging to that same society, a whole world crumbles before his gaze. The girl had left him alone in a dark room, and had opened the door to bring some fruits to the merry group in the adjoining room. And through that door he saw his father as he had never seen him before, sitting "without his jubba,[44] his shirt sleeves rolled up, swinging a tambourine and looking at the almeh -- ʿālima — with a face brimming with happiness and joy." The door remains open only a few seconds, until the girl, Zanūba, comes out again, but it is long enough for Yāsīn to become aware of a long story, "at the end of which he awoke like one who awakes from a long and deep sleep with a shock of a severe earthquake." Then he slowly begins to grasp how strange the situation is: "I am here with Zanūba and my father is in the next room with Zubeyda, both of us in the same house"! But the longer he thinks of the situation the more he likes it. All of a sudden he realizes that he is not really so different from his father as he had always believed. Yāsīn had early in life become subject to the irresistible impulse of his sexual desires. This is how he happened to come to the house where his father spent his evenings. Always he had felt uneasy that his father was so superior and so different from himself. He had wished to be assured that he was really not so bad, that there were, among the respectable people, men like himself. And now, all at once, he discovers that his own father is a man like himself, his father, "the traditional model, who for so long had troubled him — consciously or unconsciously — because he believed they were so radically different." He grew elecated with joy. At last he had a father he not only admired but whom he could imitate.

Jomier wonders [45] what the intention was in creating Yāsīn, "ce personnage dépourvu de caractère, incapable de resister à ses instincts." He suggests the following explanation: [46] "Ou bien a-t'il voulu compléter la portrait du père en montrant ce que devenait la sensualité lorsqu'elle n'etait plus contre-balancée par le sens de la dignité et de certains limites à garder"? Hardly, we would say. Jomier's interpretation would have us seeing Aḥmad 'Abd al-Jawād both the good and the evil, and would have us believe that because the good was so pronounced the evil was bearable. Such an interpretation would deprive the trilogy of its outstanding quality, that of trying to expose stifling concepts of behavior to the refreshing breeze of a more relaxed, more natural, concept of life.

The simile used by the anonymous *adīb* [47] immediately comes to mind, but the refreshing breeze so essential for the reinvigoration of the moral fabric of Egyptian society, need not be looked for beyond the ocean. It is at hand right there in Egypt, and is available to one with far less destructive consequences, by merely opening a few locked doors, a metaphor which has come to symbolize a new outlook. [48] This is why the scene of Zanūba opening the door is so rich in meaning.

Najīb Maḥfūẓ has turned this act of opening the door into a symbolic challenge to all pretense in life and to all duplicity, especially to that paralysing complex which develops from wanting to be one thing while actually being something else, which complex is what Jaques Berque considers to be the greatest predicament of present-day Arabs generally.[49] Thus Yāsīn, standing in the dark, suddenly sees a great light coming through the open door. This may not be immediately appreciated because Najīb Maḥfūẓ would not subject his story to a "thesis."[50] Yāsīn's excitement takes its natural course.

> How do you get drunk, father? How do you behave when you become boisterous? I should know in order to follow your example, in order to revive your traditions.[51] How do you make love? How do you embrace?
>
> He turned to Zanūba and saw her standing in front of the mirror smoothing the fringes of her hair with her fingers. Her armpit showed through the opening of her gown, smooth and white, its declivity joining the trunk of a breast like a round piece of dough. A stupor of excitement ran through his body, and he fell on her as if he were an elephant falling on a gazelle.

But no harm! Zanūba is going to be Yāsīn's wife, in fact the only wife, after two previous divorces who will cling to him. She will bear his children, and later, after some reluctance, will even be accepted by the family. With Zanūba at his side, Yāsīn himself will become a little more relaxed and more restrained. Has not all this something to do with the fact that she had opened the door through which Yāsīn discovered his father?

However, it will be a long time before Zanūba and Yāsin can enjoy this happiness. Before that Yāsīn and his father will go on stirring in the same stew. Zanūba will become Aḥmad ʿAbd al-Jawād's last and most disappointing mistress before Yāsin marries her, and of the three he will be the only one completely ignorant of the fact. Still earlier Yāsīn will take as mistress the elderly Umm Maryam, to whom he had gone to ask for her daughter's hand. For a while he is content to postpone marrying the daughter in order to appease the mother's passions. But eventually he will marry the daughter Maryam, against the wishes of the family, who strongly object to it on the grounds that Maryam was the girl Fahmī had loved, Fahmī the beloved son who was killed by the English in a demonstration. Fahmī had not been able to marry Maryam because his father, Aḥmad ʿAbd al-Jawād, had resented the marriage. Nevertheless, Fahmī's cherished memory would be slighted if Yāsīn should marry the girl Fahmī had loved.

Aḥmad ʿAbd al-Jawād had yet another reason to object to Yāsīn's marriage. In the past Umm Maryam had been his own mistress, and he knew that the daughter, being like her mother, was not the kind of woman his son should marry. This had been the reason for his objection to Fahmī's marrying her in the first place. But in this instance his objection carried less weight. For already he had once made Yāsīn marry a girl whom he had chosen for him, but who had bored Yāsīn so that he had turned to her maid for satisfaction. This was sufficient reason for the marriage to end in divorce. After this Aḥmad ʿAbd al-Jawād could scacely claim that he knew how to pick wives for his son, and he had to give way. Maryam turns out to be a good wife, but Yāsīn is too hard to please. So he returns to Zanūba, who can accept him again because his father had already severed his relations with her.

Thus, Yāsīn marries Zanūba. When his father learns of this he can only hope that she will be discreet enough not to tell Yāsīn anything about their own affair. And the marriage, as said, turns out to be a very good one — the best in fact, comparable to that of Khadīja, Yāsīn's half sister.

The story of Khadīja, although quite different is not without interest of its own. Through her and Yāsīn the family continues its existence, for eventually her son, ʿAbd al-Munʿīm, marries Yāsīn's daughter by Zanūba, and by the time the trilogy ends we see Yāsīn in a shop buying diapers and clothing for the expected grandchild. For ʿAbd al-Munʿim, an ardent Muslim and a member of the Muslim Brotherhood, this is a second marriage. His first marriage was to his older cousin Naʿīma, ʿĀ'isha's remaining daughter. Naʿīma, like her mother, is very pretty, with blue eyes and blond hair. Her father and two brothers had died in an epidemic of typhus, which was naturally a terrible blow to her mother, a delicate, quiet and very lovable woman. ʿĀ'isha had never really recovered after that, but at least she has her daughter with her, as the last remnant of a happy family life. But Naʿīma is a sick girl, and dies in childbirth.

What is the meaning of this meticulous extirpation of a whole branch of the family? Khadīja and ʿĀ'isha are two aspects of Aḥmad ʿAbd al-Jawād. Khadīja inherits his authoritarian character and his large nose. ʿĀ'isha inherits his sensuality and his blue eyes. Frequent mention is made of the physical characteristics of both sisters. And it is on the beautiful, blue-eyed blond that the verdict is passed that her offspring should be extirpated from under the sun. Her husband does not matter much, and may as well be wiped out with his sons, just to make sure that ʿĀ'isha produces no children. Both her husband and his brother, Khadīja's husband, are more or less degenerate remnants of the Turkish nobility which had dominated Cairo for so many generations, and formed part of the upper class. Both brothers are described as inane good-for-nothings. Their chief purpose is to enable the writer to relate the history of Aḥmad ʿAbd al-Jawād's two daughters, without being concerned about their husbands' influence on that history.

By the time Najīb Maḥfūẓ wrote the trilogy he had revealed enough of himself not to cause his readers any surprise when they read that ʿĀ'isha, the blue-eyed blond, "appeared among her family like a beautiful emblem of comeliness and attractiveness and uselessness." Her youngest brother, the ten year old Kamāl, is very fond of ʿĀ'isha.

On his way home from school, as he used to pass the Matosyan [52] tobacco shop, he would admire a poster in colors,

> depicting a woman reclining on a divan, holding between her red lips a cigarette from which a winding tread of smoke was emanating. She was leaning with one arm on the edge of a window behind whose rolled curtain was seen a view joining together a field of date-palms and a rivulet the Nile. He used to call her "sister ʿĀ'isha" because of the resemblance of the two in their golden hair and blue eyes.

This was the first of several attractions Kamāl felt during his life for foreign, unattainable, indigestible, sterile and unacceptable values, as these were later embodied in the British troops stationed for some time in their alley, then in ʿĀ'ida, [53] the French-educated, aristocratic girl he adores to the point of obsession, and lastly in Naʿīma whom he admires just as he did her mother before her. Jomier makes a very penetrating remark in this connection. [54]

> Avec Kamal, M. Naguib Mahfūz montre, d'une part la séduction d'un style de vie différent, et d'autre part celle des pensées philosophiques nouvelles, atteignant un des membres de cette famille bourgeoise. Il ne s'agit plus de contacts extériers, mais d'une influence sur le coeur et l'intellitence, avec toutes les consequences qui s'ensuivront.

The pertinence of this comment need hardly be stressed. Throughout the trilogy physical, moral and intellectual values complement each other within the structure of the appropriate milieu. There can therefore be no doubt that by identifying, in the unspoiled mind of a little boy, the painted, cigarette-smoking woman of the commercial poster with ʿĀ'isha, Najīb Maḥfūẓ wanted to indicate what ʿĀ'isha symbolizes. For all her beauty and charm she does not belong to the neighborhood, she represents something foreign, unacceptable and inessential, which cannot and need not be prolonged forever. Anything that comes from her womb must die.

We know, of course, that ʿĀ'isha is merely a continuation of what comes from her father. The fact that blue eyes and white skin can be frightful and repulsive in a domineering man, and at the same time pleasing and attractive in a beautiful woman we have seen in *Kifāḥ ṭayba*. We also surmise that both have to be rejected, no matter how much it hurts to part with the beauty and the charm. ʿĀʾisha, as we know, resembles her grandmother, who gave birth to Ahmad ʿAbd al-Jawād. Since she too might give birth to a child who may be another Aḥmad ʿAbd al-Jawād, this must stop. This element in the family's genes, so to speak, must be discontinued, just as the British soldiers with their good-looking faces must disappear and just as ʿĀʾida must eventually die. Here, too, Najīb Maḥfūẓ goes much further than Jomier suspected. He is not merely showing the seductive power of a different style of life, he is calling for a purge of something which is much more harmful but which can hardly be referred to as "different" in the same sense. The fact that the thing to be purged is symbolized by ʿĀʾisha and her daughter, the two most delicate creatures in the entire trilogy, only shows how cruel and painful the decision is. Something very deeply rooted must be uprooted, and this can never be easy. British troops, French education, these will disappear with far less pain. But it will be a much more decisive, and much more painful matter to get rid of something which has become a part of yourself, which has been absorbed into the tissue of your bones and is part of your personality.

It is not easy to define what has to be uprooted. The author does not give a clear definition, and as far as can be ascertained no Egyptian critic has ever raised the question. This fact is strange, but revealing. Because, as Lesser has pointed out,[55]

> though the story-teller deals in specifics, we expect him to spin a tale which impresses us as having wide signficance and validity...we would not be satisfied — we would not usually be interested — if a story did not cast a shadow beyond itself, if it did not possess a measure of general significance.

And here we have a tragic story of great significance, yet there are some critics who analyse the trilogy with great thoroughness and do not even touch on the cruel fate of ʿĀ'isha and her family.[56] Are we to interpret this as an indication of a fatalistic acceptance of what cannot be helped or as a whole-hearted acceptance of what is desired?

Whatever the reason this lack of any reaction is significant. For as becomes apparent, there are very few issues in life on which the writer takes an extreme, unequivocal stand. But on one issue he is decidedly uncompromising, and this is the urgent need to cleanse the soul of Egyptian society of the impurities responsible for that peculiar tenseness, or even neurosis, so often exemplified by many of Najīb Maḥfūẓ's characters. The symptoms and consequences of this unhealthy situation will be discussed later; all that we would point out now is that ʿĀ'isha symbolises whatever lies at its root — the cue for which is given in her physical resemblance to her father. Then, if we go back once more to the personality of Aḥmad ʿAbd al-Jawād, we see that what was wrong about him was his duplicity. He was whole and complete and admirable both at home and in his nocturnal exploits. In neither situation is he repugnant. But the fact that he led a double life while imposing the most severe restrictions on his family, makes him objectionable. The question is not to be regarded morally, but rather psychologically. We must ask ourselves what happens in the psyche of a man who behaves in this way. For as the writer on several occasions tells us, Sayyid Aḥmad ʿAbd al-Jawād was quite unique in this and the Sayyid himself was aware of it. He knew that people of his social status would permit their wives to leave the house occasionally, and they would even take them and their daughters for a ride into town, or to visit the more respectable places of entertainment. But he was not impressed. He adhered to his own principles, deriving moral support from the Qur'ānic verse which he kept repeating to himself: "You have your own religion I have mine."[57]

Very pointedly Najīb Maḥfūẓ relates Aḥmad ʿAbd al-Jawād's

repugnant traits to his "Turkish" physical features. In the broad sense "Turkish" is a designation applied in Egypt to all those who came to Egypt originally in the service of the Mamluks or the Ottoman Sultans, and participated in governing the land in one capacity or another. Racially these people were of diverse origins, Greeks, Albanians, Bulgarians, Russians, Circassians as well as genuine Turks. They were all of lighter complexion, and occasionally had blue eyes and red or brown or blond hair. These physical features became imprinted in the consciousness of the indigenous Egyptians to such an extent that it is perhaps possible to speak now of the Turkish archetype in Egypt. Any quick survey of the individuals of Turkish descent -- *turki al-aṣl* -- in contemporary Egyptian literature will reveal a pattern of physical features almost invariably connected with an antipathetic attitude on social and intellectual issues.

This concept of "Turk" is not new in Egypt. In the consciousness of the Egyptians, as well as in that of most Arab Muslims, the "Turk" has practically never ceased to be an enigma, ever since the Turks replaced the Arabs, first as the military establishment of the Muslim Empire in the days of Caliph al-Muʿtaṣim (died 842 A.D.) and eventually as the actual rulers of the empire. Their physical features were sometimes admired sometimes despised, but always noted as peculiar. "Poetry and later, art, accepted Turkish features as beautiful." [58] Considered as slaves the Turks, both male and female, were praised in classical days for their beauty, and their price was for that reason high. But Arabs were not too meticulous about differentiating the various racial or ethnological groups of which the so-called Turks consisted.[59] Over the years the term was gradually widened to include persons with ethnic physical features which, previously had been distinguished as non-Turkish. Thus, Ibn Buṭlān (died 1066), the famous Christian physician, distinguished between the "fair skinned" Turkish woman whose eyes "are small but enticing" and the Greek woman who is "of red-white complexion, has smooth hair and blue eyes."[60] These so-called northern features soon enough came to be associated with the privileges of authority as a result of several simultaneous processes. "All the Caliphs of the 4th/10th century were born of slave girls,"[61] who were chosen for the harems because of their outstanding beauty. Consequently, the Caliphs began to assume physical features which were not at all Arab, but rather -- in later terminology -- Turkish. Historians began to notice that they had a "reddish complexion," or a "reddish beard" or a "fair complexion."[62] These were clearly Turkish features, even in the eyes of keen observers like Jāḥiẓ (died 869).[63] To the fair complexion of the Caliphs soon were added blue eyes.[64] By the time the Buwayhids established their control in Baghdad this "stamp of northern lineage" was noticed in many rulers below the rank of Caliph,[65] mainly because Turks mingled more and more in the courts of kings and princes. It is perhaps of some significance that the Ikhshid, the Turkish governor of Egypt (935-946) and the founder of an independent dynasty, also "had blue eyes."[66] These same "Turkish" features were sometimes considered ugly, for instance by the geographer Yaʿqūbī[67] (dies 897), and the traveller Ibn Baṭṭūṭā (died 1377) who says of the Russians:[68] "These are Christians, red-haired and blue-eyed, with ugly faces." There seems to be a tendency to consider these features as beautiful in slaves and women, and less frequently so in free men or in racial groups.

Whatever the evaluation of their physical features, the Turks were admired by the Arabs for their valor in battle and for their devotion to Islam, but feared for their cruelty and despised for their vulgarity. Ever since the 9th Century this ambivalent attitude towards the Turks has been unmistakable. Their contributions to Islam and the harm they have done it have always been a matter of the most soul-searching debate among Arabs. On the negative side the consensus would seem to be that

> for more than two centuries after the year 1000 the ambitions of Turkish generals and chieftains had torn and retorn the body of Islam, devastating its lands by their misgovernment and continued warfare more effectively than any foreign foe.[69]

When all this came to an end in most of the Muslim empire, the Mongols formed the eastern lands of Islam into a province of their empire.

Egypt was spared this fate, thanks to the Turkish Mamluks who blocked the Mongol advance in 1260 at ʿAin Jālūt in Palestine. But this victory perpetuated the rule of the Turks in Egypt for another two and a half centuries until their next of kin, the Ottoman Turks, took over. These latter ruled Egypt for another three and a half centuries. Thus for practically a millenium the Egyptian consciousness identified authoritarian rule with the Turks.

This long period of Islamic history is generally considered by Arab Muslims as not really Islamic, at least not as truly Islamic as the previous period which was more Arab in nature.[70] Furthermore, there is a marked tendency among Arabs in modern times to blame the Turks for the entire downfall, or regression, of Islam as compared to Christian or European culture. Sylvia Haim points out[71] that

> Muḥammad ʿAbduh dates the decline of Islam to the day of the Caliph (al-Muʿtasim, according to Rashīd Riḍā), who suspecting the loyalty of the Arab troops of his household, made use of Turkish and Dailamite mercenaries... Under the influence of these barbarians, Muḥammad ʿAbduh explains, the intellectual civilization of Islam withered and wilted, for these barbarians 'wore Islam on their bodies, but nothing of it penetrated their soul'.

ʿAbduh's view was shared by many thoughtful Arabs. Edward Atiyah, who considers[72] the whole Ottoman period "sterile in that it imparted no new cultural values or creative impulses to the Arab world," sees the

Ottomans' only saving grace in that they "did not impinge on the Arabism of its people." With many others he would interpret important internal upheavals in Egypt in terms of a struggle against Turkish domination. Thus Egyptian nationalism, even "before the descent of the British on the scene," was in his view, "a protest by the native Arabic speaking Egyptian population against...the ascendancy, over the army and the government, of the Turkish aristocracy." [73]

But whereas throughout the Arab countries the Turks were always identifiable as different if not foreign, in Egypt they became integrated with the people. They could not be driven out of Egypt as they were driven out of Arabia or Syria, because they were practically Egyptians. Yet, for all this integration they stood apart as the ruling class,[74] the aristocracy. Therefore internal disturbances, which stemmed from a feeling of dissatisfaction with the government, assumed in part the nature of a struggle for national liberation. But this struggle could be won, not by ousting the "invaders," as had been done to the Hyksos of old, but by somehow eliminating the Turkish character of the ruling class. It can perhaps be said that this was finally achieved only after the revolution of 1952, with the abdication of the king — the last "Turkish" ruler of Egypt.

Although the grievances were real, and the struggles sincere, as far as the "Turkishness" of the ruling class was concerned it was probably more of a psychological factor than the Egyptians themselves realized. It was a struggle not only against specific persons and families, but also against a certain social outlook, a moral entity, a norm of human behavior. It was at one and the same time a struggle to redress a historical wrong, to obliterate a shameful blot, to vindicate a long-standing humiliation. By the 1930s and 1940s the issue had become much more abstruse, because there was no longer any doubt after 1919 that the innately Egyptian element of the country was on the ascent. What remained to be eliminated were the psychological and emotional "drags," or the residue [75] which still hindered the emancipated Egyptians from resurrecting that spirit of old which had disappeared when, for the Arabs "in 1258 (the fall of Baghdad), or for Egypt in 1517 (the Turkish conquest), Islamic history virtually came to an end." [76]

In the trilogy these Turkish drags are most graphically symbolized by ʿĀʾisha. They are often represented in the stories of Najīb Maḥfūẓ by women with similar features. We recall, of course, Amanarīdīs of *Kifāḥ ṭayba*. The "English" girl of *Dunyā allah*, a devilish little monster of a woman, had blond hair and blue eyes. In *Hams al-junūn* there is a story [77] of a most disgusting selfish woman, also blond and with blue eyes. In another story of the same collection, called *al-Zayf* (The Counterfeit) the woman embodying this ideosyncrasy has Turkish beauty. In *al-Qāhira al-jadīda* the father who forces his daughter to become the mistress of an influential official is of Turkish origin. In *Bidāya wa nihāya* (The beginning and the End) we read of a pretty girl, strong willed and obstinate, who of course has blue eyes and a fair complexion and is of Turkish origin.

All these "Turkish" characters are selfish, egocentric, obstinate and hard to live with. A most dramatic expression of these traits is given by Ahmad ʿAbd al-Jawād when he learns that a young police officer is exploring the possibility of marrying ʿĀʾisha. He suspects that the officer has already seen her once, which in itself is a violation of the father's honor.

> I do not want to give my daughter to a person who would taint my reputation. My daughter will never be taken to a man's house unless I shall be satisfied beyond doubt that his first motive for marriage is a sincere desire on his part to seek my relationship, mine, mine, mine! [78]

One cannot fail to sense, here as elsewhere, the father's deep concern for his family, but the significant thing is that he has no other way to express this except by a constant hammering at the one and only motive which permeates his relations with his family. We know, as his family also gradually discovers, that for all his sincerity in this respect, it is an assumed posture, that essentially it is false.[79]

ʿĀ'isha is altogether different, but she has a self-consciousness inherited from her father, together with his blue eyes. She likes to watch herself in the mirror, she enjoys her own sweet voice. After marriage she easily adopts herself to a double standard of behavior. She now does things which she used to conceal from her father, such as putting on facial make-up, smoking and drinking. In the story of her tragic fate, Najīb Maḥfūẓ evidently gave vent to his conviction that this innermost falsehood, this hypocritical stance, must be eliminated.

NOTES

1 As to his writings up to 1952 and since 1958, see Introduction.

2 *Al-Qāhira al-jadīda* (1945), *Khān al-khalīlī* (1946), *Zuqāq al-midaqq* (1947), *al-Sarāb* (1948), *Bidāya wa nihāya* (1949).

3 *Supra.*, Ch. 1, n. 2.

4 Fū'ād Dawwāra, *ibid.*, p. 17.

5 *Awlād hāritnā* was originally published serially in *al-Ahrām* from 21 September to 25 December 1959. It was first published in book form in January 1967 by Dār al-Adāb of Beirut, Lebanon. The word *ḥāra* means a quarter of a town, equivalent to the French *quartier*.

6 *Al-Liṣṣ wa al-kilāb* (1961), *al-Summān wa al-kharīf* (1962), *al-Ṭarīq* (1964), *al-Shaḥḥādh* (1965), *Tharthara fawq al-nīl* (1966), *Mīrāmār* (1967).

7 *Dunyā Allāh* (1963), *Bayt sayyi' al-sumʿa* (1965).

8 Rajā' al-Naqqāsh, *Udabā' muʿāsirūn*, Cairo, 1968, in a series of nine articles analyzing the literature of Najīb Maḥfūẓ, seems to believe

that comprehending the nature of the change which occurred between 1952 and 1958 is crucial for the understanding of his entire works.

9 *Op. cit.*, "*Shuhadā' wa muntaḥirūn* ," pp. 176-76.

10 *Ibid.*, p. 171.

11 Leslie Fiedler, "Archetype and Signature," *Sewanee Review*, v. 60, No. 2, April-June 1952, p. 261: "The word archetype...I use to mean any of the immemorial patterns of response to the human situation in its most permanent aspects: death, love, the biological family, the relationship with the Unknown etc., whether those patterns be considered to reside in the Jungian Collective Unconscious or the Platonic world of Ideas."

12 Cf. for example Sāmī Khashba, "*al-Wāqiʿiyya wa al-thawra al-thaqāfiyya fī al-riwāya al-ʿarabiyya al-ḥadītha*," *al-Adab*, May 1970.

13 Cf. Aḥmad ʿAbbās Ṣāliḥ, "*Qirā'a jadīda li najīb maḥfūẓ, al-mushkila al-mītāfīzīqiyya*," *al-Kātib*, No. 59, February 1966.

14 Anouar Abdel-Malek, *Egypt: Military Society*, New York, 1968, p. 319. A short summary of *al-Liṣṣ wa al-kilāb* (The Thief and the Dogs) is given on pp. 316-318.

15 O. Lesser, *op. cit.*, p. 46.

16 Jomier, *op. cit.*, p. 35, remarks that the name of the place evokes the time of Fatimid Caliphs who had two palaces in this quarter. The space between them retains its name although the palaces have disappeared. Perhaps the historical association made Najīb Maḥfūẓ choose this location for Aḥmad ʿAbd al-Jawād's home.

17 "*Mustashriq faransī yataḥaddath ʿan thulāthiyyat Najīb Maḥfūẓ*," *al-Hilāl*, February 1970, p. 112.

18 *Modern Islam*, p. 181.

19 Author's italics. Cf. also von Grunebaum, *Medieval Islam*, pp. 221 *seq*, on the tendency of depersonalization in classical

Muslim literature.

20 Of his readings in Western literature and his preferences, cf. Fu'ād Dawwāra, *op. cit.*

21 Jomier, *op. cit.*, p. 28."certes le cadre général de la trilogie n'est pas nouveau...Mais ce qui par contre est entièrement nouveau, c'est l'application et la transposition de tels procédés, sur une telle échelle et avec une telle maîtrise, dans le domaine de la vie égyptienne."

22 Naturally, a great deal more has been written in Arabic on the development of modern Arabic prose writing than in other languages. The phases of adopting Western techniques are dealt with by 'Abd al-Muḥsīn Ṭaha Badr, *op. cit.* A helpful review of the same aspect in English is given by Abdel-Aziz Abdel-Maguid, *The Modern Arabic Short Story*, n.d., Cairo. H. A. R. Gibb's "Studies in Contemporary Arabic Liberature." is still the most penetrating analysis of the process of adoption by Arabic literature of Western techniques. See *Studies in the Civilization of Islam*, London, 1962, pp. 246. *seq.*

23 Von Grunebaum, *Islam*, p. 244.

24 Gibb, *op. cit.* p. 286.

25 Cf. Jomier, *op. cit.*, p. 38, n. 2.

26 Adham Rajab disclosed the fact that Najīb Maḥfūẓ, having been a distingished student, was recommended to be sent to France to study philosophy, as was then the custom. But his candidacy was disapproved. Najīb Maḥfūẓ himself gives the reason: "The story is that the Palace was then persecuting the Copts because they were considered the mainstay of the Wafd party. And the Palace suspected, because of my name, that I was a Copt. I was the second in my group and the first was a Copt. So they said: one Copt will do." He was dropped also on another occasion, when he was recommended to be sent to study French. His full name is Najīb

Maḥfūẓ ʿAbd al-ʿAzīz al-Sabīljī, but he signs only Najīb Maḥfūẓ, which may also be a Coptic name. *Al-Hilāl,* February 1970, pp. 96-97. Najīb Maḥfūẓ's own feelings for the Copts is reflected in his treatment of the Copt problem in the Trilogy. This is an unparalleled example of a frank and open-minded discussion of a very painful question. Najīb Ghālī, the talented young Coptic writer (*Beer in the Snooker Club*), who eventually took his own life, assured me very vehemently, as late as 1967, that Najīb Maḥfūẓ was indeed a Copt.

27 Cf. Gibb, *op. cit.,* pp. 280-81 *seq.*

28 The two most famous literary works describing this in detail are Ṭaha Ḥusayn's *Adīb,* first published in 1935, and Tawfīq al-Ḥakīm's *ʿUṣfūr min al-sharq,* first published in 1938, both of which are discussed by von Grunebaum, *Modern Islam,* pp. 374-79.

29 The nameless *adīb* decided to divorce his wife before setting out for Europe for this reason: "I know of Europe a great deal. I have read not a few of the stories sent to us, and I heard not a little of the news about those who travel there and live there. And all this tells me that I shall not resist the European way of life and its effect on me, as a man who is faithful to his wife should." Cairo, 1961, p. 83.

30 *Op. cit.,* p. 151.

31 *Ibid.,* p. 85. *Fa man dhahaba ila faransā fa huwa kāfir aw ʿalā al-aqall zindīq.*

32 "Was I persisting in requesting to be sent to France out of a desire for learning...or out of a desire for those gateways of enticements which I could not open in Egypt, but which I do not even have to open in France because they open by themselves." *Ibid.,* p. 143.

33 The time Najīb Maḥfūẓ spent on this work, as given by Ghālī Shukrī, *op. cit.,* p. 347, is as follows; preparations: 1945-1946.

Bain al-qaṣrayn: 1946-1948; *Qaṣr al-shawq:* 1948-1950; *al-Sukkarīyya*: 1950-1952.

34 Gibb, *op. cit.*, p. 286.

35 *Op. cit.*, p. 30: "L'oeuvre qu'il vient de réaliser marquera une date dans l'histoire de la littérature arabe; elle mériterait d'être connue a l'étranger."

36 *Ibid.*, p. 29.

37 A typical example, although by no means the most extreme, of this philosophy is Aḥmad Amīn, *al-Sharq wa al-gharb*, Cairo, 1955. See particularly Ch. 11, *"Mādaiyyat al-gharb wa ruḥiyyat al-sharq."*

38 Cf. for example Muṣṭafā Luṭfī al-Manfaluṭi, *al-Mazarāt*, 4th edition, Cairo, 1923, the article *"Madrasat al-Gharām,"* pp. 237-42, where the following is said: "In the past I had prayed to God, be He exalted, for nothing more than for the progress and development of this nation, and for its attaining, in the field of civilization, such achievements as may enable her to stand side by side with the Western nations in glory and power. But I have changed, and turned into one who implores Him not to listen to my prayers and not to bestow upon her of that civilization any more than He has already bestowed upon her." On Manfaluṭī's role as a literary innovator, see Gibb, *op. cit.*, pp. 258 *seq.*

39 Cf. ʿAbd al-Ḥamīd Jawda al-Sahhār, *Jisr al-shayṭān.* A similar theme is developed by Iḥsān ʿAbd al-Quddūs, in several stories. Cf. *al-Naẓẓāra al-sawdā'*, and *Sayyida fī ṣālūn.*

40 Jomier, *op. cit.*, p. 39.

41 *Ibid.*, p. 28.

42 A follower of the rigorous conservatism associated with the name of Aḥmad Ibn Ḥanbal (d. 855).

43 Jomier, p. 29.

44 A long outer garmet with sleeves. The whole situation is not unlike that described in the book of Amos, 2:7: "and a man and

his father will go in unto the same maid..." But Najīb Maḥfūẓ certainly does not evince any prophetic disapproval of the custom.

45 *Ibid.*, p. 55.

46 *Ibid.*, p. 56.

47 *Supra*. p. 102.

48 The idea of "opening the doors" is well rooted in Islamic thought as signifying a new approach to the question of independent judgment. The traditional view was that the "doors of independent judgment" (*abwāb al-ijtihād*) have been closed forever after the first three centuries of Islam. This concept became the target for attack by all shades of "modernism" in Islam. The following is characteristic: "The present stagnation of the Musulman communities is principally due to the notion which has fixed itself on the minds of the generality of Moslems, that the right to the exercise of private judgment ceased with the early legists." Ameer Ali, *The Spirit of Islam*, London, 1967, p. 183. This book was first published in 1922.

49 Cf. R. Makarius, *op. cit.*, Préface de Jacques Berque, p. 6: "Se vouloir tel, et s'éprouver tel autre, voilà pour eux une incitation permanente à l'orgueil et au désespoir. Le déchirement, le dédoublement, la frustration accompagnent leur progrès. Un idéalisme nostalgique se cumule avec leur visées practiques. Ce qu'ils font ne recouvre pas ce qu'ils sont. Ils portent ainsi jusqu'au paroxysme un conflit commun aux hommes de notre temps."

50 Jomier is perfectly right when he says: "Cependant la trilogie n'est pas un roman à thèse," p. 84.

51 The Islamic terminology used in these sentences supports the impression that the scene should be understood in the context alluded to: *li aḥtadhī mithālaka wa uḥyī taqālīdaka*. The incisiveness of these sentences will be readily appreciated once

it is remembered that the question of following the examples of the forebears and adhering to their traditions is at the center of the whole argument about keeping the door of individual judgment closed. Reduced to mere catch words the argument is between *taqlīd* — imitation — and *ijtihād* — individual judgment. Closed doors mean the former, opened doors the latter. What Yāsīn is saying with obvious sarcasm is: now that the door is open and I see reality as it is I am prepared to imitate my ancestor. This passage is undoubtedly one of the high points of the entire trilogy.

52 A famous brand of tobacco.

53 Rhymes with ʿĀʾisha.

54 *Op. cit.*, p. 64.

55 *Op. cit.*, p. 142.

56 Cf. for example Nabīl Rāghib, *op. cit.*, who devotes three chapters to the trilogy, one for each part, and does not even mention ʿĀʾisha's tragedy.

57 *Qurʾān* 109:6, Bell's English version.

58 Von Grunebaum, *Medieval Islam*, p. 208.

59 Cf. W. Barthold, *Encyclopaedia of Islam*, V. 4, p. 903.

60 Adam Mez, *The Renaissance of Islam*, 1937, p. 162.

61 *Ibid.*, p. 364.

62 *Ibid.*, pp. 9, 10.

63 Cf. "Exploits of the Turks," *RAS*, October 1915, p. 679, where reference to the "red moustache" of the Turks is made, and p. 689 where their moustaches are described as brown.

64 Mez, *op. cit.*, p. 10.

65 *Ibid.*, p. 24.

66 *Ibid.*, p. 30.

67 Cf. Yaʿkūbī, *Les Pays*, tr. Gaston Wiet, Cairo, 1937, p. 48. Cf. also Gabriel Ferrand, *Relations de Voyages*, Paris, 1914,

pp. 423, 452.

68 Cf. *Travels in Asia and Africa,* tr. H.A.R. Gibb, London, 1953, p. 152.

69 *Ibid.,* Introduction by Gibb, p. 16.

70 Cf. W. C. Smith, *Islam in Modern History,* 1957, p. 94: "Arab Islam...is uninterested in and virtually unaware of Islamic greatness after the Arab downfall."

71 *Arab Nationalism,* ed. Sylvia G. Haim, University of California Press, 1964, p. 21.

72 E. Atiyah, *The Arabs*, Penguin, 1958, p. 48.

73 *Ibid.,* p. 75. Cf. also p. 79: "The Arabi revolt /of 1882/ was principally an attack...against the Turkish oligarchy."

74 They were indeed very harsh rulers. See Lane, *Manners and Customs, op. cit.,* indexed instances of "Tyranny of Officers of the Government."

75 The Arabic *rawāsib* is hard to render.

76 Smith, *op. cit.,* p. 95.

77 "*Nakth al-umūma.*"

78 In Arabic very often the personal pronoun is repeated after a pronominol suffix denoting the genitive. This is done for emphasis. In such a case the personal pronoun takes the nominative form. Therefore this cry in Arabic is more expressive than the English translation; it reads: " I...I...I..." So also in *Bayn al-qaṣrayn* (p. 488) where he insists that "the say in this house is my say, mine, mine, mine!"

79 Cf. *Bayn qaṣrayn,* p. 251, where Kamāl is astonished at discovering that his father can laugh like a normal human being.

Chapter Five
The Unholy Valley

Although all of ʿĀʼisha's children die, she lives on. Towards the close of the trilogy, we see her for the last time as an old-looking woman, sorely beaten by life, who has barely survived her father. Wrecked, unrecognizable, she remains alive. The writer will not let his readers indulge in the illusion that their problem is solved. The future however, augurs well. The Egyptian of the future who carries in him no trace of the inherited malady, is represented by Khadīja's two sons. Khadīja, the dark-skinned, dark-haired, fat woman with black eyes and a terrible nose, who spits profusely when she speaks, is the happy mother of the story. She is strong-willed, clear headed, confident and not in the least self-conscious. She is aware of her faults but is always ready to laugh at them. She is honest and frank and courageous. She is the only person in fact, besides Yāsīn, who is prepared to criticize her father. Before sending her to her husband's home, her father wished her to follow the example of Amīna, her yielding and obedient mother. But no woman could be more different from Amīna than her daughter Khadīja. And although her two boys are the seed of her Turkish husband, they are nevertheless the Egyptians of the future, truly her sons. They differ from one another in their convictions and philosophies. One is an ardent Muslim, the other an active Communist. But they have the courage of their convictions, they know no duplicity and have no use for it. They are frank and idealistic and eventually they are both jailed for their activities. Just before they are sent to al-Ṭūr,[1] Kamāl sees them and Aḥmad, the Communist, talks to him of the inevitability of the "eternal revolution" and the duty of men to work for the realization of "high ideals." ʿAbd al-Munʿīm, the Muslim Brother, agrees with his brother, which causes Kamāl to think that these words should be interpreted as "a call to faith irrespective of its source or aim."

These two youngsters electrify present-day Egyptian critics. They are designed to adumbrate the ideal man of modern Egypt, a man who shows a free spirit, free from the inhibitions caused by repressed emotion and ideological confusion. He is deeply committed to the well-being of his society and is prepared to make sacrifices for whatever cause he believes in. Such a man will not reject the legacy of his culture nor will he subject himself to it slavishly. He will find a way to reconcile modernism with whatever is valuable in tradition.[2] Whether the two brothers symbolize two aspects of one person or whether they merely indicate a certain similarity between the two beliefs they represent, they clearly share some basic characteristics.

This idealism has its drawbacks. As pointed out by Jomier,[3] the brothers lack psychological depth. The writer obviously used them to serve a particular ideal, but he consequently failed to develop their personalities. All of which is reminiscent of the way the writer treated the characters in his historical novels, making them comply too well with a preconveived image.

Clearly, then, ʿAbd al-Munʿīm and Aḥmad are destined for big things; but actually we do not learn very much about them because the trilogy ends when they are taken to prison. Some critics have felt that the work lacks a fourth part, dedicated to the history of these brothers. But they seem consciously or unconsciously, to miss the message of the trilogy. Najīb Maḥfuẓ could not go back to romantic writing, and portray again "perfect men." In the little he wrote of the brothers he was already utopian, but luckily this was only for a short spell. In his next literary period he will write a great deal about two young men[4] who have been released from prison. They are not at all perfect; indeed, their idealism is all too extreme and indiscriminate to do any good. They consequently die soon after they are set free. No Egyptian would consent to see in the story of these two men the fourth part of the trilogy, but perhaps it should be seen in this light. For although society may dream of the perfect man, it must resign itself to the fact that ideals can only be a source of inspiration, never a reality. The function of the two young Shaukat brothers in *al-Sukkariyya* is not to vindicate idealism but to demonstrate a certain psychological wholesomeness.

Aḥmad ʿAbbās Ṣāliḥ complains that of all Najīb Maḥfūẓ's characters, the Socialists turn out colorless and comparatively pale.[5] In 1966, this must have been considered a grave accusation, to which Najīb Maḥfūẓ hastened to reply.[6] He admits the truth of the observation, but offers three excuses. First that all his revolutionary characters play secondary roles, so naturally they should look pale next to the main characters. This he considers the artistic excuse. Second, the society he was observing in his works had no revolutionary characters, but only "disrupters and oppportunists."[7] By analyzing them the writer wished to arrive at an understanding of the crisis of his times. Third, the revolutionaries of this society actually were on the margin of society, just as they were depicted in the stories. What is more, they all came out of the *petite bourgeoisie,* who had learned the meaning of revolution by way of intellectual education, not by way of "class efforts."[8]

One cannot argue with a writer explaining his works, but on the whole Najīb Maḥfūẓ's works are replete with rebels of remarkable stature. That these should be referred to by the writer as "disrupters and opportunists" is quite revealing. In no case do they follow the standard Socialist way of thinking, or that of Islamic radicalism. Ṣāliḥ would have been much closer to the truth had he said that neither Socialists nor radical Muslims emerge as interesting characters in the works of Najīb Maḥfuẓ. Wherever we find a pale Socialist there is also to be found a pale radical Muslim. But the reason for Ṣāliḥ's complaint is clear; he has noticed that of the two it is the Muslim who signals some hope. Nevertheless, it is a fact that all social revolutionaries are insignificant, aesthetically speaking, when compared to the other types of rebels in Najīb Maḥfūẓ's stories, the so-called "disrupters and opportunities." It would appear then that in spite of the writer's preference for the Islamic tendency, both types are rather marginal in terms of human endeavor.. This impression is inescapable at the end of the trilogy. Kamāl after hearing Aḥmad's noble extortation,[9] thinks to himself: "Could you be at the same time an exemplary teacher, an exemplary husband and an eternal revolutionary?!"[10] Kamāl is a teacher, and has come to doubt his ability in this role. He is also a bachelor, approaching 40. He is not a revolutionary but he is aware of the meaning of a full, committed life and he suspects that it does not go well with being a revolutionary.

Najīb Maḥfūẓ often constructs his stories in triads, such as Aḥmad ʿAbd al-Jawād and his two sons, Yāsīn and Kamāl, Amīna and her two daughters, or the two Shaukat brothers and their cousin. In *al-Qāhira al-jadīda* the third member of the trial is a rebel. The other two, are Ma'mūn Raḍwān, the ardent Muslim, and ʿAlī Ṭāhā the Socialist. But this third, Maḥjūb ʿAbd al-Dā'im, is different from them. Faced with the problem of how to save himself from the stark poverty of the gutter, he finds the solution. Expressed in a mathematical form it reads: "Religion + science + philosophy + morals = Ṭuẓ."[11] Through rebellion he seeks to survive within society, a task which he finds extremely difficult. Eventually, he gains a fairly high rank in government service, though the price he has to pay is exorbitant. He has to cover up the illicit relations between a powerful person in the government and a girl, Iḥsān, whose father, Shaḥḥāta Turkī,has forced her to become the man's mistress. Maḥjūb married her, on condition that he vacate the house for the boss one night every week. When the scandal[12] does break

Maḥjūb and his beautiful wife have to leave Cairo and settle down to the ordinary life of a government official in the distant province of Aswān. A tragedy? When Maḥjūb graduated from college, a penniless intellectual, he had no idea how he could stay alive at all. Now he has a most beautiful girl for a wife, and the terrible boss is finally off their backs. With a government office and a pretty wife, life cannot look as bad as it did only a few months earlier. Ṣāliḥ has indeed noticed [13] that the works of Najīb Maḥfūẓ

> always begin with a search, with a situation of eagerness for an equilibrium. Then it all ends in a tragic failure. But in spite of this they leave some hope and spur /one/ on to renew the search.

In fairness it must be admitted that with refernce to *al-Qāhira al-jadīda* he says the element of hope is furnished, not by Maḥjūb's final situation, but by the uncovering of the two approaches, the secular and the religious, to the solution of society's problems. But he adds that at this point the writer "stands bewildered, unsatisfied.[14] In the last lines of *al-Qāhira al-jadīda* he places these two approaches parallel to each other, as if they would never meet!" Ṣāliḥ notices such irresolute confrontation in many of Najīb Maḥfūẓ's works. We are therefore bound to ask: where is the optimism he is referring to? Is it in the insolubility of the confrontation between two social philosophies? Not very likely. But when we examine the human situation, which for Najīb Maḥfūẓ is never the same as the ideological situation, there we do find optimism. Most of his works written prior to 1958 end with the protagonist facing the future in a somewhat more reassured state than at the beginning. There are no happy ends to be sure, but, as Ṣāliḥ so expressively put it, they all end with a spurring on to a renewed search. Before we examine the nature of Najīb Maḥfūẓ's optimism in this phase of his work, a certain digression is necessary.

In 1957 Najīb Maḥfūẓ was awarded in Cairo the State Prize for his *Qaṣr al-shawq*, jointly with Muḥammad Kāmil Ḥusayn, who received his share of the prize for his book *Qarya ẓālima* (City of Wrong).[15] It would be helpful to pay some attention to this book before proceeding. The significance of Kāmil Ḥusayn's work is that it treats the subject of the crucifixion of Christ in an unusual manner,[16] and it raises issues not of Christianity but of Islam. Kenneth Cragg sees it this way:[17]

> It is occupied with the appeal beyond conscience to the collective in human affairs, the wrong of man's slavishness to communal interest and the inability of religion or law to save man from his tragic rebellion against the truth of conscience unless they themselves, that is religion and law, are properly related to truth in the capacity of servants not masters.

This epitomized version of the book's content may not bring to mind the central Islamic issue it raises, namely the validity of the doctrine of *ijmaʿ* — consensus — one of the four recognized "roots" of Islamic jurisprudence. Underlying the concept of *ijmāʿ* is the confidence, based on a saying of the Prophet, that "never will my community be united in an error." This trust in the judgment of the community never meant that the community as a whole exercised the right to make judicial decisions. "Gradually *ijmaʿ* came to be interpreted as the agreement of those competent to judge in religious matters; it became the agreement of the learned."[18] But whatever flexibility this doctrine initially offered was practically exhausted after a few centuries of independent thinking by Islamic scholars.

> When, therefore, a consensus of opinion had been attained by the scholars of the second and third centuries on any given point, the promulgation of new ideas on the exposition of the relevant texts of the Koran and Hadith was as good as forbidden. Their decisions were irrevocable.[19]

One of these irrevocable decisions was that the "gate of *ijtihād*" was shut once and for all. The struggle to reopen the gate of individual judgment in modern Islam has been mentioned earlier.[20] But this struggle is in itself no challenge to the principle of *ijmaʿ*; it is merely a call to those in authority to exercise their judgment again, relying on the old dogma of the infallibility of the Islamic community. This however is not what Kāmil Ḥusayn is looking for. He is challenging the very principle of this infallibility. Speaking ostensibly of the Jewish Sanhedrin taking its resolution regarding Christ's crucifixion he says: [21]

> They were of all people most meticulous, sincere in their religious practice and characertized by fervor, courage and integrity. Yet this thorough competence in their religion did not save them from wrong-doing, nor immunize their minds from error...They were people who took counsel among themselves, [22] yet their counsels led them astray.

This is clearly the *leitmotif* of the entire treatise. As against this fallibility of the leaders, Kāmil Ḥusayn emphasizes the potency of the individual conscience in leading toward the good,[23] but only when it is prepared to be accountable for its decisions. Weak and unprincipled men prefer the common action of society because in such a situation

> the greatest crimes are easily and readily perpetrated, but so long as they are distributed among many the share of each individual is too insignificant for his conscience to bother about. [24]

Society being thus devoid of conscience looks to the chosen few to supply that conscience,[25] and will brook no attempts on the part of these few to shirk their responsibility. So, discovering that the Sanhedrin began to waver after first deciding that Christ should be crucified, "voices outside the meeting hall...grew louder, insisting on the death of the man and his followers. The ground of these demands was that the leaders had already so decreed. Were they not the wise and knowing people who could not agree on an error?" [26]

This digression from the writings of Najīb Maḥfūẓ has been made to show a line of thinking which expresses an extreme phase of the school of thought which is referred to as the "Modernists" by Gibb,[27] or which can be viewed as a prolongation of the liberal trend of modernism in Islam into a period in which it has ceased to have much relevance.[28] It may thus help to show the specific contours of Najīb Maḥfūẓ's own line of thinking. For the issue of individual conscience in relation to society concerns him very much in his trilogy and in all his early works. But by 1957 it was clear that his views on this subject were quite different from those of Kāmil Ḥusayn. Whatever resemblance there was could be attributed to the similarity of purpose shared by two men standing at the same crossroad, but facing different directions. Kāmil Ḥusayn's road led him directly and consistently to his next book, *al-Wādī al-muqaddas*[29] (The Holy Valley), which is a call for the internalization of individual life, and the renunciation of wordly achievement.[30]

On the basis of such an outlook it is not at all surprising to find the following:[31]

> What will show you that faith alone is sufficient to purify the soul is what you see of the purity of the pious and those who dedicate themselves to devotional service...When they base their lives on purity they wish for nothing save spiritual peace, which they achieve in this way.

This typical *Ṣūfī* attitude, is perhaps the last thing we would expect of one who has been counted among the real revolutionaries of modern Islam.[32] But such a return to Ṣufism is probably the only way open to a Muslim who rejects the authority of society. This call for an individual search for the right road to the truth, this renewed respect for self-denial[33] derives from motives similar to those of old Ṣufism which were

> a protest...against the social and political abuses which appeared to be condoned by the official Sunni ʿUlamāʾ; but its programme of reform was bound up with the awakening of the religious conscience of individuals and the consequent reaction of this spiritual revival on the social organization of the community.[34]

In Part Three of this study the problem of Ṣufism in contemporary Egyptian society will be discussed in greater depth, because it has become so central in Najīb Maḥfūẓ's later works. But it was felt important to point out at this juncture the direction Kāmil Ḥusayn's thought was already taking in his *City of Wrong*. For, as has been said, Najīb Maḥfūẓ was standing at a similar point, at which individual conscience appeared to him to be at loggerheads with society. The nature of this conflict seems to have been similarly analyzed by both writers. But the conclusions they have arrived at are diametrically opposed.

The present-day conflict between individual conscience and society is largely the outcome of the effects of the Western culture on Egypt's traditions. Invariably the conflict, as depicted by Najīb Maḥfūẓ, takes the form of a confrontation between sons and fathers. This is not surprising nor is it original in any way because, as von Grunebaum has pointed out,[35]

> At a certain stage of the acculturation process, resituating oneself, or re-evaluating oneself through a re-revalution of one's society and culture, imposes itself as a psychological obsession.

Society and culture are most easily depicted through one's father, and this is the form chosen by many Arab novelists to treat the problem. In the novels of Najīb Maḥfūẓ, a certain pattern is discernible. The conflict is either soluble or it is insoluble. If it is soluble, the son succumbs to the extent that he willingly or unwillingly strikes a road which enables him to assert himself without creating an irreparable breach with his father. If the conflict is insoluble, the son dies in a good but hopeless cause. Thus, when the scandal in *al-Qāhira al-jadīda* breaks out, Maḥjūb's old father, whom he has neglected and emotionally repudiated,[36] is present in his apartment and witnesses his son's humiliation. In this way Maḥjūb is brought back to his senses, and gets another chance.

In *Khān al-khalīlī* [37] that same motive is exploded into a full-fledged allegory in the sense that the "poet explicitly indicates the relationship of his images to examples and precepts, and so tries to indicate how a commentary on him should proceed." [38] The novel opens in September, 1941 with the story of a family who have just moved into the "old native quarter" of Cairo, Khān al-Khalīlī, after having lived for many years in the more modern quarter of al-Sakākīnī. The reason for this move is the fathers' belief that it would be safer to live closer to the holy mosque of Sīdnā Ḥusayn where the sanctity of the mosque would protect the whole quarter from German air raids. His son Aḥmad ʿĀkif, an intelligent and educated bachelor of 40 who works as a petty government official, realizes that his father's assumption is unsound. But he is nevertheless relieved at moving to the new place. We see then, the modern Egyptian, faced with the hazards of the modern world, happily even if somewhat sceptically withdrawing into the security of his traditional concepts. It is true that Aḥmad ʿĀkif is not the most modern of modern Egyptians. A namesake of his, a lawyer with social inclinations named Aḥmad Rāshid, is far more modern. He sees nothing holy about Khān al-Khalīlī. Considering it rationally, he finds nothing in this old quarter except filth, which were better removed to enable people to live a clean and healthy life. But this difference in the degree of modernity is not to be taken too seriously, for Aḥmad Rāshid too has just moved to the old and sacred neighborhood "more or less" because of the air raids. Fāṭima Mūsā comments [39] on the significance of their names:

> They are both educated. But one is *ʿākif* — obsessed — with himself and the past, and the other is *rāshid* — rightly guided — acquainted with the new learning and believes in science and is concerned with social problems.

This is generally true but there is no gainsaying that Aḥmad Rāshid is not only a minor figure in the story, he is, as are all the Socialists of Najīb Maḥfūẓ, a sterile, uninteresting character.[40] He is not even Aḥmad ʿĀkīf's anti-type. He is simply an annoying element, causing vexation and confusion. ʿĀkīf's anti-type is another ʿĀkīf, actually his own brother — Rushdī ʿĀkīf. Now, this game of names naturally invites guessing and interpretation. Rushdī and Rāshid both derive from the same verbal noun *rushd* -- good sense, reason, maturity of mind. Rāshid is the *nomen agentis,* while Rushdī is the *nomen relativum,* or a relative adjective. Obviously aware of the purpose of this verbal device Fāṭima Mūsā remarks [41] that

> Rushdī and Aḥmad Rāshid — in spite of an obvious difference between them -- are two aspects of one truth, which is youth that possesses the future as against Aḥmad ʿĀkif who is something forgotten, left behind by the past.

The direct connection between Rāshid and Rushdī is formed by making the latter replace the former as the private teacher of Nawāl. She is a girl of 16 whose feminine instincts have just become mature enough for her to begin noticing the men around her with a woman's eye. But Rāshid, her private teacher, is too insensitive to her feelings.[42] So she willingly responds to Aḥmad ʿĀkif's overtures, which, however, never go beyond looking at her yearningly from his window when she comes out on the balcony. Thus, the middle-aged bachelor, too introvert to dare, throttles this relationship with the girl at this initial phase, until his brother comes along and captures her with gusto. With the appearance of Rushdī, Rāshid disappears. But contrary to Fāṭima Mūsā's expectations Rushdī will not be present for long; in less than a year he will die of consumption. Meanwhile his relations with Nawāl develop quite rapidly, and fruition is already discerned in the expected marriage. However, it all comes to naught, because Rushdī's way of life is too individualistic, too selfish, and too inconsiderate of accepted norms of behavior. Unlike his older brother he feels no responsibility for his family. He gambles, drinks, and smokes heavily. He further exhausts himself by rising early to meet Nawāl and escort her to school. Her school is in ʿAbbāsiyya and she is used to go there by way of al-Sikka al-Jadīda, leading through al-Darrāsa [43] to the desert road. There she turns north and walks all the way to ʿAbbāsiyya. This is a symbolic journey in which place-names and geographical features are used allegorically. On the "new road" the girl goes to school. The young man meets her on this road, and they both go through the threshing machine. This leads them to a desert road, on the left side of which stretches the cemetery. They are both aware of the cemetery, where Rāshid's younger brother happens to be buried, and on their first walk together they even stop to say the *al-Fatiḥa*. [44] At the same time they try to ignore the graves and to derive pleasure from their love "without noticing the derisive contradiction between their love-talk and the speech of the grave."

The entire experience is too much for Rushdī whose health rapidly deteriorates. Soon this young and confident man dies without realizing any of his dreams. A strange comment on youth's future! It is therefore rather disconcerting to read, in the light of all this, the following lines in Fāṭima Mūsā's article:

> Rushdī's illness and then his death are...an ordained fate which the reader can sense the minute he sees his leanness and his paleness and watches his nighty exertions and contentiousness, his late return at night from Ghamra to al-Ḥusayn, [46] the road he used to take every morning with his girl through the cemetery, where the specter of the grave lingered over their love from the very beginning.

For if this could be sensed so early in the story what made Fāṭima Mūsā say that Rushdī and Rāshid both represented "the youth which possesses the future"? We must assume that she was not sincere because she obviously understood very well to whom the future belonged in this novel. In fact she quotes the very passage in the novel in which this is stated, after Rushdī's death:

> But Aḥmad -- in spite of his sorrow -- saw stars glittering over the horizon. These days people began saying that the government was going to do justice to neglected officials, and so the seventh grade now came within reach ...It made him happy that he would be placed in charge of four people apart from the messenger boy....It is obvious that life is never devoid of hope. Who knows what is hidden except God!

One of the causes of this renewed hope is the fact that after Rushdī's death, in September 1942, the family moves again, leaving Khān al-Khalīlī for al-Zaytūn, a modern suburb to the north. There, in the new apartment, Aḥmad meets a widow of 35, and there are indications that her people will welcome a proposal from him.

The son who somehow makes his peace with his father is the one who shall live to hope. Making the peace is not easy, as Najīb Maḥfūẓ knows full well,[47] and it requires a great deal of humility on the part of the son.

The story of *Zuqāq al-midaqq* (Midaqq Alley) [48] is of two friends who leave the alley to try their luck in the modern world, as embodied for them in a British Army camp during World War II. The one, Ḥusayn, leaves the alley because he hates living there, and the rift between him and his father seems irreparable. But eventually Ḥusayn returns home, penniless, disillusioned, with a pregnant wife. This is a victory for the father and a guarantee of the son's future.

The other friend, ʿAbbās al-Ḥilū, is a delicate, honest young man, whose sole ambition is to make a little money and marry the orphan girl he loves. But when he returns he finds that the girl has disappeared. She has left the alley in the Old City to enjoy the lights and adventures of the modern city. This is a great tragedy for him, and he cannot resign himself to his fate. ʿAbbās has no family, but al-Sayyid Raḍwān al-Ḥusaynī, the acknowledged moral and religious authority in the alley, advises him, just before leaving on a pilgrimage to Mecca:

> Go back to Tall al-Kabīr...[49] Work with all your zeal,

> and save as much money as you need to start a new life, God willing. Be carefull not to let your head get lost in thoughts, or your resolution be weakened in face of despair and anger. Do not think that the bad luck which has befallen you is all that awaits you in life...Get up, reinforced with perseverance,...and be delighted with the happiness of the believer who perceives that God has chosen him to join the order of the afflicted among His friends. [50]

ʿAbbās promises to follow this fatherly advice, but he cannot overcome his rebellious heart. He goes to town in search of his girl, becomes embroiled with Australian soldiers whom she was entertaining and who beat him to death. This is a sad end of the kind ʿAbbās. But life soon resumes its normal course, and every one in the alley returns to his daily worries and daily pleasures. Nothing more is told of Ḥusayn, but we know that his pregnant wife will soon give birth, and through him, the reconciled son, life will continue.

The role of the father in the works of Najīb Maḥfūẓ eludes definition. Ghālī Shukrī feels [51] that the death or incapacity of the parents, particularly of the father, usually marks the beginning of each of Najīb Maḥfūẓ's tragedies. In his view, the parents play the role of a psychological fence which protects the individual from collapse. But although this is true in some cases, there are other novels by Najīb Maḥfūẓ where the father is shown as the active cause of the children's fall. Furthermore, in the trilogy none of the tragedies are related to the absence of weakness of parents, while in most of the other novels the parents are weaklings, and usually have no say in their children's fortunes. Far from being a protective shield, in most cases they constitute liabilities which the children find burdensome. The situations are not those of children needing parental care, but of parents needing their children's aid, loyalty and devotion. In *al-Qāhira al-jadīda* and *Khān al-khalīlī* this is explicitly the situation while in *Zuqāq al-midaqq* it is an important element of the situation, and in the particular case of ʿAbbās al-Ḥilū[52] the fact that tradition is depicted also through society as a whole give it an added dimension.

Children's duty toward parents is one of the most central Islamic moral concepts, and is expressed by the phrase *al-birr bi al-wālidayn*.[53] Arabic stories and traditions, both Islamic and pre-Islamic, abound in which this specific obligation is lauded. The obligation is fairly selfless in quality as far as the children are concerned, because its fullest manifestation can take place only when the children reach the prime of their lives and the parents have sunk into complete impotence. But this absence of direct utilitarian motivation on the part of the children does not negate the utilitarian nature of the obligation in the sense that if it is neglected the consequence may take the shape of a wrathful visitation by fate. And this is indeed what happens time and again in the stories of Najīb Maḥfūẓ.

A good son's sensitivity to the respect due to his father is demonstrated in an impressively authentic episode in *al-Sukariyya*. Fu'ād, the son of Aḥmad ʿAbd al-Jawād's shop assistant of many years, whose education was made possible by Aḥmad's generosity, comes to visit the old patriarch, having just attained an impressive post at the district attorney's office. The meeting is described as seen by Kamāl, the independent minded son of Aḥmad ʿAbd al-Jawād, and Fu'ād's close friend.

> Fu'ād straightened up in his chair and placed one leg over the other. This move drew Kamāl's somewhat disturbed attention, but the Sayyid did not indicate any notice of it. Have things really come to that? True, he is a deputy district attorney — the top of the world! — but has he forgotten who is the man sitting in front of him? But good lord! not only that. He is opening a cigarette case,[54] and is offering it to the Sayyid, who gracefully declines the offer. Indeed the office of the district attorney may cause forgetfulness, but it is truly saddening to see such forgetfulness extending to the benefactor whose favor seems to have been dissipated like the smoke of this proud cigarette.

> There was no affectedness whatsoever in Fu'ād's behavior. He was an important person who got used to his own importance. Said the Sayyid, addressing Kamāl:
> - Congratulate him, for he has been promoted from assitant attorney to deputy attorney.
>
> Said Kamāl smiling:
> - Congratulations, congratulations, I wish soon to congratulate you on achieving a judge's chair.
>
> Said Fu'ād:
> - The next step, God willing.
>
> And then perhaps he will permit himself — when he becomes a judge — to urinate in front of the man sitting before him.

The novel *Bidāya wa nihāya*, written in 1943, shows a marked degree of mastery in the art of writing and in handling the material. The work is remarkable also because of its deep insight into the problems of the Egyptian society which emerged after the treaty of 1936.[55] It is the story of a young army officer of lowly origin who is admitted to the Military Academy after the liberalization of the Academy's admission policy.[56] He attains an officer's rank, only to become fully aware of his embarrassing social position among his fellow officers, most of whom come from aristocratic families. He realizes with apprehension the incompatibility between his newly gained position on the one hand, and the restrictions forced on him by his social background, on the other hand. Najīb Maḥfūẓ is certainly not to be criticized for failing to foresee in 1943 the outcome of this terrible predicament as it actually unfolded in 1952.[57] However, he clearly sensed the unsettling effects of the ostensibly minor step of admitting a small number of cadets of humble birth into the officers' ranks. He also felt quite distinctly that, faced with the problems thus created, an officer of this group might attempt to solve them destructively by denying his past, by withdrawing the respect and devotion due to parents and all they stand for.

The hero of this story, Ḥasanayn, ends his young life by drowning himself in the Nile, certain that he is left with no alternative. He had just forced his sister, a very unhappy young woman, who was caught in a police raid on a brothel, to throw herself into the Nile. This is clearly a symbolic act. Nafīsa, the sister, whose story of moral decline is externally quite flawless, is psychologically a rather "stylized figure."[58] Her allegorical role becomes apparent once it is realized that she reflects or symbolizes Ḥasanayn's own conscience, which is constantly being prostituted. His interior mologue toward the end of the novel, when he watches her dead body lying on the quay by the Nile, is thus very apposite. While standing there, noticing the most minute details of his sisters' corpse, he suddenly thinks: "O God, I am finished." Then he continues: "What right have I given myself! Am I really aroused to defend the honor of our family?! I am the worst of the whole family." And in the same stream of thought he continues: "For a long time I wanted to wipe out the past, but the past has devoured the present, for the frightening past was none other than myself."

The oft-repeated phrase "the odious past" had become an obsession with him once he saw the unbridgeable social gap between himself and the other officers. The poverty and low origin of his family, the fact that his eldest brother Ḥasan was a gangster, that his sister had to go out to work for people as a dressmaker, all these shameful features of his past had to be erased. He made his family move therefore from Shubrā to Miṣr al-Jadīda,[59] a move which is not dissimilar to the one made by Aḥmad ʿĀkif from Khān al-Khalīlī to al-Zaytūn, a suburb adjoining Miṣr al-Jadīda. But there is, nevertheless a whole world of difference between the two. The ʿĀkifs move not in rebellion, or in an effort to escape their past. Aḥmad ʿĀkif, the model of *birr*,[60] takes his parents to the new and modern place fully acknowledging their precedence and rights over him, a concept expressed by the term *faḍl*. But Ḥasanayn moves his family at night, so that the new neighbors will not see the poor furtinure they have to drag with them from the old place. Having done that he begins asking himself whether his mother and sister are equal to their new neighbors.

> He fancied the comments that would be made by the ladies after visiting his home, and his blood went to his head. He turned to his mother and said in a tone of warning:
> It is not necessary for us to meet anyone in the new neighborhood, or that anyone should meet us. We will not make any calls, and no one should call on us.

He goes on to say that he would not wish anyone of the old neighborhood to come over to see them. But here there is a problem. His fiancee, and her father Farīd Affandī Muḥammad, the devoted neighbor who has done all a man could to replace the dead father of Ḥasanayn's family, live in Shubrā. For Ḥasanayn the solution is obvious: he will end his relations with the girl. Apart from injuring the girl's feelings his calling off the engagement is a terrible insult to her father, who had unquestionable *faḍl* over Ḥasanayn.

Ḥasanayn also has that gangster brother to handle. Ḥasan is the eldest brother, and once when Ḥasanayn had urgently needed some ready money in order to register at the Military Academy he had found Ḥasan's den and had begged him for help. Now he goes there again, to try and convince Ḥasan to change. On hearing Ḥasanayn's concern for him Ḥasan says:

> A year ago you were in urgent need of money so you were not concerned at all to advise and guide me. But now that you have become an officer [61] nothing interests you more than defending this glittering star of yours.

And he concludes:

> Make no mistake. They call me the *rūsī* [62] not the noble. Now, what is the meaning of dishonorable life? All there is is life and nothing else and everyone is running after his sustenance.

This practical, pragmatic approach to life always finds a place in the works of Najīb Maḥfūẓ. But whenever we find it, we should expect its more positive counterpart. This time it is furnished by Ḥusayn the third brother, and the third person of Najīb Maḥfūẓ's ever-present triad. Ḥusayn is younger than Ḥasan but older than Ḥasanayn. When he finished high school he gave up his ambitions for further studies and, like Aḥmad ʿĀkif, assumed the responsibility for his family. He thinks positively, and he explores Socialism hoping there is nothing in it to diminish the lofty positions of religion, family and morality. And it is to him that Ḥasanayn turns after his failure with Ḥasan. Ḥusayn realizes that his younger brother is haunted by their past, and tries to reassure him:

> It is not our fault. We cannot let fear harass us all the time. We may be hit by a bullet fired by people's tongues, now or later, but we shall never be able to face life if we do not arm ourselves with a little indifference.

While all these talks are taking place, no one is aware of Nafīsa's activities. She sinks lower and lower as time passes, just as Ḥasanayn is sinking. How close their thinking has come we see when Ḥasanayn calls off his engagement to Bahīyya, and Nafīsa approves. She, the secret prostitute, and Ḥasanayn, the young aspiring officer, both believe that marriage should be a means of social advancement, which Bahīyya does not offer. Nor could Nafīsa offer such advancement to Salmān Jābir Salmān, the son of the greengrocer in Shubrā, who had seduced her then deserted her to marry a girl of property. No one in the family knew of her personal tragedy, so they could not sense the irony of her justifying Ḥasanayn's behavior. But to the reader the equation of the young ambitious officer, and the mean and vulgar son of the greengrocer is all too clear. The noble person of the piece is, of course, Ḥusayn, who rushes to Farīd Affandī to apologize for his brother's humiliating behavior. He goes there motivated by a sense of duty to a man who had stood by them like a father for so many years when they were poor orphans. He finds the good old man deeply hurt and depressed. Ḥusayn wants to help him regain his honor and his daughter's self-respect, and suddenly offers to marry Bahiyya himself. He will certainly be accepted by both father and daughter. His noble character, his dutifulness, his respect for life, for parents, for society, all these will now bear fruit. Ḥasan will soon die the death of a thief, Ḥasanayn and Nafīsa will drown in the Nile. Ḥusayn alone will marry the lovely girl, and face a future glittering with hope.

One meets with serious difficulty in attempting to classify Najīb Maḥfūẓ's characters psychologically. Maḥjūb and Ḥasanayn are very much alike in their tension and constant anxiety. They are always fearful, believing themselves to be victims of hidden forces which are constantly persecuting them. Their greatest ambition is to establish themselves as acknowledged members of a society to which they do not belong by birth. But in order to achieve this they launch themselves on a self-contradicting program. In the first instance they are convinced that anything shameful in their past and in their social background must be erased in order to qualify them to join the desired society on its own terms. But to do this they must violate the standards of honorable conduct cherished by the society to which they aspire. To escape the embarrassment inherent in such a mode of action they impute to society an intrinsic hypocricy, a pretense of cherishing all these moral values which only serve to keep the ambitious aspirant of the lower classes in his place. This can perhaps be considered a case of schizophrenic world view. The term is used here in the sense that the mental life of a schizophrenic may be described as not merely a field strewn with ruins or as an agglomeration of symptoms, but as a whole and as a *Gestalt*.[63] Can these people ever come to terms with reality? Sometimes they can, under the effect of a terrible shock, as was the case with Maḥjūb; sometimes they cannot, and like Ḥasanayn they take their own lives.

A similar problem is faced by Aḥmad ʿĀkif. He too is always tense, his ambitions are thwarted by circumstances beyond his grasp, and he therefore believes that the society to which he aspires ceaselessly obstructs his advancement. But he stops short of condemning the entire moral system of society. He escapes rather into himself and by this process of internalization he manages to resist the devastating effects of long years of frustration. Rushdī ʿĀkif, on the other hand, is quite happy with his lot, he feels no bitterness toward anyone. Only his blind egotism, his unrestrained pursuit of pleasure and his callousness to the injuries he is inflicting on the people closest to him make his early death inevitable.

A sense of satisfaction and a wholesome life are not easily attained anywhere. But in so far as they do appear in the works of Najīb Maḥfūẓ they are enjoyed either by men like Ḥusayn, whose moral integrity and courage practically guarantee his ultimate satisfaction in life, or by people who still manage to go on living as best they can within the framework of the ancient social concepts. Such a person is Yāsīn of the trilogy, whose optimism and gaiety can never be disturbed for long.

At this stage some observations on Najīb Maḥfūẓ's typology would be in place. It has been remarked that his studies of philosophy made him aware of psychoanalysis,[64] and indeed he frequently attributes certain traits of character to episodes or situations of early childhood. However, these attempts at a "reductive"[65] explanation of his characters' behavior usually fail to produce a satisfactory psychological sequence. Blaming the dead father for Ḥasan's and Nafīsa's depravity in *Bidāya wa nihāya* or making Aḥmad ʿĀkif's introversion the consequence of some event in childhood, can hardly be accepted as conclusive. Similarly by alluding to Kamāl's forceful removal from his mother's bed at the age of six or seven, his later hesitations about marriage are not made any more comprehensible. One feels that by these psychological hints Najīb Maḥfūẓ is misleading his readers in order to allay anxieties which are aroused by his stories. The probability of this is enhanced when one notices the casualness of his psychological explanations. Certainly, a man's behavior can to some extent be traced to events of his young days. But as Jung has indicated[66]

> A man is only half understood when we know how everything in him came into being...Life is also tomorrow, and today is understood only when we can add to our knowledge of what was yesterday the beginnings of tomorrow...The symptoms of a neurosis are not simply the effects of long-past causes, whether 'infantile sexuality', or the infantile urge to power; they are also attempts at a new synthesis of life — unsuccessful attempts, let it be added in the same breath, yet attempts nevertheless, with core of value and meaning. They are seeds that fail to sprout owing to the inclement conditions of inner and outer nature.

This Najīb Maḥfūẓ seems to have fully realized, and the anxieties, or neuroses, of his heroes are no less the result of fear of what is coming than of complexes created by what has happened in the past. He also seems to have realized that his heroes

> are mostly of a type whose surface herosim is an infantile defiance of a fate greater than they, or else a pomposity meant to cover up some touchy inferiority.[67]

The crux of the psychological difficulty, in Jung's terms, is probably that it does not lie in the power of man to transfer disposable psychic energy at will. "Psychic energy is a very fastidious thing which insists on fulfilment of its own conditions."[68] The consequence is that often a voluntary transformation of psychic energy fails dismally, "and all that happens is a new repression."[69]

For the psycholoanalyst this is usually a predicament of an individual. For the historian this may sometimes be the predicament of a generation, or a civilization.[70] For a writer telling the story of his generation and describing the recurring frustrations of individuals, this must become the central issue of his writing. It should be recalled that basically the desired transformation which is so difficult to bring about is an emergence from the traditional Muslim culture and the development of a modern Muslim culture. As observed in the individual, the psychological process at work is almost exactly that described by Jung when he explains [71] the tension between the conscious and the unconscious and their peculiar relations in the two main opposite types singled out by him, namely the introvert and the extravert.

Jung emphasizes [72] "that not a few of the great spiritual controversies rest upon the opposition of the two types." But the important point for our present discussion is that "each individual has a share in this opposition of types." [73] This, as Jung explains, means that every person has both attitudes in him and it follows "that with the introvert extraversion lies dormant and undeveloped somewhere in the background, and that introversion leads a similar shadowy existence in the extravert." [74] The significance of this dualistic psyshic content which hides under the surface of each individual "persona" [75] is that "in the introvert the influence of the object produces an inferior extraversion, while in the extravert an introversion takes the place of his social attitude." [76] The "inferior counter action" thus initiated produces sensitivity, a sure sign of inferiority, which "provides the psychological basis for discord and misunderstanding, not only between two people, but also in ourselves." If the "inferior function" is repressed too long undesirable consequences may follow:

> the extravert loses his indispensable relation to the object, and the introvert loses his to the subject. Conversely, it is equally indispensable for the introvert to arrive at some form of action not constantly bedevilled by doubts and hesitations, and for the extravert to reflect upon himself, yet without endangering his relationships. [77]

All this has direct bearing on the problem faced by present-day Muslims. In the final analysis the dilemma which the cultural confrontation with the West in all its ramifications poses before the Muslim was defined very concisely by H. Saab as that of remaining a Muslim or becoming nothing at all.[78] The attitude toward the challenging object, namely, Western culture, easily brings out the persona in each individual Muslim in so far as he happens to be consciously confronted by it at all. And then, one or the other of two typical attitudes seems to prevail. The difference between these two attitudes is basically the difference between that of the reflective nature of the introvert which makes him slow to act and hesitant, and the positive attraction to novel situations of the extravert which makes him quick to act and impatient with misgivings. And very often, after one such attitude has been crystalized, a reaction sets in, sometimes with rather damaging consequences. Frequently we find the Muslim, who went forward happily to meet and embrace Western culture, experiencing, even while he is still enjoying the excitement of the acquaintance, the beginning of the "inferior reaction." This reaction may take the form, in spite of his conscious wish, of a strong impulse to revert to his former self. Modern Arabic literature amply reflects this reaction. Tawfīq al-Ḥakīm, for example says[79] of his hero in *ʿUṣfūr min al-sharq* that while living in Paris he

> had always felt that he did not live alone on earth, that his life was extending also to heaven, where he had friends and loved ones and protectors...He would never forget the pure Lady Zainab[80] and the benevolence she has shown him in time of adversity. She had real existence in his life.

But perhaps the most conspicuous example of how these conflicting attitudes affect a single individual is furnished by the personal history of Muḥammad Iqbāl.[81]

He went all the way toward Western culture and reached the highest peaks of Western philosophy. Yet, in later years he reverted to an incorrigible Muslim fanaticism in which all people were divided, according to the concept of early Islam, into two kinds: Muslims and nonbelievers.[82] Furthermore, he came to consider any conscious need for Western wisdom and guidance as a shameful act of *su'āl* -- begging. He considered any vestige of cultural borrowing not only harmful, but humiliating; traces of Platonism in Islamic theology were damaging,[83] and to require any assistance from a foreign culture was as humiliating as riding, baby-like, on a woman's back, or like eating charity at another man's table.[84] The only way to be strong and honorable, he thought, that which negates *su'āl*, is expressed by the term *ʿishq* — love,[85] used here in a modified meaning of love for Muḥammad and his message.[86] This repeated emphasis on emotional attachment to the cultural legacy is in itself very indicative, showing as it does the type-attitude involved in this reaction. In other words, it is a reversion to introversion which lies at the root of this kind of reaction. After an initial extravert type-attitude, a going all out toward the new object, the foreign culture, the extravert feels a growing resistance to the object and becomes the prisoner of his own ill-humored subjectivity.[87]

But in the literary world of Najīb Maḥfūẓ there is no safe return for these types, and as soon as the reaction sets in they have to die. In other words, he sees no way of self-redemption as recommended by Iqbāl. *Taṣawwuf*,[88] as Kamāl says, is just another way of escaping, it solves nothing. Therefore, it is as good as death. As seen by Najīb Maḥfūẓ, an individualistic and egocentric outburst of passion for a new culture can only result in another sort of individualistic and egocentric introversion, of the type recommended by Iqbāl or, indeed, Kāmil Ḥusayn. There may be a world of intrinsic difference between the two ambitions, that of the extravert and that of the extravert turned introvert. But they are both equally sterile and hopeless.

The other process, always leading toward a viable situation of living-in-society while at the same time moving forward, is that depicted in the development of Aḥmad ʿĀkif, or of Maḥjūb of *al-Qāhira al-*

jadīda and Ḥusayn of *Zuqāq al-midaqq*. But the ideal type is most decidedly Ḥusayn of *Bidāya wa nihāya*, the latest of this series of novels. It therefore comes somewhat as a surprise that the next main character of Najīb Maḥfūẓ is Kāmil Ru'ba-Lāẓ of *al-Sarāb* (literally Fata Morgana). He is a highly introverted type, almost a total failure in his personal life, who, only after many ordeals, begins to see the light of hope. Perhaps the explanation for this reversion of Najīb Maḥfūẓ can be found in the fact that Ḥusayn of *Bidāya wa nihāya* is after all too perfect to be real or interesting. He lacks depth, he lacks the grating quality of individualism which "means deliberately stressing and giving prominence to some supposed peculiarity, rather than to collective considerations and obligations." [89] As much as Najīb Maḥfūẓ cares for constructive harmony between the individual and society, he apparently felt that too nearly perfect a harmony must slough off so much of the individualism of a person that life itself may become devoid of interest. This is a very interesting literary phenomenon, which has been illuminated by Kenneth Burks: [90]

> A writer may *profess* to a certain cause, for instance, but you find on going over his work that the *enemies* of this cause are portrayed with greater vividness than its advocates. Here is his 'truth' about his professions of belief.

There is no doubt that the searching, complicated introvert is Najīb Maḥfūẓ's type. In real life this is, in his view, the reliable type, the one on whom cultural continuity depends. But he must at a certain point give way to his dormant extraversion, cut short his hesitation and step forward.

Kāmil Ru'ba-Lāẓ is such a type. The novel in which he is delineated seems to have been constructed consciously on the basis of Freud's article, "The Most Prevalent Form of Degradation in Erotic Life." This is a story [91] of a very acute case of psychical impotence, in a man of a strongly libidinous nature. From childhood his libido turns away from reality into the creation of phantasy (introversion), becomes fixated to unconscious ideas of an incestuous sexual object -- his mother. The sensual current of feeling now attached to this object is discharged in onanistic acts. Having at puberty been deprived of sexual enjoyment, offered him by a rather dirty and ugly servant girl, he experiences lack of potency and satisfaction when his sexual desires are later given free rein in marriage. This is naturally his main difficulty, for he refuses to lower his primary sexual object by applying his sexual instincts to the girl who represents it. It can now be added that his mother is of Turkish descent, tall, slim, with green eyes. The unhappy son who looks exactly like his mother, lives separated from his Turkish father, who has divorced his mother several times. Kāmil's unhappy young wife tried to find happiness with another man, an extravert young physician who happens to know her husband's predicament, and who later causes her death by attempting on her an abortion for which he is not qualified. Soon after, Kāmil's mother dies, too, and thus he is relieved of all the miseries brought on him by the two women he has loved most. But even before this happens he meets a middle-aged widow, rather ugly and vulgar, who attracts him sexually at first sight. Soon she has him in her car, where she practically forces him to make love to her. He then realizes that his desire for her is not less than his desire for life, "nay, it is life itself, and pride and manliness, confidence and happiness." In her arms he feels as if he is wallowing in dirt, "but it was a good dirt, compassionate dirt, giving lavishly confidence and happiness. And then I realized the mistake of my past." Noticing his state of mind "she flicked my nose with her finger and asked me: Satisfied? I replied with all my heart: Very much."

Although this novel has appealed to the public, and has gone through eight editions since its first publication in 1948 [92] Egyptian literary criticism at first paid scant attention to it. Ghālī Shukrī felt initially [93] that the novel's framework was too inflated for the rather small idea it offers. Later, [94] however, he admitted that *al-Sarāb* constitutes an important milestone in the literary development of Najīb Maḥfūẓ in that it forms "a natural conclusion to the previous stages of the epopee of downfall and collapse." [95] As Ghālī Shukrī sees Najīb Maḥfūẓ's works, up to this novel, they all form a continuous endeavour to show the futility of the efforts made by the *petite bourgeoisie* to deliver itself from its plight by any other way save that of a Socialist revolution. According to this view the emphasis is placed on the conflict between the individual and the external world, in which the individual is crushed because of his inherent weakness, rather than on the internal conflicts of the individual, from which he can emerge victorious if he can "pull himself together." Ghālī Shukrī's interpretation is convincing only as long as he neglects to note — as he most certainly does — the obvious repugnance displayed by the writer toward Socialism's message bearers.

Unless it is understood that the area in which Najīb Maḥfūẓ is operating is that of the individual's internal conflicts, the significance of all that he has written cannot be fully comprehended. This explains why Ghālī Shukrī came to the mistaken conclusion that *al-Sarāb*'s importance is in pointing out that all the various ways [96] tried by the *petite bourgeoisie* for solving its problems must end in a *fata morgana*. This conclusion is just as wrong as considering *al-Sarāb* an end of any one phase in the writer's development. Aḥmad ʿAbbās Ṣāliḥ undoubtedly penetrated much deeper into the meaning of the novel, when he pointed out [97] that it is the story of a person emerging from his own closed, interior world into the objective reality of the outer world. And because this is the way Ṣāliḥ saw it, he also realized that this is a recurring theme not only in Najīb Maḥfūẓ's previous works, but also in his later works.

Al-Sarāb is undoubtedly an important literary *étude* unique in its directness of approach. A measure of its uniqueness to the writer is perhaps the fact that this is the only novel of this period written in the first person. The dilemma of the modern Egyptian is twofold: how to guard his past, and how to liberate himself from his past. The liberation of Kāmil Ru'ba-Lāẓ, is at one and the same time a liberation from his fears and inhibitions as well as from his heritage. That his shackles take the form of a beautiful Turkish mother need cause no difficulty at this stage of our discussion. But the Oedipal tangle need not blur our view of the deeper meaning of the novel. The message seems quite clear: the modern Egyptian must shed his fears, his illusions, in short, he must relax his introverted attitude and adapt himself more willingly to changing circumstances. His concepts of beauty, loyalty, loftiness, baseness and the rest must be adjusted, and the world of dreams must be replaced by the world of reality. It is perhaps no accident that the automobile, so often the symbol of evil, [98] has become in *al-Sarāb* the locus of deliverance. Things do have different aspects, and rigid conceptualization will not do. The depth of the modern Egyptian dilemma is for the first time laid wide open. Given that change is inevitable and that renouncing the historical heritage is suicidal, the problem is how far change can be admitted and what part of the heritage is to be relinquished. Identifying all that has to be given up of the past as "Turkish" may serve as a guideline, but then the personal decision has to be made as to what is "Turkish" enough to be given up. Persistent introversion will not do, because some action must be taken. The attempts, made by al-Manfalūti, Tawfīq al-Hakīm [99] and others, to escape into the world of dreams and imagination are no more than Kāmil Ru'ba-Lāẓ's onanistic delusions. The importance of *al-Sarāb* is not that it shows the futility of a non-revolutionary solution, as Ghālī Shukrī feels, but rather in that it shows the futility of escaping into *fata morgana*. *Al-Sarāb* is a call to face reality.

Kamāl ʿAbd al-Jawād is rightly considered the culmination of Najīb Maḥfūẓ's portrayal of character. And, as mentioned, the Mahfuzian type is the introvert working his way slowly to extraversion. Perennial introversion is sterile just as spontaneous extraversion is deadly. At the risk of being flippant, we venture to say that the perfect Mahfuzian type is the negation of the *Ṣūfī* Perfect Man,[100] in the sense that the former is constantly endeavouring to move away from the state of the latter. The Mahfuzian type, however, is not the antipode of the Perfect Man, for this would be the spontaneous and complete extravert.

Najīb Maḥfūẓ's positive characters, that is, those who end up by being re-encouraged, indicate a tendency which has a very important bearing on the problem posed by the present state of Egyptian Islam, as a religion and a culture.[101] What has rightly been said of all Arabs today, has a reinforced relevance with regard to the Egyptians, namely, that [102] "the special quality of the Arabs today lies less in the problems with which the world has confronted them than in the attitude with which they confront the world and respond to those problems." Or, put differently by the same writer, the aggression felt by the Arab as being carried against him by the West is accompanied by a feeling of "internal, subjective incrimination. The attack is interiorized; and thereby gains its anguish." [103] Psychologically this reaction is not dissimilar from the reaction of masses of Arab Muslims to the upheavals and misfortunes of the late Middle Ages, when "an Islam that, impregnated with Ṣūfism, had learned to survive the misfortunes of the thirteenth and fourteenth centuries, was not so concerned to appropriate to itself the earthly glories of the fifteenth and the sixteenth." [104] The retreat into Ṣūfism in times of adversity has not yet been thoroughly studied, just as the *Ṣūfī* movement has not yet been fully studied and analyzed.[105] What can safely be assumed is that psychological stresses in the past have produced reactions similar to present day reactions to stresses of similar nature. [106]

The historical tension between Ṣūfism and orthodoxy in Islam need not be discussed here, but there is no doubt that, psychologically the similarity between the two has increased remarkably since the 12th century. This similarity is well illustrated in that portion of the teaching of al-Ghazālī (died 1111)[107] which reintroduced the element of fear into the consciousness of Islam. "It was no time, he held, for smooth, hopeful preaching. The horrors of Hell must be kept before man."

The fact that at some midway point in the history of Islam a fundamental change in its psychological attitude took place is commonly recognized Very indicative in this respect is the opening remark made by Iqbāl in his preface to *The Reconstruction of Religious Thought in Islam:*

> The Quran is a book which emphasizes 'deed' rather than 'idea'. There are, however, men to whom it is not possible organically to assimilate an alien universe by re-living, as a vital process, that special type of inner experience on which religion ultimately rests.

In this short passage there is a typical attempt to gloss over the fundamental change alluded to, which in itself is very much in line with the nature of this very change. That the *Qur'ān* emphasizes deed is quite true.[108] But by attempting to re-interpret "deed" as if it referred to the Sūfic notion of "assimilating the universse," Iqbāl is demonstrating one of the main consequences of this great change, which he describes, rather inaccurately, only a few pages later, where he explains[109] that early Muslims

> read the Quran in the light of Greek thought. It took them over two hundred years to perceive — though not quite clearly — that the spirit of the Quran was essentially anti-classical, and the result of this perception was a kind of a revolt, the full significance of which has not been realized even up to the present day.

The nature of this "revolt" as understood by Iqbāl, is the acceptance of the *Ṣūfī* concept of God and the world:[110]

> The great point in Christianity is the search for an independent content for spiritual life which according to the insight of its founder, could be elevated, not by the forces of a world external to the soul of man, but by the revelation of a new world within his soul. Islam fully agrees with this insight and supplements it by the further insight that the illumination of the new world thus revealed is not something foreign to the world of matter but permeates it through and through.[111]

It is quite clear that Iqbāl's reconstruction of Islamic thought consists in reviving *Ṣūfī* emotionalism, reinforced by a typical modernistic reinterpretation of the *Qur'ān* is a way which would lend rational support to most of the *Ṣūfi* concepts of religious experience. It is therefore interesting to see how Fritz Meier describes the development discussed by Iqbāl.[112]

According to Fritz Meier, the essential conflict between orthodoxy in Islam, as initially conceived, and Islamic mysticism, lay in the concept of the relationship of man and God. In orthodozy, mankind and the godhead never wholly coincide, and the Muslim is called on not to imitate God but to obey him. For the mystic, however, this is a painful isolation, for mysticism is actually an attempt to tear open the ego, in which man marks himself off from God, and let the godhead flow in, or even eliminate the ego altogether. Consequently, the way in which Islamic mysticism describes the result of overcoming the duality of man and godhead, is extremely contradictory. The mystic never speaks of the ominous 'union' (*ittiḥād*) with God, but only of the harmless 'attaining' (*wiṣāl*). The notion of man receiving God into himself (*ḥulūl*) is rejected. The Islamic mystics preferred the idea that the human person becomes nothing in the presence of God or is destroyed by him, so that in the end only God exists."[113]

It is easy to see then that in Islam the original relationship between God and man which recognized man's rights and obligations as those of a self-assured created of God, turned into a relationship whereby man's independent existence was conceived as a challenge to God's omnipotence.

The complete abnegation of man, though reaching the highest expression in Ṣūfism, occurs in orthodozy as well. As Fritz Meier points out,[114] al-Ashʿarī (died 935) [115] "held that God was behind man's evil as well as his good strivings, for nothing happens without the will of God." Orthodoxy too came to accept the elimination of man's independence even if through a different line of reasoning. So much so that the very choice of belief and disbelief was denied to man.[116] According to this concept man can evidently contribute very little toward his fate in the world to come. The *Ṣūfī*, however, with his heightened intuitive faculties, was quick to realize that with the elimination of man's potency Paradise and Hell ceased to be what the *Qur'ān* meant them to be — a reward and a punishment for man's voluntary decisions.[117] Thus the *Ṣūfī* claimed to be motivated by nothing but his selfless love for God. This absolute dissolution of man in God, considered by Ṣūfism as "the greatest of all gifts of grace," has not been admitted by orthodoxy, to be sure. And a more humble reduction of man, to the status of a helpless object of God's inscrutable will, was conceived as the only solution to the dilemma of man's relation to God in times of incomprehensible adversity. What is common to both of these concepts are the indications that "introversion has attained it highest goal." [118] Fritz Meier now reached the final conclusion of his analysis: [119]

> If we consider Ṣūfism as a whole we must admit that introversion was predominant and that this excess of introversion was largely responsible for its downfall. This is its weak point, and it is here perhaps that we must seek one of the causes of the decline of Islamic culture in the modern era.

Much as the analysis of Fritz Meier is to be admired for its lucidity and insight, these concluding sentences may be hasty. There can be no doubt that the present state of Islamic culture is closely tied to the introversion both in Ṣūfism and in orthodoxy. But the "downfall" of Ṣūfism is liable to prove more of an illusion than a fact. Morroe Berger has found recently [120] that in Egypt Ṣūfism "may still be considerable, although perhaps expressed differently today" and that, therefore, "if we are interested in contemporary social life we cannot continue to ignore this aspect of popular religious belief and conduct." "Popular religion" is a particularly apt phrase, not only because Ṣūfism has been for centuries the form of belief most prevalent among the masses, but mainly because this phrase points to the source of present-day strength of Ṣūfism in Egypt. Although Ṣūfism no longer produces literary and intellectual giants as in the past, it still nourishes the needs of many people in every-day life, and not necessarily those lacking modern education or sheltered from exposure to the West.[121] And it is indeed hard to conceive of orthodoxy, whatever turn it takes, parting substantially from Ṣūfism, as long as Ṣūfism continues to be viable. Therefore, the assertion regarding the downfall of Ṣūfism, and the implied hope expressed therein for Islam as a culture seems premature. In any case we may assert that for Najīb Maḥfūẓ the problem posed by Ṣūfism is as alive today as it ever was. Without it his entire work since 1958 cannot be understood, just as a great deal of his previous work may seem irrelevant without understanding that basically it is an attempt at a literary psychotherapy of this problem.

If one were to seek a literary character personifying all the psychological conflicts of an ancient culture faced with the challenges of the modern world and beset at the same time by the paralyzing effects of the idealistic introverted character of Ṣūfism, no better example could be adduced than Kamāl, of the Cairo trilogy. In childhood he is perfectly healthy and happy, an unrestrained extravert. With adolescence he becomes highly introverted, and his life turns into a long series of frustrations and disappointments. But toward the end, by sheer power of will and intellect, a sort of self-therapy seems to be taking place. Circumstances help. That giant of a father and that angel of a mother both die, and he realizes that his problem is indeed the incessant conflict within himself. Like Jung's imaginary patient [122] he realizes that

> this mysterious part of his personality that hides under the father-and-mother images, making him believe for years that the cause of this trouble must somehow have got into him from the outside,

that this

> is the counterpart to his conscious attitude; and it will leave him no peace and will continue to plague him until it has been accepted.

Being an adult, in the second half of his life, when this realization occurs, it is so perfectly sensible that

> the development of the function of opposites lying dormant in the unconscious means a renewal; but this development no longer proceeds via the solution of infantile ties, the destruction of infantile illusions and the transference of old images to new figures: it proceeds via the problem of opposites. [123]

When we leave Kamāl at the end of the Cairo trilogy he has not changed much. Only the first signs of renewal are noticeable. His last act is buying a new black tie for his mother's funeral, his old one having become worn out from excessive use after his father's death. But somehow, the fact that his brother Yāsīn is there with him, buying diapers for his expected grandchild, and coming out of the shop they both walk together, side by side, -- the last scene of the trilogy -- helps create a feeling that Kamāl has finally started moving toward the outer world with increased confidence. Having lingered for so long in the depths of the unholy valley of extreme subjectivity, of stifling introversion, Kamāl seems to have found the strength to set into the wide open world.

NOTES

1 A small town on the coast of Sinai where political prisoners were detained in a concentration camp.

2 Jomier, p. 85, rightly stresses Aḥmad's adherence to the family group in spite of previous verbal denigration in the usual Communist terminoloty. As for ʿAbd al-Munʿīm, as a Muslim Brother his basic approach is to revive Islam and make it the foundation for life in modern Egypt.

3 Jomier, p. 82. The same criticism is made by Nabīl Rāghib, *op. cit.*, pp. 128, 188 *et passim*. Jomier's influence on Egyptian criticism of Najīb Maḥfūẓ is all too obvious.

4 In *al-Liṣṣ wa al-kilāb* and *al-Shaḥḥādh*.

5 "*Al Mushkila al-mītāfīsīqiyya*," *op. cit.*, p. 67; "What causes great astonishment is that Najīb Maḥfūẓ has not penetrated until now the revolutionary personality. Always he touches it from a distance." "Revolutionary" here means Socialist.

6 Najīb Maḥfūẓ, "*Mulaḥaẓāt ʿalā al-mushkila al-mītāfīsīqiyya*," *al-Kātib*, No. 60, March 1966, p. 92.

7 *Mumazziqūn wa intihāziyun*.

8 *al-Muʿānāt al-ṭabaqiyya*, perhaps we should understand the expression as "class struggle."

9 *Supra*, p. 127.

10 The term "revolutionary" here clearly applies to the Muslim Brother as well to the Communist.

11 See S. Spiro, *Arabic-English Dictionary of Modern Arabic of Egypt*, Cairo, 1923: "*ṭuz* -- phaw!"

12 The novel was originally published as *A Scandal in Cairo*.

13 Aḥmad ʿAbbās Ṣăliḥ, "*Qirāʾa jadīda, al-mawqif al-trājīdī*," *al-Kātib*, No. 51, December 1965, p. 80.

14 *La tanqaʾu lahu ghulla*.

15 Jomier, p. 27, n. 1. *City of Wrong* was translated into English by Kenneth Cragg and published in Amsterdam in 1959. The report in

al-Ahrām of December 13, 1957, states that Najīb Maḥfūẓ was awarded the prize for "the story of *Bayn al-qaṣrayn.*"

16 Introduction by K. Cragg, *op. cit.*, p. ix.

17 *Ibid.*, p. xiv.

18 Von Grunebaum, *Medieval Islam*, p. 150.

19 H.A.R. Gibb, *Mohammedanism*, London, 1957, p. 97.

20 *Supra*, Ch. 4, n. 48.

21 *City of Wrong*, p. 3.

22 A clear reference to the principle of *shūrā* in Islam, which is considered a safeguard against error in judgment.

23 *Ibid.*, p. 21: "The individual conscience is the most potent factor inducing us toward the good. It is in fact the sole means of guidance into truth."

24 *Ibid.*, p. 27.

25 *Ibid.*, p. 56: "Society lacking a conscience of its own chooses individual persons to take common counsel in the hope that these individuals will act in the name of society with due regard to conscience."

26 *Ibid.*, p. 66. The concluding sentence is a verbatim repetition of the saying attributed to the Prophet on the infallibility of the Islamic community.

27 *Supra*, p. 164.

28 Albert Hourani, *Arabic Thought in the Liberal Age, 1798-1939*, London, 1962, p. 352.

29 Muḥammad Kāmil Ḥusayn, *al-Wādī al-muqaddas*, Cairo,1968.

30 *Ibid.*, p. 11 "If you must choose between success and purity, it is better that you choose purity."

31 *Ibid.*, p. 18.

32 Cf. Kenneth Cragg, *Counsels in Contemporary Islam*, Edinburgh, 1956, p. 109.

33 *Aḥda al-ṭuruq ila al-ḥaqq*, *Zuhd*, and the whole tenor of the passage

referred in n. 31 are so much part and parcel of *Ṣūfī* terminology and style that the conclusion is self-evident, although the term Ṣufism is not used.

34 Gibb, *Mohammadanism*, p. 134.

35 *Modern Islam*, p. 349.

36 "His life was bleak and dreary, his heart dark and his mind in constant rebellion. He had a philosophy which he borrowed from different minds according to his whims, and a philosophy of freedom as he understood it, of which *ṭuẓ* was the best motto, which meant becoming free from everything, from value and ideals, from dogmas and principles, free from the entire social heritage! If my family could bequeath me nothing to make me happy, it is not right that I should inherit from them what can make me only miserable.'" (p. 25)

37 "Le quartier le plus pittoresque du Caire" — Vaucher, *op. cit.*, p. 34.

38 Frye, *op. cit.*, p. 90.

39 Fāṭima Mūsā, *"Najīb Maḥfūẓ wa taṭawwur fann al-riwāya al-ʿarabiyya,"* *al-Kātib*, No. 90, September 1968, p. 84.

40 Ghālī Shukrī, *al-Muntamī*, p. 214, considers this to be a severe defect in the entire dramatic structure of the novel.

41 *Ibid.*, p. 85.

42 The insensitivity of Najīb Maḥfūẓ's Socialists to feminine emotions is noteworthy, Cf. also ʿAlī Ṭaha's relations with Iḥsān in *al-Qahira al-jadīda*.

43 *Al-Sikka al-jadīda*, literally The New Road, was cut through the city in the days of the Mamluks. *Al-Darrāsa*, literally the threshing machine, or the threshing floor, is a place-name.

44 The first Sūra of the *Qur'ān*, said on almost all solemn occasions.

45 *Ibid.*, p. 87.

46 Ghamra, the name of the Casino he used to frequent. Al-Ḥusayn,a

common reference to the area around the mosque of Ḥusayn, used here obviously to emphasize the incompatibility involved in Rushdī's nightly trips.

47 Najīb Maḥfūẓ's close friend Adham Rajab writes of the writer's father: "He was so stern at home that we — the lifelong friends of Najīb Maḥfūẓ — never entered his home during his childhood and adolescence." *Al-Hilāl*, February 1970, p. 99.

48 Translated into English by Trevor le Gassik, Beirut, 1966.

49 The location of large British Army installations in World War II.

50 The concluding words are of particular force since the Sayyid himself was afflicted with the loss of all his children.

51 *Op. cit.*, p. 151 *seq.*

52 *Supra*, p. 138.

53 Meaning filial piety.

54 Adham Rajab, *op. cit.*, p. 99 tells of Najīb Maḥfūẓ's older brother, Ibrāhīm ʿAbd al-ʿAzīz, who at the age of 70 did not dare light a cigarette in his mother's presence.

55 The treaty between the Wafdist Government and Great Britain acknowledging Egypt's full independence.

56 See Vaucher, *op. cit.*, pp. 1, 87 *seq.*

57 The revolution of 1952 was the work of officers of humble origin who were admitted to the Academy in the first few years after 1936. See Vaucher, *op. cit.*, for a detailed account of these officers.

58 Frye, *op. cit.*, p. 304: "The romancer does not attempt to create "real people" so much as stylized figures which expand into psychological archetypes."

59 Shubrā is an old quarter of Cairo, adjoining Būlāq. Miṣr al-Jadīda is a modern suburb of Heliopolis.

60. See n. 3 *supra*.

61 It is a fact that after 1936, for various considerations, the

Egyptian Government reduced the period of training in the Military Academy. See Vaucher, *ibid.*

62 There is a pun hidden in this name. *Rūs* is the plural form of *rās*, the dialectial word for head. But *rūs* also means the Russians. *Rūsī* would be the Russian or the one of the heads, i.e. he who inflicts blows with the head in fist fights.

63 Quoted by Henri F. Ellenberger, " A Clinical Introduction to Psychiatric Phenomenology and Existential Analysis," *Existence*, p. 124, from Nafred Bleuler "Researches and Changes in Concepts in the Study of Schizophrenia."

64 Jomier, *op. cit.*, p. 38.

65 C. G. Jung, *Two Essays, op. cit.*, p. 56 refers to both Freudian and Adlerian theories as reductive.

66 *Ibid.*

67 *Ibid.*

68 *Ibid.*, p. 63.

69 *Ibid.*

70 Cf. Jaques Berque, *supra*, Cf. 4, n. 49.

71 *Op. cit.*, pp. 63-64.

72 *Ibid.*, p. 64.

73 *Ibid.*, p. 65

74 *Ibid.*, p. 66.

75. Defined by Jung as the mask an individual puts on knowing that it corresponds with his conscious intentions while it also meets with the requirements and opinions of his environments. *Psychological Types*, Pantheon, 1964, p. 590.

76 *Two Essays*, p. 68.

77 *Ibid.*, p. 68.

78 *The Arab Federalists of the Ottoman Empire*, 1958, p. 206.

79 Tawfīq al-Ḥakīm, *ʿUsfūr min al-sharq*, Cairo, 5th edition, p. 107.

80 Sayyida Zaynab, the daughter of Imām ʿAlī and grand-daughter of the Prophet. Her mosque in Cairo is one of great sanctity.

81 D. 1938. "The most outstanding and exasperating figure in twentieth

century Islam in the sub-continent" of India. K. Cragg, *op. cit.*, p. 59.

82 Cf. Nicholson's introduction to Iqbal, *The Secrets of the Self (Asrār-i khūdī)*, tr. Nicholson, pp. x-xi.

83 *Ibid.*, Verses 74-80.

84 *Ibid.*, Verses 434 *seq.*

85 The concept of *ʿishq* is manifestly Ṣūfic, expressing "the highest and purest love in which there is no lover or beloved, since both have passed away in the love that is God's very essence." See R. A. Nicholson, *Studies in Islamic Mysticism*, Cambridge, 1967, p. 102.

86 *The Secrets of the Self*, Verses 844 *seq.*

87. Thus Jung described the process in the example of the "two youths rambling in the country," *Two Essays*, p.66 *seq.*

88 Meaning the *Ṣūfī* way of life.

89 Jung, *Two Essays*, p. 183.

90 Quoted by Stanley Edgar Hyman, *The Armad Vision*, New York, 1955, p. 343.

91 The following characterization is couched in terms used in Freud's article. Somekh, *op. cit.*, p. 103, feels the novel has been "tailored to suit one...psychological concept -- the Oedipal situation." This comment seems to ignore the deeper recesses of the psychological tangle which the novel uncovers, which explains, perhaps, Somekh's further comment that Kāmil's affair with ʿInāyāt has no deeper significance than that of demonstrating the protagonist's complexes. *Ibid.*, 104.

92 According to the list of Ghālī Shukrī *al-Sarāb* was written in 1944, after *Bidāya wa nihāya*, but its first publication preceded the latter by one year. Its eighth edition came out in 1972.

93 Ghālī Shukrī, *"Maʿna al-jins ʿind Najīb Maḥfūẓ," al-Kātib*, No. 22, January 1963, p. 140, reproduced in Ghālī Shukrī's book

Azmat al-jins fī al-qiṣṣa al-ʿarabiyya (The Crisis of Sex in the Arabic Story), Beirut, 1962, pp. 81-126. Toward the 1970s greater appreciation of this novel became evident in critical writing. Cf. Muḥammad Ḥasan ʿAbdallah, *al-Wāqiʿiyya fī al-riwāya al-ʿarabiyya,* Cairo, 1971, pp. 469-74. Also Ṭaha Wādī, *Madkhal ila ta'rīkh al-riwāya al-miṣriyya,* Cairo, 1972, pp. 112-15.

94 *Al-Muntamī,* pp. 176 *seq.*

95 Cf. *op. cit.,* p. 85, where he expounds the following idea: "*Al-Qāhira al-jadīda* is the first stage in the creation of the epos of Najīb Maḥfūẓ's novelistic works, which began in 1939 and concluded in 1944 with *al-Sarāb.*"

96 Described *ibid.,* pp. 131, 144.

97 A. ʿA. Ṣāliḥ, "*al-Mawqif al-trajidi,*" *ibid.,* p. 83.

98 In *Zuqāq al-midaqq,* Ḥamīda's downfall occurs after a taxi ride in the modern parts of Cairo. In *Bayn al-Qaṣrayn* Amīna is the victim of an automobile accident.

99 Cf. al-Manfalūṭī, "*Siyāḥa fī riḥāb,*" *al-Naẓarāt,* pp. 355-64. Also, Tawfiq al-Ḥakīm, *ʿUṣfur min al-sharq,* p. 69.

100 The definition of the Perfect Man by Ibn al-ʿArabī (d. 1240) includes the following: "He is the mirror by which God is revealed to himself, and therefore the final cause of creation." Cf. *Shorter Encyclopaedia of Islam,* Nicholson's article.

101 W.C. Smith, *Islam in Modern History,* p. 93, observes that "the Arabs sum up in concentrated intensity the modern crisis of the whole Islamic world. Yet they do so in a specifically Arab fashion. It is their Arabness that gives poignancy and pith to their Islam." But within this Arabic framework Egypt surely has a very unique position. This is generally recognized in the books treating of Egypt as an Islamic sub-unit, but unfortunately no substantial work has brought out as yet the peculiarity and uniqueness of Egypt as an Islamic community.

102 *Ibid.*, p. 97, n. 5.

103 *Ibid.*, p. 99.

104 *Ibid.*, p. 37.

105 Cf. Gibb, *op. cit.*, p. 211.

106 This has been recognized by Morroe Berger, *Islam in Egypt Today*, Cambridge, 1970, p. 75: "The very broad social needs that first impelled Muslims to follow Ṣūfism and to establish the orders may be much the same today."

107 Cf. Gibb, *Mohammedanism*, p. 140, where Macdonald's summery of al-Ghazālī's influence is reproduced.

108 Gibb, *op. cit.*, p. 123, where Islam is described as the "most worldly and the least esoteric" of the great religions of Western Asia.

109 Iqbāl, *The Reconstruction of Religious Thought in Islam*, London, 1934, p. 3. The attribution of Greek characteristics to early Islamic thought is quite in line with Iqbāl's later attitude (cf. *supra* p. 150). But in itself the assertion blurs the great difference between early Islamic thought and the Islamic thought of ʿAbbāsid times.

110 *Ibid.*, p. 8.

111 This seems to bear out von Grunebaum's assertion that "almost all personal devotion of the individual Muslim down to this very day is somewhat tinged with Ṣūfism and thus inclined,be it ever so lightly, toward pantheism," *Medieval Islam*, p. 138.

112 Fritz Meier, "The Transformation of Man in Mustical Islam," in *Man and Transformation*, Papers from the Eranos Year Books, Bollingen Series XXX. 5, Pantheon, 1964, pp. 37-68.

113 *Ibid.*, p. 41.

114 *Ibid.*, p. 47.

115 A prominent theologian, "generally regarded as marking a turning point, or the completion of a stage, in the history of Islam." Cf.

W. M. Watt, *Free Will and Predestination in Early Islam,* pp. 135 *seq.* Sunnite orthodoxy is generally recognized as Ashʿarite orthodoxy.

116 Watt, *op. cit.,* pp. 142-43.

117 Cf. F. Meier, *ibid.,* p. 57.

118 *Ibid.,* p. 58. In the text this conclusion is applied strictly to Ṣufism, but it is valid for orthodoxy as well, as Fritz Meier admits on the next page of his study.

119 *Ibid.,* p. 59.

120 *Op. cit.*, p. 62

121 *Ibid.,* p. 77 *seq.*

122 Jung, *Two Essays*, p. 70.

123 *Ibid.*, p. 71.

Chapter Six
The Old City

It has been maintained that no change is ever as abrupt as it seems to be and the change that occurred between 1952 and 1958 in the writing of Najīb Maḥfūẓ is a case in point. If we start with the distinction, made by Rajā' al-Naqqāsh, between the two periods of Najīb Maḥfūẓ's writings,[1] the large novel, *Awlād ḥāritnā*, marks the first period's last phase and the beginning of the second period. In this novel, relating the history of a place, both place and history acquire symbolic value. The place is the neighborhood, that part of town which was the "physical environment" of no fewer than five novels and many short stories, and whose history is told in terms of the history of civilization.

Examining the literary history of Najīb Maḥfūẓ from the vantage point of the present, it seems inconceivable that the old quarter of Cairo was for him at any time merely a convenient locale for his stories. He is undoubtedly the writer of his town, and the old quarter obviously has mystical significance for him. The flow of life in the quarter is seen with eyes that take in everything: the beauty and the ugliness, the humane and the beastly, the sacred and the profane. Nothing is overlooked or ignored. The large amount of cruelty and suffering in that old quarter seem to give it a transcendental quality, turning it into God's own backyard, where life is reduced to its most elementary or primeval phase. That is the phase where the relationships of man to man, of man to God, of man to society are forged. The peculiar history of the old quarter made the scene look if anything,more natural, for in spite of being for centuries the seat of great dynasties, its people, the neighborhood, so to speak, lived a life entirely removed from all that attracted the attention of historians. Manifestations of formal government were rarely noticed and then only as visitations of some evil power, which was better avoided, as so many of Najīb Mahfūz's stories show.

In spite of all these apocalyptic elements, life in the old quarter was good and enjoyable. It had the quality of fullness even when hardships, disappointments and sorrows were taking their toll. Life seemed to have a purpose, a direction which held great hopes for those who could adjust themselves to its pulsebeats. And yet, with *Awlād ḥāritnā* this aspect of life seems to have disappeared. The question that has been raised by some critics and which we would also like to discuss is: how does this novel relate to all those which preceded it?

There is something uncanny about *Awlād ḥāritnā*. Some critics quite clearly prefer to ignore it,[2] and others hardly know what to make of it. Reaction against this novel, immediately after its publication in 1959, was severe.[3] Ghālī Shukrī who believes that Najīb Maḥfūẓ's preceding long silence was due to his feeling that he was not free to say what he wanted, asserts that when Maḥfūẓ finally resumed his writings he was still under the impression of a deep crisis in Egyptian society, "the crisis of freedom and cultural backwardness."[4] He therefore "turned to symbolic form in *Awlād ḥāritnā* only because he had not yet freed himself of the feeling of constraint under this crisis." In plain words Ghālī Shukrī feels that Najīb Maḥfūẓ tried to say something, but owing to the suppressive atmosphere in his society he first kept silent and then attempted to say it under the guise of symbolic writing.

His central idea, according to Ghālī Shukrī, was as follows: the Egyptians are lagging in their intellectual capacity behind the Europeans, and consequently "there develops in the intellectual of our country a crisis of inconsistency between his intellectual inclination toward the West and the backward cultural make-up of the East." [5] In other words, there is a feeling in Egypt of living in the 20th Century without participating in its culture. Faced with this situation, Najīb Maḥfūẓ conceived of the following remedy:

> From the very beginning Najīb Maḥfūẓ has felt that religion forms the central pillar in the structure of values in which we are living in the East. And through religion he wished to penetrate into our spiritual world until he would be able -- while inside that structure — to replace this great pillar of our life, by another one which had already found its way into the civilized world a long time ago. And that new pillar with which Najīb Maḥfūẓ tries to replace the old one is science.

Naturally if this is what the novel was meant to do, the "Neighborhood" must symbolize, if not the entire world, then at least the whole of Egypt.[6]

Whether or not Najīb Maḥfūẓ did have in mind this very intricate plan to replace religion by science in Egypt's value-structure is a question we shall have to examine in due course. There is indeed a widespread feeling among Egyptian critics that this is what he actually did, but that it somehow has not been able to quite fit in with anything else he has written, either earlier or subsequently.[7] It is interesting therefore to note what he himself had to say about it on several occasions. On one occasion, he said: [8]

> But what is the artistic form of *Awlād ḥāritnā?* Perhaps — I say perhaps — it is the converse of what Swift did in his famous journey. Whereas he criticized reality by means of a fable, I am here criticizing a fable by means of reality. I have dressed the fable in the garb of reality in order to increase our understanding and our hope...

On another occasion answering a question regarding the relationship between society's plight and the plight of the individual, he said:[9]

> ...I have already said this in *Awlād ḥāritnā*. I said

> that curing social evils by means of Socialism drives man into preoccupation with his first predicament, which is death; and if the people of the neighborhood -- Jabalāwī's[10] neighborhood — would change, thanks to the distribution of the endowment equally, justly and humanely, they would all have the opportunity to become magicians (learned) and to devote themselves to the solution of the problem of death!
> So, the solution of society's predicament may solve in the end the predicament of existence, or alleviate it; in any case it will give life a meaning worth living for.

Almost a year later Najīb Maḥfūẓ was asked to write an article for the Cairene literary magazine *al-Kātib* discussing the future of the novel, with particular reference to his own new trend as seen in all his novels beginning with *Awlād ḥāritnā* up to *al-Ṭarīq* (The Way).[11] In this article,[12] entitled "My New Direction and the Future of the Novel," he says;[13] with reference to *Awlād ḥāritnā:*

> In this novel science[14] presumed that it had no need for Jabalāwī and therefore killed him. This end leads it to emptiness...which is the result Camus arrived at when he believed that there was no meaning to life...
> From the thematic point of view, the denial of the higher meaning in life is a moral fault, which may lead men to the most extreme degrees of despair.

Noting that when faced with new problems the novel discovers new artistic forms which are more compatible with these problems, he goes on to explain the nature of symbolic writing:

> When life becomes a problem man is no longer a specific individual, but merely a human being. He is not a specific person who differs from all others in his own details and identity. Therefore the details disappear and enumeration disappears and the dispute gets priority over all other elements.

Asked on another occasion[15] whether *Awlād ḥāritnā* was written with a certain philosophical idea in mind Najīb Maḥfūẓ said:

> It can be considered a novel which is based on a philosophical idea, and those who consider it so say that it is an attempt to place Socialism and science on

> a basis which is not devoid of mysticism. But I should confess that this idea never entered my mind with such clarity while I was writing the novel.

For a writer who is unusually so reticent about his own writings, the number of things he agreed to say on one single novel of his is remarkable. As a novelist he was clearly faced with new problems which obliged him to turn to a new form of writing. The problem that stands out in it is the relation of science to "higher meanings in life," and even for one who is not yet acquainted with the details of the novel, enough has already been said to make it clear that the murder of Jabalāwī symbolizes the rejection of these "higher meanings," and that this is "a moral fault." The reason why such problems have to be treated in an abstract, symbolic way is that these problems are raised when belief in society is badly shaken. We know that Najīb Maḥfūẓ believes that his writing up to that time was realistic. But he feels that realistic writing is basically optimistic, whereas symbolic writing is at best a symptom of grave doubts. As he explains in his article on the future of the novel, these doubts relate to society's ability to solve its problems, and to enable the individual to turn finally to the problem of his own existence. The main source of doubt seems to be the excessive belief in science.

When Maḥfūẓ obliquely indicates some reservations to that interpretation given to *Awlād ḥāritnā*, advocating the establishment of Socialism and science on a basis not devoid of mysticism, we do not really know to what exactly he is taking exception. Socialism in the sense of an aspiration for social justice is quite innocuous, and there is no doubt that he believes in the blessings of science.[16] Possibly he dislikes the dogmatism which so often accompanies ideological formulae. Indeed, a consistent disinclination on the part of Najīb Maḥfūẓ to be harnessed into any "frames of acceptance," [17] has long been one of his traits. However, he has said enough to leave no doubt as to why he turned to symbolic writing and what he felt to be the most urgent issue to be dealt with in his first novel after six years of silence.

Briefly, this novel is the story of the "Neighborhood," that is the old city of Cairo. By the time the novel was written, this neighborhood had already become an heirloom of Egyptian literature by virtue of its being the locale of so many of Najīb Maḥfūẓ's novels and short stories. But in this novel the neighborhood is plucked out of its own rich and colorful history. It is shown as an isolated community whose dull, sad, uninspiring and aimless history is sketched in terms purporting to be those of the history of human civilization. The recorder of the history tells us that being one of the few among his people who could write, he was asked to put on record the story of the Neighborhood as told for generations by the transmitters — *ruwāt* — of this ancient lore. By so indicating the "source" of his story, the writer is alluding to a definite genre of popular literature which has reigned supreme in the coffe houses of Cairo since the 15th century.[18]

This device enables Maḥfūẓ to feel unhampered by real history as well as to have recourse to the simple style of a popular transmitter who reduces historical events to their barest essentials. The monotony of the events recounted helps to throw into relief the senseless sufferings of the people; the repetitive nature of the story makes history fall into a pattern of inertia; even the sporadic attempts at reform, because of their insignificant consequences, are seen as mere silverlining on the eternal dark hopelessness which is life.

Jabalāwī,[19] the founding father of the Neighborhood, has tremendous wealth which he has administered from his house for many years. When he becomes older, he appoints one of his sons, named Adham,[20] to administer the property. The eldest son Idrīs — to rhyme with Iblīs or Satan — protests vigorously and is ordered to leave the house. A few years later, Adham too falls into disgrace and is expelled from the house. His crime is that he has attempted to read Jabalāwī's secret will. He does this in a moment of weakness, under pressure from his expelled brother and his own wife, both of whom are impatient to know the provisions of the will. These two brothers are the first to live outside the big house, and this is the beginning of the Neighborhood. Adham is never forgiven and he never returns to the house with its beautiful garden. But before his death, Jabalāwī comes to see him and promises him that the endowment will be for his descendants. His descendants are the children of his son, Qadrī, and the only daughter of Idrīs. The fact that the people of the Neighborhood are the descendants of Adham and Idrīs is of the greatest importance, as a future reformer, Qāsim, will point out a few generations later. The suffering and misery of the descendants of Jabalāwī is thus a curse which nothing can purge, because the sin for which they are punished inheres in their very blood. This concept is not unlike the old Islamic doctrine that "God creates the unbelief and sin of men."[21]

And, indeed, the descendants of Jabalāwī hardly know any happiness. The endowment property is administered by supervisors, who are presumably appointed by Jabalāwī himself[22] to carry out the ten provisions of the mysterious will. But the supervisors, who follow each other over the generations, ignore the rights of the people, and are protected by groups of thugs -- *futuwwa* -- who are given a share in the profits in return for keeping the people down. Over the generations only three men have dared to challenge the supervisors with partial and temporary success. These have been Jabal, Rifāʿa and Qāsim, representing respectively Moses, Jesus and Muḥammad all of them concerned with establishing a more equitable administration of the endowment. But in so far as they are successful, their success is not a lasting one, and with their deaths the supervisors regain control. Then comes ʿArafa,[23] an orphan, who is motivated by a desire to avenge his mother's sufferings at the hands of the thugs. He is well equipped for this job, having served as an apprentice to a magician. After an absence of some years he returns to the Neighborhood, accompanied by his brother Ḥanash and inspired with a plan to free the people. But unlike the reformers who preceded him, who were motivated by an unquestioning belief in Jabalāwī and his infinite goodness, and who were actually encouraged by him to fight for their reforms, ʿArafa acts out of confidence in his own power. He has no need for guidance or inspiration from Jabalāwī because he has ceased to believe in him. Always there has been this mystery about the great father who entrusted his affairs to the supervisors and kept sending messages to fight his own officers. As for the few bright spots of the past, the days of the great reformers, these ʿArafa dismisses by saying: "The past will not return." He has no great admiration for their temporary achievements, and he himself aspires for a change that will last. This he hopes to achieve by eliminating the thugs, and by making all the people magicians, like himself. He feels he knows the way to achieve this goal, but first he wants to enter the big house and see the will, and perhaps Jabalāwī himself. Why? He develops the theory that Jabalāwī's will is also a book of magic, which contains the secret of Jabalāwī's power. Being a magician himself, he has learned that he cannot believe in anything unless he sees it with his own eyes and touches it with his own hands. And so he breaks into the big house one dark night like a burglar, but before seeing the will he is discovered by one of Jabalāwī's servants. He has no choice now but to kill the servant and escape without seeing the will or Jabalāwī. It later transpires that, on hearing what happened to his servant, Jabalāwī himself died. When the frightful tidings reach ʿArafa he has a terrible feeling of guilt and decides that the great magical power he possesses should be used to bring back to life "Jabalāwī, whom it is easier to kill than to see." This will be achieved by ʿArafa himself becoming a Jabalāwī.

So ʿArafa begins to fight the thugs, using a mysterious explosive device which makes obsolete all other weapons. The supervisor, however, out-smarts ʿArafa and uses him to get rid of the thugs and to remain the sole master of the endowment. ʿArafa does not go unpaid, but he becomes practically a prisoner of the supervisor, and has to live a life of moral decline until he reaches the lowest levels of depravity.

One night, when he returns home from the supervisor's house after the usual debauchery, an old black woman approaches him, whom he immediately recognizes as Jabalāwī's maidservant. She tells him that Jabalāwī died in her arms, and she has now come to ʿArafa in order to carry out Jabalāwī's last request. "He said to me just before the divine secret departed from him:[24] 'Go to ʿArafa the magician and say to him that his grandfather died very pleased with him'." ʿArafa is astounded, because this is the formula, by which, according to the polemical literature of Islam, the authority of the dying Prophet is claimed to have been bestowed by him on his successors -- *khulafāʾ* or Caliphs.[25] The change which this information works on ʿArafa is traumatic. Now that he, too, has received Jabalāwī's message he decides to run away and start his own revolution. But his difficulties are enormous. And like Jabal, Rifāʿa, and Qāsim, he, too, has to begin by first converting the people closest to him. But he has no time left for that; the supervisor's men pursue him, equipped with the magic weapons he has invented, and he dies without accomplishing anything. Still, before dying, he throws away his notebook in which all his secrets are written in code. Ḥanash, his brother, has been seen searching for it, and rumor has it that he has found it. A new hope is thus born, that one day Ḥanash will return and deliver his people from their misery. The supervisor now tries to discredit ʿArafa by spreading the information that he killed Jabalāwī. But the people's reaction is amazing. They say: "We are not concerned with the past, and our only hope is ʿArafa's magic. If we had to choose between Jabalāwī and the magic we would prefer the magic." Faced with this defiant attitude, the supervisor tightens his control over the Neighborhood, and life becomes worse than ever. But the people's new hope sustains them in their sufferings.

In a way this is a terribly iconoclastic story, in which life is seen as an endless dark road leading nowhere. Hope, which feeds on man's agony, will accommodate itself to the most bewildering upheavals, and never cease. But it is a sterile hope, bound to symbols which acquire in daily life the "compensating function of dreams,"[26] the most characteristic feature of which is their repetitive occurrence. Yet some critics maintain that already in the trilogy, the most extensive work depicting the Neighborhood, we can see that this is the way the writer has all along seen his neighborhood. Ghālī Shukrī believes that the unhappy end of the trilogy foretells the story of *Awlād ḥāritanā*.[27] Aḥmad ʿAbbās Ṣāliḥ is more explicit and maintains that ʿArafa is Kamāl ʿAbd al-Jawād of the trilogy.[28] This is a very far-reaching observation which should be analyzed carefully.

The inconsistency of ʿArafa's behavior is clear. First he maintains that Jabalāwī does not matter any longer, the truth of which assertion reality has amply sustained. Yet, before taking any action he feels he has to discover Jabalāwī's mysterious powers, and by searching for them he causes Jabalāwī's death. With Jabalāwī dead ʿArafa himself is deprived of all moral efficacy, and allows himself to become a mere tool in the hands of the supervisor. Only when he learns that Jabalāwī approved of him is his moral courage revived. For ʿArafa, then, the final moral authority rests with Jabalāwī. But this is more than the simple people of the neighborhood can grasp. For them ʿArafa's magic and Jabalāwī's authority are beyond reconciliation and they follow ʿArafa. It is clear that Jabalāwī stands for God as a psychological fact formulated to express a concept of "the independence and sovereignty of certain psychic contents which express themselves by their power to thwart our will, to obsess our consciousness and to influence our moods and actions." 29 In this sense Jabalāwī represents God. And what is described in the story of ʿArafa killing God is a symbolic situation comparable to situations observable elsewhere namely, that the transformation into abstraction indicates a sense of

> fear, despair, aggression and mockery that sounds like a cry from many works. The 'metaphysical anxiety' that is expressed by the distress...may have arisen from the despair of a doomed world...In other cases, the emphasis may lie on the religious factor, on the feeling that God is dead. There is a close connection between the two. 30

In *Awlād ḥāritnā* we clearly have both elements. Perhaps for Najīb Maḥfūẓ the world's doom is not so much a contingency as a concrete situation, a state of having experienced the worst already. Therefore, the death of God becomes inevitable, for such a dark vision is incompatible with God's existence. What may be beyond God's death is, therefore, again, not so much a matter for speculation as a matter simply to be described. Do the people of the neighborhood now believe in something higher than God? Hardly. They place their trust in a rumor saying that ʿArafa's notebook of magic formulas may have been found by Ḥanash in the garbage dump. And on this meagre information human hope now hinges. Instead of a rational reliance on science, as some Egyptian critics suggest, it is more likely that this indicates a reversion to the age of superstitions.

How far does all this relate to the real Neighborhood? This question is important on two counts. The first is that the writer identifies the physical neighborhood by name and feature. The second is that when Aḥmad ʿAbbās Ṣāliḥ says [31] that ʿArafa is a continuation of Kāmal ʿAbd al-Jawād he means that the intellectual and psychological development of the latter leads inevitably to the attitudes symbolized by the former. The question is evidently very important for understanding the development of Najīb Maḥfūẓ's work since 1958 and its relation to his previous works. We shall therefore discuss it in greater depth in the following Epilogue.

NOTES

1 See *supra*, p. 98.

2 Nabīl Rāghib, *op. cit.*, who discusses every novel of Najīb Maḥfūẓ up to 1966 apologizes for not being able to discuss *Awlād ḥāritnā* because he could not get hold of the *al-Ahrām* issues in which it was published serially. At that time it had not yet come out in book form. Ibrāhīm ʿĀmir, *ibid.*, explains his omission of this novel from his review of Najīb Maḥfūẓ's novels by pointing out that the book has not been published in Egypt. It had been published three years earlier in Lebanon. Rajā' al-Naqqāsh, perhaps the most outspoken of Egyptian literati, mentions the novel in his book, but does not stop to discuss it. Perhaps all this is not unrelated to the fact that so many years after it was published serial[illegible] it has not yet been published in Egypt in book form. There are critics who are less diffident with regard to this novel, [illegible] will be seen presently.

3 See Ghālī Shukrī, *op. cit.*, p. 231.

4 *Ibid. Azmat al-ḥuriyya wa al-takhalluf al-ḥaḍārī*, meani[illegible]ereby that there was no freedom but there was cultural backw[illegible]s.

5 *Ibid.*, p. 230. On the "conflict of opposites," cf. ch.

6 *Ibid.*, p. 231.

7 Aḥmad ʿAbbās Ṣāliḥ, "*Qirā'a jadīda li najīb maḥfūẓ, a[illegible]dima,*" *al-Kātib*, No. 56, November 1965, p. 57.

8 *Ḥiwār*, *ibid.*, p. 72.

9 *Ibid.*, pp. 73-74.

10 The founding father of the Neighborhood, who went[illegible]ng for

several generations, secluded in his "big house."

11 That is, from 1958 to 1964.

12 Najīb Maḥfūẓ, "*Ittijāhī al-jadīd wa mustaqbal al-riwāya,*" *al-Kātib*,

13 *Ibid.*, pp. 21-22.

14 The word science — *ʿilm — here*, as elsewhere in Arabic, should be taken in its wider sense of knowledge or learning. When the term Science in the more precise sense of natural sciences is meant, it would usually take the plural form of *ʿulūm*.

15 Fū'ād Dawwāra, *op. cit.*, p.10.

16 *Ibid.*, p.12. *Al-Hilāl*, February 1970, p. 41.

17 The term is used here in the sense given to it by Kenneth Burke, *Attitudes toward History*, New York, 1937, V. 1, pp. 2-3, of "a more or less organized system of meanings by which a thinking man gaugs the historical situation and adopts a role with relation to it."

18 Cf. Muḥammad Sayyid Kīlānī, *Al-Adab al-maṣrī fī ẓill al-ḥukm al-ʿuthmānī*, Cairo, 1965, pp. 22-23.

19 Literally, "the mountain dweller."

20 The name is meant to rhyme with Adam. Literally it means "the black one," a clear reference to the story of the creation of Adam, *Qur'ān* 15:26 "And surely We created man...of black mud..."

21 M. Watt, *Free Will and Predestination in Early Islam*, London, 48, p. 142.

22 s matter is never explicitly mentioned in the novel.

23 name, derived from the root *ʿrf*, is clearly used to bring to the idea of knowledge.

24 pression describing the moment of death: *qāla lī qabla ṣuʿūd rr al-ilāhī*.

25 or instance Abu Bakr ibn al-ʿArabī (1075-1148), *al-ʿAwāṣim awāṣim, taḥqīq Muḥibb al-Dīn al-Khaṭīb, Cairo 1375 (H.)*,

p. 178: *"qultu li abī mūsa: mā tara fī hādhā al-amr? qāla: ara innahu fī al-nafari alladhīna tuwaffiyya rasūlu allāhi ṣal'am wahuwa 'anhum rāḍin." Al-amr* meaning, of course, the right of succession, cf. p. 175. So also, cf. Aḥmad b. Ḥajar al-Haythamī, *al-Sawā'iq al-muḥriqa,* Cairo, 1965, p. 63, where 'Alī is reported to have said, defending the titles of Abū Bakr and 'Umar: *qubiḍa [rasūlu ilāhi ṣal'am] wa huwa 'anhumā rāḍin.*

26 C. G. Jung, "Approaching the Unconscious," in *Man and His Symbols,* ed. C. G. Jung, New York, 1970, pp. 37-40.

27 *Op. cit.,* p. 231.

28 *"Qirā'a jadīda," al-Kātib,* No. 57, December 1965, p. 82.

29 C. G. Jung, *Two Essays on Analytical Psychology,* New York, 1970 p. 250.

30 Aniela Jaffe, "Symbolism in the Visual Arts," in *Man and His Symbols,* ed. C. G. Jung, p. 314.

31 Cf. n. 28 *supra.*

Epilogue to Part Two

The question has been raised whether we can see in ʿArafa of *Awlād ḥāritnā* the continuation of Kamāl ʿAbd al-Jawād of the Cairo trilogy.[1] It is hoped that enough has been shown of both characters to appreciate that if this is possible then Kamāl must have made progress indeed since we last saw him in 1952. ʿArafa, it will be recalled, is the God-killer, a man of resolution and definite convictions, a man whose belief in God's existence is firm, as is his conviction that God has outlived His usefulness. As a result of his daring raid into Jabalāwī's sanctuary ʿArafa quite logically brings about his death. Later, hearing that Jabalāwī had expressed his approval of him just before his death, ʿArafa decides to undertake the fight in the way of God as previous bearers of divine messages have done before him. But what happens to all of Najīb Maḥfūẓ's extraverts, happens also to ʿArafa. When he realizes to what lengths he has gone in his drive for personal assertion and decides, out of sheer fright, to return, he finds it is too late for him either to do any good or to save his life.

So this is certainly not Kamāl. Kamāl could not kill God in the first place because he is too uncertain as to His meaning. Secondly he would not kill God, because he is not convinced, as ʿArafa is,[2] that the past has ceased to have any meaning for the present. As against ʿArafa the pragmatist, the realist, the dare-devil Kamāl vanishes into thin air. The best description of Kamāl would probably be that of the exact opposite of ʿArafa, indeed the description of Egyptian man by the Egyptian poet ʿAbd al-Raḥmān Shukrī (died 1958):[3]

> L'Egyptien a peu de volonté, mais beaucoup de reves, d'éspoirs. Il passe ses jours à rêver au lieu de s'appliquer à ses tâches. Il a peur, son courage est rompu. Son courage a honte de lui-même. Le jeune Égyptien est troublé dans ses sentiments, plein d'illusions, de rêves et d'espoirs. Nulle confiance en soi...En lui, malgré toutes ses illusions, regnent la perplexité, le doute de soi.

Nevertheless, it is a fact that Egyptian critics do see a continuation of Kamāl in ʿArafa.[4] The reading of these critics [5] is clearly influenced by their desire to see in Najīb Maḥfūẓ the propagandist for their political philosophy. Aḥmad ʿAbbās Ṣāliḥ puts it very explicitly: [6]

> Najīb Maḥfūẓ defined his political belief in *Awlād ḥāritnā* and realized that the interpretation of humanity's history offered by scientific Socialism is the right interpretation...

Oddly enough, the critic feels that this was also the conclusion of Kamāl at the end of the Cairo trilogy. In Kamāl's last meeting with his his two nephews,[7] he heard them speak of the necessity of believing and acting for the cause believed in. He admitted, thinking of himself, that although it may be easy enough to live shut up within one's selfishness, "it is difficult to be happy in this state if one is really human..." The great difficulty for him was that the problem of belief was still without a solution. "All I can console myself with is that the battle has not ended, and shall not end."

Based on this very frank admission of hesitancy Aḥmad ʿAbbās Ṣāliḥ does not hesitate to write: [8]

> At the end of the trilogy Kamāl ʿAbd al-Jawād had chosen the road of Aḥmad Shawkat,[9] the road of eternal revolution.

And then follows the statement:

> And Kamāl continues with all his remaining strength on his new road. And as soon as *Awlād ḥāritnā* was published it became certain that Najīb Maḥfūẓ had already reached the summit, regarding the belief for which he was searching.

The feeling that *Awlād ḥāritnā* is an expression of faith in scientific Socialism stems from the assumption that ʿArafa represents knowledge of science — *ʿilm*, which is conceived as a current in Islamic intellectual history that has always competed with religious faith.[10] Najīb Maḥfūẓ is seen, therefore, as putting his weight on the side of *ʿilm* as against religious faith, by having ʿArafa kill Jabalāwī. Ṣāliḥ does not ignore Jabalāwī's last message to ʿArafa but feels no scruple in saying:[11]

> Whatever was ʿArafa's attitude toward this strange message which reached him from the dead Jabalāwī, Najīb Maḥfūẓ has already arrived at the truth which is that Socialism is the ultimate solution...and that the road of Socialism is the road of *ʿilm*.

It should be pointed out that the word *ʿilm* with reference to ʿArafa's qualifications is never mentioned in *Awlād ḥāritnā*. ʿArafa's qualification is that of possessing *siḥr*, magic or glamor.[12] It is true that years after its publication Najīb Maḥfūẓ implied that what he meant by this term was *ʿilm*.[13] The question could be discussed at length whether the author's later interpretations should be taken as conclusive evidence as to his original intentions. A few remarks may be appropriate. Frye's dictum,[14] that "a poet's primary concern is to produce a work of art, and hence his intention can only be expressed by some kind of tutology," would tend, if taken too literally, to deprive the work of art of its "external fiction which is the relation between the writer and the writer's society, that is of its thematic significance. As Frye points out, the reader is entitled to ask "what's the point of this story?" which indicates "that themes have their elements of discovery just as plots do."[15] Which is to say that in so far as the question is raised in relation to the theme of a work or art, the issue of intention must be admitted as perfectly legitimate. Wellek and Warren, make the following observations:[16]

> 'Intentions' of the author are always 'rationalizations', commentaries which certainly must be taken into account

> but also must be criticized in the light of the finished work of art...
> Artists may be strangely influenced by a contemporary critical situation and by contemporary critical formulae while giving expression to their intentions, but the critical formulae themselves might be quite inadequate to characterize their actual artistic achievement.

The influence of "contemporary critical formulae" is of course many faceted. Just as the persecution of ideas may cover "a variety of phenomena, ranging from the most cruel type as exemplified by the Spanish inquisition, to the mildest, which is social ostracism," [17] so also the force of contemporary critical formulae may be such as would limit the writer's freedom of expression in varying degrees depending on the nature of the society in which the formulae are accepted. Therefore, it must be assumed that occasionally a writer who chose to write in a way which did not comply with these critical formulae, will in later years try to prove that he had in fact complied with them. Conversely, it may happen that his work was, indeed influenced by contemporary critical formulae, but in his later commentaries he tries for some reason to prove that it was not. The question of the writer's intentions may be of particular importance in understanding a work of art that develops two separate dimensions, the esoteric and the exoteric. The problem of distinguishing, in this case, between plot and theme, as described by Frye,[18] may develop into a matter of reading the lines and reading "between the lines," [19] either of the work itself or of the commentaries offered by the writer.

The extent to which such considerations are relevant to the literary climate in present-day Egypt will not be explored here. But it seems at least possible that when Najīb Maḥfūz referred to ʿArafa's *siḥr* — magic — as *ʿilm* — knowledge — he offered a commentary which was meant to legitimize his *Awlād ḥāritnā* in the eyes of a certain part of the public. In itself, this construction of the story goes against the grain not only of *Awlād ḥāritnā* itself, but of almost all that had earlier been written by Najīb Maḥfūẓ. To appreciate how difficult it is to accept ʿArafa's *siḥr* as *ʿilm*, it must be realized that *siḥr* according to the *Qur'ān* is that which Satan taught men in order to dissuade them from accepting the true message of God.[20] The great commentators of the *Qur'ān* are agreed that Satan is the source of magic.[21] But to avoid being sidetracked by extraneous images we must point out that the story of ʿArafa's stealing into Jabalāwī's big house in order to stealthily read the secret will, and of his escape therefrom, follows with amazing fidelity the Qur'ānic story of Satan attempting to penetrate into heaven in order to learn there, by stealth, God's secret words.[22] Satan, just like ʿArafa, was disturbed on approaching heaven by the lighted lamps which illuminate heaven. This is how the story of ʿArafa is told: "He came to a long corridor illuminated by a lamp in a niche in the wall." From this we know that ʿArafa penetrated heaven, for this is unmistakably the image described in the famous verse[23] which reads:

> His light is like a niche in which there is a lamp;
> the lamp is in a glass and the glass is like a
> shining star.

We are not told in the *Qur'ān* that this is the lamp Satan saw when he stole into heaven, but we are told that all the lamps he saw looked like stars.[24] When Satan made his escape the bright light disturbed him, and similarly, the light with ʿArafa saw, when escaping from the big house, "blinded his eyes."

It would appear then that ʿArafa is presented in the image of Satan perpetrating one of his most outrageous and ignoble acts. Why therefore was ʿArafa given that noble name?[25] For the name is noble and was probably chosen for that reason, and it is only through this name that the concept of *ʿilm* can enter the discussion at all. Only by giving the person administering *siḥr* the name of ʿArafa can the issue of *ʿilm* be raised. But it must be realized that when Najīb Maḥfūẓ introduces the concept of *ʿilm* in this context — in interviews given after the publication of the novel — it is a peculiar kind of *ʿilm* he is talking about, an *ʿilm* devoid of "the higher meanings of life."[26] Indeed it is not the concept of *ʿilm* as evolved in Islamic culture over the centuries. It is probably true to say that this kind of knowledge, deprived of those values or, to put it differently, knowledge which is not derived from God but from natural forces, is *ipso facto*, *siḥr*, in Islamic terminology.[27]

The following discussion of a concept which does not appear in the novel may seem strange, but it is important to clarify the issue. The missing concept of *ʿilm* is very conspicuous by its absence. ʿArafa is curing sick people, he develops a bomb, he has medicaments to revive waning manhood. All these crafts could very well be referred to as *ʿilm*, a term which has always been wide enough to include natural science of non-Islamic origin.[28] The question is unavoidably raised why have these crafts been referred to in this case as *siḥr*, which is ungodly knowledge.

In order to understand the importance of the question it should be pointed out that

> *ʿilm* is one of those concepts that have dominated Islam and given Muslim civilization its distinctive shape and complexion... *ʿilm* is Islam.[29]

This statement of Franz Rosenthal will help the reader to realize the deep significance of the absence of the term *ʿilm* from a novel which attempts to depict science as a dominant social force. This force is introduced in the novel as devoid of the most important features of *ʿilm*, namely its emanation from God.[30] *ʿIlm* is irrevocably impressed on the Muslim mind because of the acceptance of the assumption permeating the *Qur'ān* "that human knowledge, that is, true human knowledge, is to be equated with religious insight."[31] Consequently faith itself follows on knowledge, and "believing" and "being given knowledge" become parallel expressions[32] because "those who have come to believe know" (*Qur'ān*, 2:26).

All this applies to human knowledge that has some real value and truly deserves to be called "knowledge."[33] Such knowledge, as indicated, stands in very special relation to God:

> There can be no human knowledge secular or religious without the knowledge possessed by the deity. On the other hand, the reason for the existence of divine knowledge as well as its final destination are, in a manner of speaking, man and his need and desire for knowledge.[34]

If in the light of all this we examine ʿArafa's message, and his crafts, it becomes quite obvious that the term *ʿilm* cannot be used to describe them because, as exercised by him, they have no affinity to knowledge. The only other so-called knowledge in possession of man, that which does not derive directly from God, is Satan's knowledge, namely *siḥr*. The fact that Najīb Maḥfūẓ lumped together under this term such crafts as medicine and the production of explosives clearly reveals his criterion. It is not the nature of the sciences which decides whether they are godly or satanic, but the spirit in which they are employed. The spirit of ʿArafa, from the very beginning, is condemned by applying to it the term *siḥr*. It will be recalled that his three predecessors, unlike ʿArafa, believed in Jabalāwī and respected his inscrutable wishes. This unquestioning faith is totally absent in the history of ʿArafa. Therefore, in spite of the fact that he brings with him a kind of knowledge which is technologically superior to that of the three previous messengers of Jabalāwī, he is nevertheless rejected. What is more, after each one of the three great reformers — let us call them prophets — the situation did indeed deteriorate again, yet humanity was somehow enriched by their experience; but after ʿArafa, humanity is much morse off than before, and all that people have to fasten their hopes onto is the rumor that Ḥanash may have saved ʿArafa's *siḥr* and will one day put it at their dispoal. A definite set-back for numanity as a whole.

The remaining question now is the meaning of Jabalāwī's last message to ʿArafa, expressing his approval of him. The episode is told in a manner which leaves it open as to whether the message was really delivered or whether it was merely an hallucination of the drunken ʿArafa in the morning after a nigh-long debauchery. The situation is certainly not a typical one for prophetic inspiration. It can be assumed that the event never actually happened, and that it was merely an apparition produced by ʿArafa's disturbed conscience, that is by his feeling of guilt. If, "remorse is the reaction to a forbidden deed of aggression"[35] the episode can really be looked on as repeating essentially the sensation of remorse experienced by Ḥasanayn of *Bidāya wa nihāya* after forcing his sister to jump into the Nile. The death which soon follows this sensation completes the equation of the two cases, which in turn provide us with Najīb Maḥfūẓ's characteristic pattern of the extravert's life-cycle.

But there is no need to exclude the other interpretation which assumes that the message was really sent by Jabalāwī. In that event the all-knowing Jabalāwī can be said to have approved of ʿArafa's basic ambition to help his people in their plight, but this ambition, stripped of higher values, proved to be of no avail. Even Jabalāwī's approval could not save it from failure. Thus we see that ʿArafa, in spite of his initially admissible motives, is finally rejected.

But if ʿArafa is the negative, the rejected apostle, Satan exercising *siḥr*, we may ask who is Najīb Maḥfūẓ's true apostle?

After reading the Cairo trilogy the impression is unmistakable that Kamāl might develop in stature and become the positive model of his generation. He has grown up and lived all his life in the Old City, but he comes out and exposes himself to all that the New City has to offer. He is captivated by foreign beauty and he is sufficiently intrigued by the Western intellectual challenge to master Western philosophy. But eventually he comes to realize that foreign values are of diverse grades, and that in themselves they may prove to be the undoing of Egypt's society. By the same token he finds that his own society's native values are much more worldly and much less idealistic than he had thought. After many tribulations he emerges not unscarred, but fairly composed. His faithfulness to his native culture is still firm even if no longer naively uncritical. His admiration for Western culture is still considerable but no longer raptuous. Some sort of an emotional balance seems to have been achieved. Kamāl is no longer that introverted young man, looking at the beautiful, French-educated and rich ʿĀʼida, as Kāmil Ruʼba-Lāẓ used to look at his wife, with impotent admiration. He is no longer that young man so conscious of his ugly nose and funny-looking head. By now Kamāl is deriving great physical pleasure from his association with a young mother of two, who is making a living by working in a whore-house run by his father's old mistress. This is still a far cry from actually being able to marry a woman and start a normal fruitful life. But at least he recognizes that sensual fulfilment must accompany spiritual satisfaction to make life meaningful. His notion that "those who really love do not marry" has disappeared by now. There is no trace of the young man who stood out in the desert on the night his adored ʿĀʼida married, looking at the lighted window of her room, wondering "into what corner on earth now has ʿĀʼida's pride crawled?"

But having somehow established an emotional balance, Kamāl is still far from capable of taking his bearings in the world he inhabits. He had already indentified the values to be renounced, such as egocentrism,

Sūfism, "negative belife in *ʿilm*."[36] He also knows now, in general terms, what should be done positively. "Therefore action is inevitable, and there is no action without faith.[37] The problem is how can we create faith worthy of life." Again we see how these twin terms -- knowledge and faith — become crucial. The line of thinking we see here is, of course, essentially Islamic, for we immediately notice the implicit equation of *ʿilm* and *imān*, knowledge and faith.[38] The concept of a "negative belife in *ʿilm*" is clearly to be understood as *ʿilm* devoid of *imān* — faith. Obviously, therefore, a man who has no faith, or for whom the problem of faith is still unsolved,[39] can believe in *ʿilm* only in a negative manner, that is in *siḥr*. In traditional Islam, any attempt to separate knowledge from faith is condemned:

> Those who felt that faith was to be kept separate from knowledge were the ones who were inclined to favour rationalistic or esoteric knowledge and to play down the importance of formal faith...On the other hand, the vast majority of Muslims were conditioned by the *Qurʾān* and the history of the term *ʿilm* to see 'faith' as a function of 'knowledge', or vice versa...[40]

When faith is in any way separated from knowledge the result is loss of certainty — *yaqin*. "While knowledge is the firm belief that a thing is as it is, certainty is one's satisfaction with, and assuredness of, what one knows...Certainty is the knowledge whose owner is not beset by any doubt *(rayb)* whatever. It is a knowledge which does not fall prey to doubts."[41] And this is exactly what Kamāl does not possess, even after reaching emotional balance. His failure at this stage consists in his being in doubt, and "doubt in whichever way indicated became the true pariah and outcast of Muslim civilization. It stands for all that is to be shunned like a plague."[42] For the consequences of prolonged doubt may be the embracing of satanic disbelief. Thus, we see Kamāl, in one of the last scenes of the great trilogy, in a position traditionally held as the lowest a Muslim can reach. His is not the useful doubt, leading to certainty after search, which is sometimes lauded even in Islam,[43] but rather a way of life which has always been "banned from Muslim society."[44]

Also, quite in line with Islamic thinking, Najīb Maḥfūẓ specifies, as a crucial consideration, that doubt, or lack of faith, precludes positive action. The basic Islamic concept which makes *ʿamal*[45] dependent on *īmān* is clearly adhered to by Kamāl and is at the root of his predicament. Having restored his emotional equilibrium, Kamāl is now faced with the task of restoring his intellectual self-reliance on which his redemption depends. If we view Kamāl as the symbol of his civilization, the message of Najīb Maḥfūẓ seems clear. The way for Egypt to extricate itself from its present cultural distress is to regain emotional composure and intellectual confidence, both of which are of the essence of its Islamic heritage, in its original, unadulterated form.

That the Cairo trilogy does not end with an unequivocal promise of success is self-evident. But it has shown a way and a direction. That six years later Najīb Maḥfūẓ could see nothing more heartening happening in the Old City than the dismal failure of ʿArafa, is a measure of the crisis he felt Egypt was undergoing.

NOTES

1 *Supra*, p. 180.

2 *Supra*, p. 177.

3 Translated by Jacques Berque, *L'Egypte*, Paris, 1967, p. 369.

4 *Supra*, p. 180.

5 Mainly Ghālī Shukrī, and Aḥmad ʿAbbās Ṣāliḥ.

6 "*Qirā'a jadīda*," *al-Kātib*, No. 56, November 1965, p. 60.

7 *Supra*, p. 127.

8 *Ibid.*, p. 59.

9 The Communist brother. Ṣāliḥ simply ignores the other brother who was an ardent Muslim.

10 Ṣāliḥ, *ibid.*, p. 59.

11 *Ibid.*, p. 60. Ṣāliḥ reports that Najīb Maḥfūẓ was making references in private talks to the escape of Western scientists to the Soviet Union "a matter which resembles ʿArafa's attempt to escape." It is not clear whether the similarity is indicated by Najīb Maḥfūẓ or is a conclusion of Ṣāliḥ.

12 Cf. *siḥr* in the *Shorter Encyclopaedia of Islam*, article by D. B. Macdonald.

13 See *Supra.*, p. 173.

14 *Anatomy*, p. 86.

15 *Ibid.*, p. 52.

16 R. Wellek and A. Warren, *Theory of Literature*, New York, 1956, p. 148.

17 Leo Strauss, *Persecution and the Art of Writing*, Clencee, 1952, p. 32.

18 *Supra*, n. 15.

19 Strauss, *op. cit.*, p. 30.

20 *Qur'ān*, 2:102.

21 Macdonald, *op. cit.*

22 *Ibid.*, *Qur'ān* 37, 9,10:72, 89.

23 *Qur'ān*, 24, 35. The translation is by Goldziher, as given in the *Shorter Encyclopaedia*. S. V. Nur. Niche in the *Qur'ān* is *mishkāt*. The word used in the novel is *kūwa*.

24 Macdonald, *ibid.*, *Qur'ān*, 37, 10.

25 Cf. ʿArafa in the *Shorter Encyclopaedia of Islam*. On Ibn ʿArabī's discussion of *maʿrifa*, cf. Franz Rosenthal, *Knowledge Triumphant*,

Leiden, 1970, p. 116. Cf. also *supra*, Ch. 6, n. 23.

26 Cf. *supra*, p. 173.

27 Macdonald's article in the *Shorter Encyclopaedia of Islam* on *siḥr*:"In regard to the magical work of al-Būnī (d. 622/1225)... in which the author tried to draw up a system of licit magic, Ibn Khaldūn held that it was illicit magic, because it professed to derive its forces from natural powers and not from Allāh."

28 Cf. von Grunebaum, *Islam*, "Muslim World View and Muslim Science."

29 F. Rosenthal, *op. cit.*, p. 2.

30 "All human knowledge specifically comes from God," *ibid.*, p. 29.

31 *Ibid.*

32 "Allah will exalt those of you who believe and who are given knowledge (*ʿilm*)," *Qur'ān*, 58, 11.

33 Rosenthal, *op. cit.*, p. 30.

34 *Ibid.*, p. 31.

35 Theodor Reik, *Myth and Guilt*, New York, 1970, p. 22.

36 *al-Imān al-salbī bi al-ʿilm.*

37 *La budd li al-ʿamal min imān.*

38 Franz Rosenthal, *op. cit.*, p. 97. "Knowledge" (*ʿilm*) and "faith" (*imān*) are equated in the *Qur'ān.*"

39 *Supra*, p. 185.

40 F. Rosenthal, *op. cit.*

41 *Ibid.*, p. 168.

42 *Ibid.*, p. 300.

43 *Ibid.*, p. 304.

44 *Ibid.*, p. 308.

45 *Supra*, n. 36.

Part Three

WHISPER OF MADNESS

Chapter Seven
The Rebel

Najīb Maḥfūẓ's novels, after *Awlād ḥāritnā*, are relatively short and each revolves mostly around a single episode in a man's life. The writer's interests have noticeably narrowed to a study of those episodes in the lives of individuals which show the inevitable defeat of individualism in its encounter with forces supporting society's immutable prerogatives. This may not be surprising in an age that witnessed the final collapse of 30 years of the so-called liberal experiments in Egypt. But an irritating dissonance is sensed by some Egyptian critics in the way society is represented in these novels as opposing the rebelliousness inherent in radical individualism. For the basic assumption of many Egyptian intellectuals in the last three decades or so has been that the social revolution which Egypt is undergoing should, of itself, satisfy all the cravings for rebellion. A conflict between the rebel and contemporary society is thus a contradiction they find hard to accept. Oddly enough, they tend to consider such a conflict to be a novelty in the works of Najīb Maḥfūẓ. But when this is seen in the light of Najīb Maḥfūẓ's previous writing, his belief that the era of conflict between individual and society had not ended, should not cause astonishment. What would seem to be a novelty in the warmth and sympathy with which he presents those compulsive rebels who, in the past, were rarely meant to gain the readers' sympathy. To be sure, his rebels are still doomed and their defeat is just as unavoidable. But now they are striving for values which the reader can accept as worth fighting for and possibly even dying for. In this light, it becomes understandable at least why some critics wonder. For the change is remarkable and the historical context in which it has occurred can hardly be overlooked.

But this is not the only change which marks Najīb Maḥfūẓ's writing in the 1960s, which have been variously described:

> The stress is now on moods, situations, and symbols rather than on naturalistic or psychological studies. The existential moments gain prominence. Both the characters and events in these novels are evocative. They have a significance which transcends the bare statement of experience. Very often they can be described as double-layered stories. [1]

This change in style, coupled with the continuation of theme, creates the greatest difficulty for the Egyptian critic. Although, as has been justly pointed out by another observer:[2]

> The forlorn alienated person, who wanders about in search of meaning did not appear in the stories of Maḥfūẓ only after the revolution. When the Arab literary critics emphasized that the post-revolution novel *The Thief and the Dogs* represented a totally new approach, Maḥfūẓ remarked that this was not the case and noted that the third part of this triology *al-Sukkarīya* (completed before the revolution) had some similar features.

Therefore a formal description which would tend to isolate his post-1960 work can be acceptable more as a matter of emphasis than as a definitive division. Nevertheless, the difference between the two periods is unmistakable, for reasons already alluded to: first, the writer's greater empathy with the individualistic rebel; and second, his increasing predilection for pensiveness and abstraction.

It is true that *al-Sukkarīya*, in some parts at least, gives notice of a possible development of this nature, but less so probably than *Bayn al-qasrayn* where the first sympathetic rebels are encountered, and their inevitable failure is so movingly described.

The two episodes may be recounted summarily. The first rebel is, of course, Amīna, the submissive and obedient wife of Aḥmad 'Abd al-

Jawād. One Friday when the formidable father journeys to Port Saʿīd on business, the wily Yāsīn suggests that she should go and visit the mosque of Sīdna Ḥusayn whom she revers so much. The mosque is only a few minutes walk from the house, but for 40 years she has never been permitted to go out and visit it. Her reaction is unexpected, and mostly to herself.

> She did not know how the adventure appeared possible, even tempting and compelling. Indeed, the visit to Ḥusayn appeared to be a powerful excuse — it had the attribute of sacredness -- for the easy leap [3] for which her heart yearned. But this was not the only source of her desire, for its call was answered in the depth of her soul by repressed currents eager to be let loose, just as instincts craving for battle respond to the summons of war with the pretence of defending freedom and peace.

Amīna wants to rebel and she, therefore, succumbs to the temptation. The next stage, however, is rather strange. Although this is to be the first time in 40 years that Amīna goes out, no one undertakes to join her, to show her the way and protect her, except Kamāl, the little boy less than ten years old. But for the purpose of the following allegory this is an excellent device. For although "they all — without knowing it — participated in the rebellion against the will of the absent father" it was the little inexperienced boy — *ghulām* — who led Amīna, explaining to her whatever they saw on the way, "proud in the role of a guide — *murshid*." [4]

The detailed description of the actual visit to the tomb cannot be related here, but the vast gap of feelings and thoughts between the compulsive rebel and her opportunistic-guide is clearly brought out. As against Amīna's perfect sincerity of faith and selfless devotion to the ideal she worships, Kamāl's expectations are downright materialislistic and his hopes are heightened by the prospects of enlisting the holy saint's support for their realization. On the termination of the visit, the mother, elated and excited, wishes to return home, but the child, who wants to turn the adventure to his own benefit, pleads with her to walk just a little further, up to al-Sikka al-Jadīda — The New Road.[5] Once on this crowded and busy thoroughfare, Kamāl again asks her to walk with him along the street westward up to al-Ghūriyya[6] Street, where he intends to make her buy him some pastry. The original purpose of the excursion is by now completely forgotten. Amīna is confused and overwhelmed by the noise and traffic; as if to say that the revolution declines, as it must, once its high ideals are perverted by childish desires into materialistic goals. Thus suddenly a car hits Amīna, she falls and the whole adventure, so gaily and courageously begun, comes to a tragic end.

It is hard to say why Amīna's rebellion fails. Is it for the reason that all rebellions are bound to fail, or is it because of the perversion of its original purpose.

Not unrelated to this episode is Fahmī's martyrdom. We remember Najīb Maḥfūẓ's words on "instincts craving for battle" responding "to the summons of war with the pretence of defending freedom and peace." Well, Fahmī did feel the powerful summons of events leading to the victory of Saʿd Zaghlūl in 1919.[7] But he joins the demonstrations against his father's wish. Not only that. After Saʿd Zaghlūl has been released and victory achieved, he comes to his father, apologizes for his behavior and promises not to take part in such activities again. Aḥmad ʿAbd al-Jawād sees through the ruse and distrusts his son's sincerity. He is right. The same morning Fahmī again engages himself in organizing a peaceful and legal demonstration.

This is a tremendous demonstration, and Fahmī feels great satisfaction at seeing such a huge crowd coming to participate in this symbol of victory. As they march, he sees a few high ranking British officers at the head of their troops silently watching the demonstrators. One of them, a deputy chief of police, is reputed to be a most hateful official. Fahmī cannot recall his name and the name Julian comes to his mind. Julian was a British soldier who flirted with Maryam, the girl Fahmī loved, but was not permitted to marry. Now Fahmī is disturbed: memories of the past distract his attention from his immediate task. He tries to shake off the "dust" of past memories:

> We live for the future not for the past. Geese. Mister Geese, Mister Geese, that is the name of the deputy chief of police, God's curse on him. Get back to the cheers to shake off this uncalled for dust.

As the demonstration comes within sight of the Azbakiyya gardens, a shot is fired. Then another shot, and the demonstration begins to disperse in disorder. But Fahmī cannot move. Soon he begins to lose consciousness. Everything becomes blurred before his eyes. He sees the sky. "The sky? stretching high above. Nothing but the sky, still and smiling, and peace dripping from it." [8]

In both cases we already sense the writer's altered feeling for his rebels. He sympathizes with them, but the faults causing their final defeat are revealed with precision. Basically they are the same as those of the previous rebels: disrespect for authority, a passion to break away from the past, a displacement of one set of values by another.

But before 1960 all this was no more than an element in a broad plot which always had other characters whose fates were different, and who lent the stories a measure of realism and hope. Since 1960 only the gloomy and hopeless element prevails. This is a matter for serious reflection on the part of both writer and reader.

Rebellion in any shape or form seems to be ruled out, regardless of motive. One cannot help thinking of the deep-rooted Islamic suspicion of all shades of dissent. "All those who foment disturbances (*fitna)* are innovators (*muḥdith*)" said Ḥasan al-Baṣrī, [9] and innovation, of course, is the anathema of traditional Islam. Najīb Maḥfūẓ's rebels, at least up to 1952, are not politically motivated, with the obvious exception of Fahmī, whereas Islam's traditional suspicion of disturbance is decidedly political in nature. But since the distinction between political issues and non-political issues is practically unrecognized in Islam, Najīb Maḥfūẓ's rebels are all political, even though they are distinctly so only since 1958. What is unique in the later works is that no matter what the hero's grievances are, whether personal in nature, or caused by social difficulties or intellectual or emotional stress, they soon develop into a conflict between the individual and the body politic. This new tendency is already clear in *Awlād ḥāritnā* which, in a sense, is a thoroughly Islamic work, in which political, social, moral and religious issues are all treated without discrimination. Everything is tied into one whole system describable as "a religious way of life."[10] Consequently all issues, such as people's rights, their relations to their ancient father (God), and to the government, are naturally settled between the Prophet and the Supervisor. After this work, no novel[11] ends without the political authorities intervening as final arbiters in the crises described.

Such a change must be looked into carefully. There is no doubt that the distance between the individual and the government of the land has been reduced. The individual now has much less leeway than before; as soon as he strays, the state intervenes. In other words, the individual has lost his liberty to be in error for any length of time, and society has become less tolerant, in so far as the political power represents society. To be sure, formerly, too, the political authorities of the land existed and were recognized, but they were so distant from daily awareness that they hardly mattered.

It has been remarked that Najīb Maḥfūẓ's short stories often bring out the quintessence of an idea or a situation. In the collection *Bayt sayyiʾ al-sumʿa*[12] (The House of Ill Repute) there is a short story called "*al-Khawf*" (Fear). The story consists of three parts.[13] The first depicts a quarter in old Cairo at the beginning of the century, which remains unaware of the authority of the central government, and submits to the tyranny of the local gang leaders. Two of the gang leaders wish to marry a local beauty, and the competition between them threatens to embroil the quarter in a fierce struggle.[14] In the second part of the story a police station is providentially established in the quarter just before the battle breaks out and a young and energetic police officer, employing modern techniques of fist-fighting, manages to overcome the gangsters and expel them from the quarter. In the third part, the police officer proceeds to repress the peace-loving inhabitants of the quarter who at first welcomed the police. He does so under the pretext of fighting gangsterism, and eventually anyone with self-respect or ambition is forced to flee the quarter. In time, the officer having suppressed the people and removed all opposition to his authority, loses his vitality. Thus the establishment of a central governmental authority over the old quarters of Cairo ends in a mood of futility and lack of purpose.

Obviously the distance between the individual and the police has diminished. The gangsters, under whose cruel tyranny life was often miserable enough, are gone, but at the same time the little one had of personal freedom and pride is also gone. Are the people better off? Were they really so miserable previously? An answer of sorts to these questions is given in the short story, *Rūḥ ṭabīb al-qulūb* (The spirit of the Healer of Hearts).[15] There the guardian of the sacred tomb interrogates a poor girl of the streets who visits the sanctuary trying to find out what made her come.

> - Are you happy with your life?
> She said with enthusiasm:
> - Life is beautiful, in spite of all these fights.
> - So the fighting is worrying you?
> - Not at all, it only adds taste to life.

The girl was referring to the fights of the gangs of thugs. Her reply reflects exactly what the people of the quarter feel after their deliverance by the police. Life has become devoid of much that was worth living for. There can be no doubt that living in constant terror of the gangsters was miserable, and the need and hope for delivery could not be felt more strongly. But how agonizing it must be, when the hoped-for change does arrive, to discover that life has become even more senseless than before? What is one to do in such circumstances? To despair and yield to this cycle of tyrannical powers hopelessly, succeeding each other, and to murmur: "What has been written shall prevail?"[16] The problem is not the lack of an ideal, but rather the disappointment following its realization. This is not an isolated or a passing phenomenon.

> No aspect of Muslim civilization lends itself more convincingly to the demonstration of that grandiose and sublime failure to strike a balance between aspiration and achievement, that incapacity to institutionalize with reasonable adequacy the divinely revealed principles of the body politic so keenly grasped and so unrealistically pursued by the legists.[17]

The complete dependence of the people on the whims of whoever happens to be the ruler has been recognized in Islam with perfect resignation. A famous tradition attributes to the Prophet the following saying:[18]

> After my death rulers will rule over you. The righteous will rule according to his righteousness and the wicked will rule according to his wickedness. Listen to them and obey them. If they shall be good, it will be good for you and for them; and if they shall be bad, it will be bad for you and for them.

This concern for complete obedience stems, as has been mentioned, from Islam's horror of dissent.[19]

The right and obligation to oppose the evil acts of the rulers are not, however, ruled out in Islam. On the contrary, it is specifically stated that

> He among you who sees somthing displeasing to Allah, must change it by force, if he is unable -- by his work; but if not even that, then at least in his heart.[20]

This is a very practical advice, for in most cases the last measure was the only one that could be resorted to. In fact it goes very well with the concept of *taqiyya*[21] (disguise) which is the term for dispensation from a requirement of religion under compulsion or threat of injury.

All this has not prevented successive attempts to dislodge lawful rulers, some of which failed and were therefore condemned both on practical and on theoretical grounds. But some attempts succeeded and could always be similarly justified on practical and theoretical grounds.[22] A Qur'ānic commandment which could be utilized by an aspirant to power was that which calls on all Muslims to urge doing what is good and to restrain what is disreputable.[23] This was normally the basis for acts executed by the state to protect public and private morality.[24] But occasionally it was turned into a rebellious slogan, and a justification for seizing power by force.[25]

Thus one may obtain an idea of the inherent conflict in traditional Islamic thinking between the duty of obedience and the duty of opposing the wrongdoings of the state. The supreme consideration of preserving the community from the hardships of civil war operates in favor of both the established ruler and the usurper who manages to establish effective control over any part of the land. Therefore the final decision as to whether a rebellion is justifiable or not rests with the rebel himself, who will be judged according to the results of his action. He will be praised if he is successful, and he will be condemned if he is vanquished. And it is on this moral issue that we find Najīb Maḥfūẓ's position after 1960 unique. He evaluates the moral issues on their own merits, regardless of success. This should not come as a surprise, because, in his past works moral issues were never judged by the criterion of success. Nevertheless, the actual relationship between moral justice and success was eclipsed by the fact that success always came finally to those who were morally just, which is of course not the same as saying, as Islamic political theory does, that success is proof of the justness of a cause.

After 1960 Najīb Maḥfūẓ makes it quite clear that success in itself is no necessary token of the moral rightenousness of the successful. And perhaps this is what lies at the root of the anxiety caused by his works. For the situation can now be described as follows. A confrontation develops between an individual and society as represented by the agencies of government. Society inevitably wins, and the individual is vanquished. But in spite of his failure the individual may still be the upholder of what is just. Society may therefore be wrong in spite of its victory, and this stigma is attached directly to the formal representative of society, namely the state. Besides being rare, this notion has always been intolerable on practical grounds. It is, therefore, of the utmost interest to see how Aḥmad ʿAbbās Ṣāliḥ,[26] has quite frankly attempted to formulate a concept that would allow literature to be openly critical of the state without too obviously overstepping the traditional concepts of the relative positions of the individual and the state.

> /Some people may think that/ since literature must by its very nature be in opposition (*muʿāriḍ*)[27] therefore literature which opposes Socialism is the true literature. This conclusion, naturally, is utterly false.
> And yet, literature, because of its nature, cannot but be in opposition. How can literature oppose the Socialist revolution and still remain...within the purview of the revolution?
> Indeed, literature does not oppose the revolution. It only opposes the errors in application; it opposes deviation.

He then goes on to explain that the writer is in advance of society in the search for revolutionary solutions to the problems created by the revolutionary circumstances. And alone in the wilderness where no solutions have yet been found, the writer experiences personally the agonies of a search which must be followed by all with interest and sympathy.[28] By thus taking a very independent line of thinking Najīb Maḥfūẓ has evidently created a situation which permits a degree of forbearance in judging the individual in his conflicts with society.

Al-Liṣṣ wa al-kilāb was written in 1960 and was influenced by the single-handed fight against society of a criminal whose exploits had arrested the public's attention during March and April of that year.[29] The exploits of the hero of the novel, Saʿīd Mihrān, follow in a general manner those of the criminal, who sought to take revenge on his unfaithful wife and her paramour, made an attempt on the life of his own lawyer, and finally took refuge in the house of another woman where he was found and shot by the police.

It is impossible to say whether *al-Liṣṣ wa al-kilāb* has its source only in this episode,[30] but the link between the real events and the novel is obvious. Clearly the interest of the novel is not in the repetition of a story well known to the public; it lies in the way the novel idealizes the criminal. The theme of the betrayal of a man by the people closest to him is very conspicuous in the novel, but equally conspicuous is that of the betrayal of an ideal. And the ideal is the one cherished by the pre-1952 revolutionaries, who are now enjoying their success but have not much more use of their ideal. Consequently the grudge of the betrayed hero is no longer personal in nature, but transcendental; it is a grudge against society for having failed to live up to its ideals.

The novel opens with the following sentence:

> Again he breathed the breath of liberty, but in a dusty choking air and an unbearable heat.

This is the kind of liberty Saʿīd Mihrān finds after four years of imprisonment. The occasion of his release is the anniversary of the revolution, which is not yet four years old. His arrest comes about when the police catch him in the act of committing a robbery, having been tipped off by his closest associate ʿAlīsh. After that his wife Nabawiyya obtains a divorse and marries ʿAlīsh Sadra, which convinced Saʿīd that this was the purpose of ʿAlīsh's betrayal. Now, after his release from prison, he goes to see his little daughter Sinā', who does not accept him, sharing her family's deep suspicions of him. Saʿīd also notices that ʿAlīsh and his new family are protected by the police.

Having found liberty so stifling, Saʿīd turns to the *Ṣūfī* Shaykh ʿAli al-Junaidī, whom he has known since childhood. This is the first time we meet a veritable Ṣūfī shaykh in Najīb Maḥfūẓ's stories, and he virtually dominates the scene.

Najīb Maḥfūẓ is deeply concerned with the role of Sūfism in modern Egyptian society. In 1961 he published the story *Zaʿbalāwī*,[31] which is a quest story of a person who was afflicted by "a malady for which no one had a remedy." Hoping that Zaʿbalāwī, one of the holy men -- *walī* -- would be able to cure his disease, the hero sets out to find him. He never does find Zaʿlabāwī, but is nevertheless determined to go on searching for him.

It has been suggested [32] that "the search for cure is in fact a quest for religious faith" and that "the incurable illness from which the hero suffers represents the anxiety of the human condition." And both these elements, of anxiety and quest, are more prominent in the works of this later period than before. Another important difference is that the men of the earlier works, who ventured out alone in search of a goal, were far less metaphysical in their thinking and their ways led them nowhere near religion. Yet the differences cannot conceal what is common to these two kinds of quests. In the first place, all of Najīb Maḥfūẓ's searchers fail -- inevitably. Secondly, no matter how close they approach to Ṣufism in the later period, they finally do not wholly embrace it, and at the end of their search, they are as far from the mainstream of society as were their forerunners of the earlier period.

Therefore it is quite true to say that the story of Zaʿbalāwī may serve "as an introduction to the world of Najīb Maḥfūẓ." [33] At the same time there is no reason to assume that the story reflects Najīb Maḥfūẓ's own view of the place of man in the world. This story, like most of his short stories, should be looked on as an experimental study of an idea, a situation or a motive which, at a later point, is almost sure to find its way into one of his major works. [34] It is usually an indication that the idea, motive or situation has engaged the writer's attention to a considerable extent, which in itself is very significant. *Zaʿbalāwī* would never have been written had the writer not felt the resurgence of *Ṣūfī* sentiments in Egypt of the 1950s, [35] a development which is reflected also in *al-Summān wa al-kharīf*. [36] The story of Zaʿbalāwī and the novel, *al-Liṣṣ wa al-kilāb* were written more or less at the same time, which may indicate that the episode of Mahmūd Amīn Sulaymān [37] has been used merely as a framework for ideas which engaged Najīb Maḥfūẓ at the time. Both stories seem to convey the same message: that chasing *Ṣūfī* happiness may seem to be a colorful adventure, but it is never more than the pursuit of an illusion.

When Saʿīd Mihrān approaches the simple abode of Shaykh al-Junaidī, his memories take him back to the days of his childhood, when he used to accompany his father to the *Ṣūfī* gatherings at the shaykh's place.

He takes the shaykh's hand and kisses it, sits down and tells the old man that he has come to him because he has no place on earth except this house. "You mean the walls not the heart," says the old *Ṣūfī* Saʿīd explains to him that he has just come out of prison and the old *Ṣūfī* answers:

> 'You have not come out of prison.' Saʿīd smiled. The same expressions of the old days are repeated again, where every word has a meaning other than its meaning. He said:
> - 'My lord, any prison is easy, but the government's prison'.

He looked at him with a clear eye and muttered:
- 'He said any prison is easy by the government's prison'.
Saʿīd smiled again. He almost despaired of a meeting of the minds.

The discussion continues at cross-purposes:

- 'My lord, I came to you at a time when my daughter disavowed me'.
Said the shaykh with a sigh:
- 'He places his secrets with the meanest of His creatures!'
He then said with emotion:
- 'I said to myself, if God has granted him old age I shall surely find the door open.'
Said the shaykh calmly:
- 'And how have you found the door of heaven?'
- 'But I have found no place on earth and my daughter disavowed me.'
- 'She is so much like you.'
- 'How my lord?'
- 'You are looking for a house not an answer.'
He rested his frizzly head on his dark lean hand and said:
- 'My father used to come to you at times of distress, so I found myself...'
He interrupted him with the calm that never left him:
- 'You want a house, nothing else.'

This talk worries Saʿīd and he protests:

- 'Not only a house,more than that. I wish to say: God be pleased with me.'
Said the shaykh as if reflecting:
- 'Said the heavenly lady: 'Aren't you ashamed to ask that He with Whom you are not pleased be pleased with you?!' 38

Saʿīd suspects that the shaykh does not welcome him after all, and he asks the shaykh if he does. The shaykh evades the question and Saʿīd demands:

- 'But you are the owner of the house!'
He said with a sudden gaity:
- 'The owner of the house welcomes you, as he welcomes every creature and everything'. Saʿīd smiled, encouraged. But the shaykh added:
- 'But I am the owner of nothing.'

Later the shaykh's demands are not only metaphysical. He says to Saʿīd:

- 'Take a volume /of the *Qur'ān*/ and read.'
Saʿīd was embarrassed and said apologetically:
- 'I left the prison only today and have not yet had an ablution.'
- 'Perform the ablution and read.'
He said in a complaining tone:
- 'My daughter disavowed me, and shied away from me as if I were Satan. And before her her mother betrayed me!'
The shaykh said again softly:
- 'Perform the ablution and read.'
- 'She betrayed me with a contemptible one of my gang, an apprentice who was standing before me like a dog. She demanded divorce on ground of my being in prison, and then she married him.'
- 'Perform the ablution and read.'
He persisted:
- 'And my property, the cash and jewelry, he took it all and with it he became a master as big as the world, and all the cowards of the alley became his men.'
- 'Perform the ablution and read.'
Sternly with veins bulging on his forehead:
- 'I was not caught because of the cleverness of the police. No. As always I was confident of escape. The dog tipped them off, with her consent he tipped them off. Then the disasters came following each other until my daughter disavowed me.'
Said the shaykh reproachfully:
- 'Perform the ablution and read.'

And he goes on to specify what Saʿīd should read and recite of *Ṣūfī* wisdom which would express complete subjection and resignation before God's inscrutable will. Saʿīd does not comply. He thinks of his first night of freedom, "with the shaykh who is absent in heaven, repeating the words which cannot be comprehended by one who is approaching fire.[39] Yet, is there any other shelter where I can seek refuge?"

So ends the first meeting between a Mahfuzian hero of the writer's third literary period and the first real *Ṣūfī* to appear in his works, and it does not augur well for Ṣūfism. In the passage, Ṣūfism is described forcefully as a clear and well-defined way of life, that brooks no compromise. In times of distress men may feel that Ṣūfism offers a temporary shelter, but what they seek truly cannot be attained through Ṣūfism. The message of this chapter of *al-Liṣṣ wa al-kilāb* lends itself to no other reading.

Saʿīd will return to the *Ṣūfī* twice before the novel ends. The first time is after Saʿīd has experienced failure and the second after attempting to kill his rival, ʿAlīsh Sadra. The failure consists in being caught by his old friend and teacher, Ra'ūf ʿAlwān, when he breaks into his house at night. This is a senseless attempt, motivated by a newly discovered hatred for the man who has become so satisfied with his new position as a newspaper editor,[40] after the revolution, that he has forgotten his own ideals. Saʿīd sees in Ra'ūf, the man who had taught him to be a revolutionary, the symbol of treason, a man whose betrayal is more unpardonable than the betrayals by his friend and by his wife.

> I do not know, Ra'ūf, which of you is the greater traitor, but your crime is the more hideous you the master of reason and history.

After this, he attempts to kill ʿAlīsh Sadra, but unknowingly kills an innocent person. He now returns to the *Ṣūfī* shaykh, whom he finds wide awake at night reciting unintelligible words. Suddenly he hears the shaykh recite a verse expressing a very involved *Ṣūfī* notion relating to the experience of God and truth.[41] It appears that this verse Saʿīd does understand, and the shaykh follows it with another: "Their hearts' eyes opened, then their heads' eyes saw." But quite obviously Saʿīd is not impressed. On hearing this last verse he scoffs:

> This is why he does not notice me.

The shaykh indeed behaves as if he notices nothing. But when morning comes he gets up, spreads the *sajjāda*,[42] takes his place on it and asks: "Won't you pray the morning prayer?" But Saʿīd is too tired, and "disappears from existence."[43] This is the final rejection of the *Ṣūfī* way to salvation by the man alienated from modern Egyptian society. One may even sense in this description a severe condemnation of the insincere attempts to escape into Ṣūfism which the writer seems to observe in his society.

That this hankering after *Ṣūfī* peace of mind has no relevance to what is troubling our hero is increasingly manifest in the scenes where Saʿīd and the shaykh keep talking at cross purposes. In his sleep Saʿīd sees the shaykh asking him for his identity card, as he dreams that he comes to the *Ṣūfī* meeting "to hide from his pursuers." This is contrary to what actually happened in real life, but the dream stresses what in essence Saʿīd felt the shaykh to be demanding of him all along. For the shaykh, who is very much idealized in the novel, does actually pressure Saʿīd to be truthful. Nevertheless, Saʿīd returns to him once again. This happens after he has committed several more misdirected crimes and after the disappearance of Nūr -- light -- the prostitute who loves him and in whose apartment he has hidden after leaving the shaykh for the second time. Again he came to the shaykh. "He found himself thinking of Shaykh 'Ali al-Junaidī's abode as a temporary harbor." He comes in hungry and disturbed. The shaykh notices his disquiet.

> -'When will you achieve peace of heart under the law?'
> Answered Saʿīd with a sigh:
> - 'When the law will be just.'
> - 'It is always just.'

The situation is now very desperate. The police have surrounded the area, looking for Saʿīd. And every minute, the gap between the *Ṣūfī* shaykh and Saʿīd becomes wider. Saʿīd talks of the scoundrels who have betrayed him and the shaykh speaks of God. The shaykh offers Saʿīd bits of *Ṣūfī* wisdom and Saʿīd frankly admits his inability to understand. But no matter what the *Ṣūfī* says Saʿīd is confident in the rightness of his actions. It is this self-confidence which the shaykh finds hard to leave unchallenged:

> -'Said my master: I look at the mirror several times every day lest my face has blackened!' 44

- 'You?!'
- 'Nay, my master himself!'
So he asked with irony:
- 'And how do the scoundrels look at the mirror every hour?!'
The Shaykh bowed his head and recited: 'It is naught but your temptation.[45]

Saʿīd sleeps all day and when he awakes in the following evening, the *Ṣūfī* gathering is already under way. He listens to a recitation of a poem by Ibn al-Fārid (d. 1234), the great Egyptian *Ṣūfī* which, in a sense, sums up not only Saʿīd's own fate, as he feels it, but draws the curtain on the passing episode of the ill-fated juncture of Ṣūfism with the estranged rebel of modern times.

At this moment a melodious voice ascended reciting:[46]
- *'Woe to me that time has passed in vain*
I failed to meet my loved ones.[47]
No hope of solace for him whose life is two days:
One day of hate and one day of withdrawal.'
Sighs spread all over, then another voice was heard reciting:[48]
- *'Enslaved, abundant is my anguish:*
Ahead is my passion and behind me death.'

The poem as a whole is written in an elegiac mood, expressing a desire for the unattainable, and Saʿīd, having in his childhood taken part in many a meeting where these poems were recited, probably appreciates the meaning of what he hears.

Happy childhood memories of the *Ṣūfī* flood his mind, but the effect of the *Ṣūfī* poem is now in exactly the opposite direction; opposite, that is, to the *Ṣūfī* tendency. In a passage of interior monologue Saʿīd abuses *Ṣūfī* ideas, and reaffirms his own:

When solace can be hoped for? Time has passed in vain and I have missed. Now death is behind me. This pistol in my pocket still has a mission. It must overcome treachery and corruption. For the first time the thief will chase the dogs.

He steals out of the house and goes out to fight. He reaches the cemetery which is adjacent to Nūr's apartment. He goes to the northern edge of the cemetery from where he can see Nūr's window. It is lit, and he makes out a woman's head at the window. "He could not see its features, but it reminded him of Nūr." He wants to call her and ask her to look after Sinā', but a dog's barking is heard.

> Finally came the dogs and the thwarting of all hope. So the scoundrels are saved, at least for a while, and life has said its final word, that it is all in vain. It became impossible to define the source of the barking which filled the air in every direction. There is no hope escaping from darkness by running away in the darkness.

And so he dies, killed by the police in the cemetery, under Nūr's lighted window. Just before his death he sees a "gleam of light" but it offers no hope,[49] for it comes from a policeman's flashlight.

Running away in the darkness in order to escape darkness probably summerizes Najīb Maḥfūẓ's appraisal of his rebel's attempt to solve his problem. The alleged escape to Ṣūfism is clear indication of how futile this way appeared to Najīb Maḥfūẓ. This is not to say that he denies the sincerity in *Ṣūfī* escapism.[50] In *al-Summan wa al-kharīf*, for instance we meet a person whose escape to Ṣūfism is both sincere and rewarding. But in order to achieve that he had to give up his former hopes and ambitions. Above all, he had to give up his rebellion.

The Mahfūzian rebel cannot, Sufi-like, give up his urge to try to influence the flow of history. But do we know what it is he wishes to change, or what it is that makes him dissatisfied? Saʿīd in *al-Liṣṣ wa al-kilāb* is fighting the "dogs," and ends up being pursued and defeated by dogs. That dogs should be instrumental in taking revenge on a man who sets himself to thwart the ordained course of history is not so hard to comprehend.[51] But identifying the "dogs" presents greater difficulties. One critic suggests that the novel's name should be read "The Thief and the Traitors," on the basis that both ʿĀlish Sadra, who tipped off the police and married Nabawiyya, and Ra'ūf ʿAlwān, who betrayed the revolutionary ideals, are all referred to as "dogs." But the term is applied also to people in a more extended sense. When in the last scene, at the cemetery, the police officer calls on Saʿīd to surrender and says: "Surrender, and I promise that you will be treated humanely," Saʿīd reflects: "Like the humaneness of Ra'ūf and Nabawiyya and ʿĀlish and the dogs!" He definitely does not mean humanity at large. On the contrary, Saʿīd feels great affinity to the people generally. He notices that as his exploits become famous the people's admiration for him increases. He feels certain that the people support him. So much so that when he approaches for the second time the villa of Ra'ūf ʿAlwān, "the symbol of treachery," he says to himself:

> ...My true tragedy is that in spite of the support of the millions I find myself without a helper.

On another occasion, in the course of a long soliloquy Saʿīd says:

> Whoever shall kill me shall kill the millions...

All this still does not offer a clear definition of who the "dogs" are, but it is probable that the term refers to "officialdom." Fighting all these "dogs" is madness, as Saʿīd himself realizes, if only because there is no hope of winning. But on the other hand, the novel does not ever question the feeling of frustration and there is no glossing over the treachery of the "dogs."

Nūr, the prostitute who shelters Saʿīd and loves him selflessly, wants him to escape and to cease fighting. Like the *Ṣūfī* shaykh she advocates giving up the struggle, and Saʿīd quite consistently rejects her advice just as he has rejected the shaykh's. But the road he chooses is just as futile, and ends in death. Very emphatic is the symbol of the graveyard which gradually becomes the arena of Saʿīd's ideological and physical struggle. We cannot find in the novel any advocacy of the *Ṣūfī* way of life, but there is a loud condemnation of the alternative chosen by Saʿīd, the way of an individual and reckless defiance of society. In this respect, it might be stressed again, there is no difference between the Najīb Maḥfūẓ of pre-1952 days and that of the later period. However, there is a difference in the moral evaluation of the motives for the struggle. Starting with a story of personal treachery the author gains sympathy for his hero with a public that considers treachery the most hideous crime. Soom this sympathy is carried further to encompass the hero's betrayed ideals, and the main object of hatred becomes a specific person whose treachery is emphatically stressed.[52] Almost unawares the reader's outraged feelings are then turned against a much larger object, poorly but unmistakably identified. And when the hero gives up the fight, overcome by death, the reader feels that a truly devoted martyr has died. This feeling of identity had never before been cultivated by the writer to such an extent, not even in the story of Fahmī's death.[53]

But it must be stressed that *al-Liṣṣ wa al-kilāb* is unique among Najīb Maḥfūẓ's laṭer novels in its clarity of exposition and its comprehensiveness. The other novels tend to be less extended in scope and vaguer in exposition. Nevertheless, if we consider them chronologically a fairly clear profile can be traced. *Al-Summān wa al-kharīf* (1962) is the story of a privileged person of the old regime, who is now alienated by the revolutionary regime, and cannot find a way to make his peace with the new society. Unlike the hero of *al-Liṣṣ wa al-kilāb* his dissatisfaction stems from being deprived of his former privileges. His struggle therefore is much more internalized, and naturally he is not troubled by feelings of betrayal. His dilema is whether to forget and "get on the band wagon" or to continue in his rather comfortable sullenness. *Al-Ṭarīq* (1964) is again concerned with the problem of Ṣūfism, as it name would indicate. *Ṭarīq* or *ṭariqa* means road, way or path and is one of the most richly weighed *Ṣūfī* terms, expressing both "moral psychology for the practical guidance of individuals who had a mystic call" and "the whole system of rites for spiritual training" of *Ṣūfī* communities.[54] The "way" is both ascetic and mystic,[55] and *The Way* is a neatly structured "double-layer" story, written with the purpose of denying the viability of the "way" both in its practical and its mystical sense. The *Ṣūfī* way consists of stages — *maqāmāt* — and steps leading to the unity or encounter with God.[56] The hero of the novel, too, proceeds through various stages on his way to meet his mysterious father, significantly named "Lord Lord Merciful."[57] Ṣābir, of *al-Ṭarīq*, resembles in many respects Saʿīd of *al-Liṣṣ wa al-kilāb* and the various stages of his way are similarly defined. Eventually he is sentenced to death for murder, without ever seeing his father.[58]

Al-Shaḥḥadh (The Beggar; 1965) is the development of an idea which is still embryonic in *al-Ṭarīq*,[59] and the hero of which is a spiritual beggar. Having made a fine career as a lawyer, ʿUmar al-Ḥamzāwī, loses interest in his work and in his family and searches for a new meaning in life. Finally he arrives at the conclusion that he must abandon everything and live a secluded life of asceticism and mysticism. At this point the story would have contributed little to the literary world of Najīb Maḥfūẓ and it would be correct to observe that "the basic tune in this story is the same that Najīb Maḥfūẓ has already played and made known to us in the story of *al-Ṭarīq*.[60] But there is an interesting addition in *al-Shaḥḥadh* which makes it probably the most spiritually reassuring of the novels to date. At a certain stage, before ʿUmar completely rejects all his acquired values in the search for new ones, an old friend of his is released from prison. This friend, ʿUthmān Khalīl, was arrested and sentenced under the previous regime for revolutionary activities, and in spite of the revolution of 1952 had to serve his full term. Now, however, the situation is rather embarrassing, for ʿUthmān is still a great believer in the revolution, whereas ʿUmar has replaced the books on Socialism in his library with others on mysticism. ʿUmar tries to offer excuses and says that there is nothing to fight for any more, since the revolution has already taken place and the ideal has been realized. But ʿUthmān maintains that the revolution has not occurred yet and ʿUmar is forced to admit that he is merely lying to himself. ʿUthmān continues to fight, trusting that even if fighting is madness, the world, nevertheles, owes a great deal to this kind of madness. But consequently ʿUthmān is killed by the police, in circumstances similar to those in which Saʿīd Mihrān was killed. But before this happens ʿUthmān, the irreconcilable revolutionary, marries Buthayna the daughter of ʿUmar the mystic, and when he dies she is already pregnant with his child.

This development is significant. For the first time a Socialist revolutionary begets a child in a Mahfuzian novel. But the circumstances are very peculiar. Buthayna is a symbol of cross-cultural breeding, the two cultures being represented by a Muslim father, lately turned *Ṣūfī* and a Christian mother who remains a model of sobriety and good sense. Begetting a child has always been Najīb Maḥfūẓ's symbol of continuity and hope.[61] All this is not in itself surprising or unusual.[62] But that ʿUthmān Khalīl should have a child by Buthayna calls for special attention, for it bespeaks some significant changes of attitude. As mentioned, no Socialist revolutionary in his stories had before been so fortunate as to beget a child. ʿUthmān's only qualification for this privilege may be that he consistently fought for his ideals under two different regimes. The same sort of sympathy shown to Saʿīd in *al-Liṣṣ wa al-kilāb* is shown here to ʿUthmān. Buthayna, too, indicates a change. She has in herself that foreign element which for a long time Najīb Maḥfūẓ could not bring himself to "perpetuate" through fictive descendants. Perhaps the fact that the foreignness in this case is not purely Turkish but Christian makes it easier to accept.[63] Furthermore, she is pregnant by a man who represents an idea which, until now, Najīb Maḥfūẓ never qualified as being fertile. Indeed he must die for being a rebel but not without leaving some hope for the future.

No less hopefully does the story of ʿUmar the mystic end. Although in the closing scene of the novel we hear him utter a *Ṣūfī* verse expressing characteristic disappointments

If you really wanted me why have you abandoned me,

he is already on the road to recovery when he chants the verse. Therefore, he will see his grandchild grow. And thus, without yielding any of his own articles of faith, Najīb Maḥfūẓ just manages to find an opening for a future born of the confluence of all those irreconcilable currents assailing modern Egypt's consciousness.

NOTES

1 S. Somekh, "Zaʿbalāwī -- Author, Theme and Technique," *Journal of Arabic Literature*, V. I, 1970, p. 25.

2 Menahem Milson, "Nagib Mahfuz and the Quest for Meaning," *Arabica*, T. Fasc. 2, 1970, p. 181.

3 *Li al-tafra al-yasāriyya*, could also be translated, out of the immediate context, of course -- as "the leftist leap." This is a typical example of "the fine equilibrium that is maintained between the two layers of the story," which Somekh finds so characteristic of the writer's post-1960 writing, cf. *op. cit.*, p. 31.

4 The inherent absurdity of the situation is indicated by the use of the terms *ghulām* and *murshid*. The first reflects youth and inexperience, the second old age and a great deal of experience and wisdom. *Murshid* is the term used also for spiritual guide, master of a *Ṣūfī* order.

5 The continuation of this street, bearing west, becomes the Muskī, leading into the more modern parts of Cairo in the vicinity of of the Azbakiyya gardens. That this is a dangerous road, symbolizing the way of moral downfall, we have seen before. Along this road Ḥamīda of *Zuqāq al-midāqq* first experienced the temptations of the outer world. Cf. also n. 43, Ch. 5, *supra*.

6 This is one part of a street stretching from Bāb al-Zūwayla in the south to Bāb al-Futūḥ in the north, cutting the Old City down the middle. It changes its name 13 times according to Douglas Sladen's *Guide of Oriental Cairo*. Al-Ghūriyya is the name of that part of the street nearest to the mosque of al-Ghūrī which lies to the south of al-Sikka al-Jadīda. It would not be too far-fetched to assume that the walk westwards of Amīna and her son up to al-Ghūriyya — which derives from the same radical letters forming the nown *ghawr* (bottom or depth, into which one can conceivably fall) — is an essential part of the allegory we are following.

7 Now referred to as the revolt of 1919, which forced the British to release the leaders of the *Wafd* party, and practically to permit them to assume the government of the country.

8. Cf. Tolstoy, *War and Peace*, p. 301-302, where the scene is described of Prince Andrey falling wounded on the battlefield of Austerlitz: "Above him there was now nothing but the sky...'How quiet, peaceful, and solemn; not at all as I ran',thought Prince Andrey — 'not as we ran, shouting and fighting...There is nothing but quiet and peace'."

9 See L. Gardet, *fitna* in *The Encyclopaedia of Islam*, New Edition. Ḥasan al-Baṣri (728), a famous preacher of the Umayyad period in Baṣra, disapproved of any rebellion, maintaining that tyrants were a punishment sent by God, that could not be opposed by the sword but must be endured with patience. He is revered by *Ṣūfīs* for

his ascetic piety. Cf. H. Ritter's article "Ḥasan al-Baṣrī," *ibid.*

10 "Islam is a religious way of life," E. I. J. Rosenthal, *Political Thought in Medieval Islam,* Cambridge, 1962, p. 2.

11 This is certainly true of the six novels published between 1961 and 1967.

12 First published in 1965.

13 The following resumé follows the English summary of the main articles of *ha-Mizrah he-Hadash* (The New East) V. XVI,1966, No. 3-4, pp. vii *seq.* "The Views of Najīb Maḥfūẓ on the Arttibutes of Political Power" — *Demūt ha-shilṭon be-ʿeiney najīb maḥfūẓ* — by the present writer.

14 The devastating effects of such a fight in the neighborhood are described in "*al-Majnuna*" (The Crazy One) in the short story collection *Khumārat al-qiṭṭ al-aswad* (1968).

15 First published in *al-Hilāl,* February 1970.

16 *Al-Maktūb maktūb* the expression used in "*al-Khawf,*" meaning that fate is inexorable.

17 Von Grunebaum, *Medieval Islam,* p. 153.

18 See al-Māwardī, *al-Aḥkam al-sulṭāniyya,* al-Maktaba al-Maḥmūdiyya al-Tijāriyya, Cairo, n.d., p. 30.

19 Cf. Gibb, *Studies on the Civilization of Islam*, p. 165. Al-Ashʿarī's statement: "We maintain the error of those who hold it right to rise against the Imams whensoever there may be apparent in them a falling away from right. We are opposed to armed rebellion against them and civil war."

20 Quoted by E. I.J. Rosenthal, *op. cit.,* p. 97

21 Cf. *Shorter Encylopaedia of Islam, "Taqiyya."*

22 "Every forcible deposition may have been accompanied by a *fatwa* [a legal opinion given by a Mufti who is a canon lawyer of standing] authorizing it on various moral or religious grounds."

Gibb, *Studies on the Civilization of Islam*, p. 161. But this was pure formality. The practical justification for obeying a ruler who seized power was that "necessity dispenses with stipulations which are impossible to fulfil." *Ibid.*, p. 164. Cf. also Louis Gardet, *La cité musulmane*, Paris 1954, p. 98 where he remarks that this law of necessity opened the way to mechiavellianism of the worst kind. The usual theoretical justification of the act of usurpation is that it was dictated by the precepts of Islam.

23 E.g. *Qur'ān*, 3, 103; 31, 17.

24 Cf. Levy, *The Social Structure of Islam*, pp. 334 *seq.*

25 This is recognized in Islamic political theory as *imārat al-istīlā'*, Amirate by Seizure. cf. Gibb, *ibid.*, pp. 162 *seq.*

26 *"Qirā'a jadīda, al-muqaddima,"* pp. 64 *seq.*

27 This characteristic of literature has been elaborated at length earlier in the article. "Socialism" and "revolution" in this context are synonyms of "state" and "society".

28 Ṣāliḥ's attempt to broaden the scope of critical literature seems to go far beyond the limits defined subsequently by Ḍiyā' al-Dīn Dā'ūd, at that time secretary of the Permanent Committee of Education, Thinking and Guidelines, of the Central Committee of the Socialist Union of Egypt. Cf. *al-Hilāl*, October 1970, pp. 6-11.

29 See Fū'ād Dawwāra, *"al-Liṣṣ wa al-kilāb, ʿamal thawrī,"* (The Thief and the Gods, A Revolutionary Work), *al-Kātib*, No. 22, January 1963, pp. 80-95.

30 The episode of Aḥmad Amīn Sulaymān, the criminal who was killed by the police, is detailed in *Akhbār al-Yawm*, beginning on March 12, up to April 1, 1960, the day he was killed.

31 Later incorporated in the collection *Dunyā Allāh* (1963). For an analysis of this story, see Somekh, *ibid.*

32 Milson, *ibid.*, p. 179.

33 Milson, *ibid.*

34 Some outstanding examples can be mentioned. The story *al-Sharīda*, where a scene of a wife finding her husband at night with a strange woman in the house, both very drunk, is later utilized in *Qaṣr al-shawq*. The story *Ḥayāt li al-ghayr*, is a preliminary study of a situation developed in *Khān al-khalīlī*. Both stories are printed in the collection *Hams al-junūn*.

35 See M. Berger, *op. cit.*, pp. 62 *seq.*

36 *The Quail and Autumn* (1962). The pertinent passages are given in Milson's article, *ibid.*

37 Cf. n. 30 *supra*.

38 The following is told of Rabīʿa al-ʿAdawiyya, a *Ṣūfī* woman (d.801); "It was asked of Rabiʿa al-ʿAdawiyya: when is a man to be considered pleased?" She said: When a mishap gladdens him just as comfort does." Cf. *al-Risāla al-qushayriyya*, ed. ʿAbd al-Ḥalīm Muḥammad and Maḥmūd b. Sharīf, Cairo 1966, p. 424.

39 Traditionally "fire" means hell. Here it could mean the firing squad.

40 The unprincipled newspaper editor, who uses the revolution for his personal advancement, is also the theme of the larger novel by Fatḥī Ghānim, *al-Rajul alladhī faqada zillahu*, four volumes, Cairo, August-September 1969, tr. by Desmond Stewart, *The Man who Lost His Shadow*, London, 1966. This novel was first published serially in 1961, and came out only eight years later in book form. For a comparison of the two novels, see Yūsuf al-Sharūnī, *Dirasāt*, pp. 161-175.

41 The verse recited by the Shaykh is the first of the following couplet of Abū Bakr al-Shiblī:

al-wajdu ʿindī juhūd | *ma lam yakun ʿan shuhūdī*
wa shāhidu al-ḥaqqi ʿindī | *yunfī shuhūda al-wujūdi*

The couplet has been rendered into French by Anawati and Gardet as follows:

Je renie mon extase
tant qu'elle ne vient pas de mon témoignage;
Et le Temoin de la Vérité
aneantit le temoignage de l'extase!

See *Mystique Musulmane*, Paris, 1961, p. 180. Cf. *ibid.*, for the meaning of the terms *wajd* and *shuhūd* as used in *Ṣūfī* poetry. For the Arabic version, cf. *Diwān abī bakr al-shiblī*, ed. Muṣṭafā al-Shaybī, Baghdad, 1967, p. 100, couplet No. 24.

42 A prayer rug.

43 *Ghābā ʿan al-wujūd*. The word *wujūd* concludes the second verse in the couplet of al-Shiblī, which the shaykh did not recite. But the use of this word by Najīb Maḥfūẓ in this context to describe Saʿīd's falling asleep is too intentional not to be noticed. Therefore it seems legitimate to read this description of Saʿīd falling asleep as his finite answer to the challenge implied in the second, unrecited, verse (cf. n. 41). Naturally the word '*wujud*' in the story means primarily existence, but this playing with words should by now be familiar to readers of Najīb Maḥfūẓ. *Wujud* in the *Ṣūfī* sense is the presence of God (cf. Anawati and Gardet, *ibid.*). So Saʿīd, by falling asleep while the shaykh invites him to pray is, in *Ṣūfī* terminology, turning away from God. And indeed, this is what Saʿīd was doing.

44 Cf. *al-Risāla al-qushayriyya, op. cit.*, p. 66: *wa yuḥkā ʿan /al-qasṭī/ al-sirrī annahu qāla: anā anẓuru fī anfī al-yawma kadhā wa kadhā marra, makhāfata an yaswadda ṣūratī limā ataʿāṭāhu.*

45 *Qur'ān*, 8, 28: "And know that your wealth and your children are a temptation, and that Allah is He with whom there is a mighty reward."

46 The following verses are from a *qasīda* by Ibn al-Fāriḍ. Cf. *Diwān ibn al-fāriḍ*, ed. al-Bustānī, Beirut, 1962, pp. 110, 122.

47 *Uhyalu mawaddati* interpreted as *al-qarībin min maḥabbatī* by al-Burīnī, Marseilles, 1853, p. 288.

48 This is the concluding verse of the *qaṣīda*.

49 *Wa jafalat sinā' bila amal.* Sinā' it is remembered, was the name of Sa'īd's daughter; and the meaning of *sinā'* is a gleam of light.

50 That Ṣūfism is an escape is the verdict of Kamāl at the end of *al-Sukkarīyya*.

51 The story is told of Euripides' death by being torn to pieces by the King's hounds. These hounds were the offspring of a Molossian hound whose death at the hands of some Thracian villagers went unavenged through the playwright's intercession with the King. See G. Murray, *Euripides and his Age,* Home University Library, p. 169 *seq.* The notion that a breach of accepted rules cannot go unavenged seems to underlie both stories. Making the dog the bearer of society's wrath is generally an indication of the heinous nature of the offense thus punished. See the biblical curse in I Kings, 14,11; 16, 4; 21, 24. By the same token, the inquiry to which a victim is subjected is often expressed by calling the executioner dog. So Psalms 22, 15: "For dogs have compassed me," which may be suggested as the motto for *al-Liṣṣ wa al-kilāb*.

52 The way the hatred for Ra'ūf 'Alwān is built up deserves close scrutiny. Beginning with his journalistic publications which demonstrate vividly an intellectual degradation, we are then shown his large and inhospitable office. His villa on the banks of the Nile is identified as one which previously — before the revolution — had belonged to a rich Pasha. The first meeting between Sa'īd and Ra'ūf in the villa is designed to provoke the abhorrence of the reader at the sight of a past fighter for liberty so quickly immersed in the pleasures of a rewarding revolution. Nothing of his laudable past seems to have left a trace on his new personality.

53 Cf. Rajā' al-Naqqāsh, *op. cit.*, pp. 203 *seq* for an almost lyrical description of the sympathy felt by the reader toward Najīb Maḥfūẓ's criminal heroes, including that of *al-Liṣṣ wa al-kilāb*.

54 See *Tariqa*, *Shorter Encyclopedia of Islam*.

55 Anwati and Gardet, *op. cit.*, p. 42.

56 *Ibid.*, pp. 42 *seq*. Cf. also Annemarie Schimmel, *Mystical Dimensions of Islam*, Chapel Hill, 1975, pp. 98-100.

57 Sayyid Sayyid al-Rahīmī. The translation of the name is suggested by Milson, *ibid*.

58 Again, the *Ṣūfī* exasperating experience: "I failed to meet my loved ones," cf. *Supra* n. 46.

59 Rajā' al-Naqqāsh, *op. cit.*, p. 218, believes that *The Beggar* magnifies the beggars of many of Najīb Mahfūz's works, but he does not specify.

60 Rajā' al-Naqqāsh, *op. cit.*, p. 220. Rajā' al-Naqqāsh admits that the later story is not a mere repetition of the earlier, but he fails to specify what else *al-Shaḥḥādh* offers.

61 The giving of birth to a child is the subject of several stories by him. *"al-Samt"* in *Bayt sayyi' al-sumʿa* (1965), and *Walīd al-ʿanā'* (The Child of Agony), *al-Ahrām*, 8 May 1970. (Reprinted in *Shahr al-ʿasal;* 1971).

62 On the various aspects of the child archetype see C. G. Jung, "The Special Phenomenology of the Child Archetype," *Bollingen Series*, xxii, 1949. This archetype in the works of Najīb Maḥfūẓ is employed in a rather limited but consistent role of symbolizing continuity.

63 Riyād Qaldas of *al-Sukkarīyya* is a Copt, and something of his character Kamāl wishes to find in his future wife. Perhaps Buthayna combines in herself the diverse qualifications to bear Egypt's child of the future. Her mother, whom she resembles very

much, was originally a Christian. Therefore, Buthayna's green eyes may indicate a slackening of the writer's resentment against Turkishness.

Chapter Eight

On the Waterfront

Najīb Mahfūz's scale of values can be depicted geographically as extending from the desert in the east to the water in the west. The movement from east to west, from desert to water, is morally a decline. The desert is not saintly to be sure, but it is the place where saints have been seen. On the edge of the desert the City has been built, and the Neighborhood had thrived. In the desert men get their inspiration, and from the desert came men in the past with heavenly missions. In the desert,too, people are buried so that desert and cemetery seem to symbolize, as it were, two sides of the same coin. It is a topographical fact that north and east of Bāb al-Naṣr stretches the great cemetery of "Neighborhood," but one cannot fail to notice how Najīb Maḥfūẓ loads this geographical coincidence with deep symbolic meaning. [1] "The crossroads of success and failure" he once called the cemetery of Bāb al-Naṣr.

Inside the City, by the desert, life flows ceaselessly. It is not idealized in any way, yet its proximity to the desert lends it a certain quality which precludes downright perversion and depravity. There is a subtle but well-marked distinction in the stories of Najīb Mahfūz between the depravity and corruption which disintegrate the moral fabric of society and the common immorality or repression which does not. The former is to be found next to water, the latter is on the edge of the desert.

The special ennobling and protective quality of the desert, has been acknowledged by the ancient Near East world-view since Biblical days, and is equally admitted in Islamic thinking.[2] The association of west (and occasionally north) with water is a natural consequence of the geographical disposition of the heartland of the Islamic world. It is therefore, an altogether indigenous Egyptian outlook which reflects that suspicion of foreignness by placing irreparable depravity near the water in the west.

We have seen Ḥamīda going west to be lost for ever in the city of depravity. No less impressive is the change in the locus of Aḥmad ʻAbd al-Jawād's nightly exploits; after the death of his son Fahmī the place of his nocturnal meetings is a floating house — *ʻawwāma* — on the Nile. And only there do these nocturnal activities begin to look degrading. His final humiliation as a man and as a representative of a value system takes place in his own *ʻawwama* which he has bought to secure for himself the charms of Zanūba.

In later works the geographical west and the proximity of water merge to form a symbol of corruption and depravity, the antithesis of which is the Old City on the edge of the desert. In *al-Liṣṣ wa al-kilāb* the movements of Saʻīd between Nūr's apartment or the shaykh's abode, both of which are located on the desert edge, and Ra'ūf's villa on the bank of the Nile, become the symbolic voyages between the loci of good and evil. In *al-Ṭarīq* the contradiction between good and evil is depicted by Cairo and Alexandria. Ṣābir goes to Cairo to escape the degradation inevitably awaiting him if he remains in Alexandria. In *al-Shaḥḥādh*, too, the realization of his frustration with life comes to ʻUmar on the sea coast of Alexandria, far from Cairo. And it is in the desert, near Cairo, that he experiences his moment of exaltation. This moral polarization thus symbolized geographically, reaches extreme dimensions in the short story, *al-Khalā'* (The Emptiness). Sharrshāra [4] is a gangster who returns from Alexandria to his old neighborhood in Cairo to settle old scores. Some 20 years earlier the local gangster forced him to divorce Zaynab, his newly-wed wife, on the night of their marriage. Humiliated and disgraced Sharrashāra then migrated to Alexandria, where he nurtured his passion for revenge. Now he is coming back to force his enemy to divorce Zaynab, and thereby compensate himself for his long agony. But Sharrshāra soon finds out that Zaynab is a widow and a mother of several grown up children. What is more, she is completely indifferent to his passions and memories. Ashamed and bewildered he turns away "toward the empty desert."

Sharrshāra is a typical Mahfuzian character; he is haunted by his past, and devotes his whole life to erasing the shame of it. But what is new in *al-Khalā'* is the definite association of the useless waste of a lifetime in senseless dreams of revenge with Alexandria, and of a normal, meaningful life with old Cairo. Thus we read of "a thirst for revenge of 20 years of banishment, far from wakeful Cairo, in the obscurity of the port of Alexandria." This identity of the indigenous evil of vengefulness with the symbols of foreign evil namely water in the west, is the emphasis added in this story.Here we also see the line of redemption: from water to desert [5] which, in given geographical circumstances, means the movement from west to east.

Najīb Maḥfūẓ does not write much about water. His occasional mention of water, almost invariably hints at hostility or danger. In the short *Thalāthat ayyām fī al-yaman*[6] (Three days in Yemen) the travel by sea from Egypt to Yemen is hardly described, except for a passing remark referring to it as

> a long voyage in which the heat exhausted us...over the surface of angry sea, under a pallid sky extending silently into the horizons, among packs of dolphins.

This reads like a description of a mortuary voyage which, it may be observed, fits very well with the whole tenor of the story.

Water is always associated with a dark experience. When the Nile is looked at, it is with the idea of committing suicide[7] and when it is used for boating the purpose is to commit a crime or to conceal a crime.[8] The idea of death is always present when water, mostly the Nile, is mentioned; and any activity that takes place on the Nile, usually occurs at night. Bachelard's observations seems to be largely applicable to Najīb Maḥfūẓ when he says:

> Chez plusiers poètes apparait aussi une mer imaginaire qui a pris ainsi la nuit dans son sein. C'est la Mer des Tenèbres — Mare Tenebrum, où les anciens navigateurs ont localise leur effroi plutôt que leur experience.

We know too little of Najīb Maḥfūẓ's personal biography to speculate on the reasons [10] for this combination of water and gloom in his stories. But if we note that "l'eau est épiphanie du malheur du temps" [11] and that "l'eau dans la nuit donne une peur penétrante,"[12] then the imagery that emerge would be as follows: Water represents misfortune, and travelling on water is therefore ominous. Water is found on the west side of the conceptual world, therefore going down into the water is doubly unfortunate since it is both perilous and immoral. Activities of Egyptians on the water are therefore seen as taking place at night, that is to say in an atmosphere of fear.[13]

The foregoing may well serve as a general background for the discussion of two very controversial novels by Najīb Maḥfūẓ: *Thar-thara fawq al-nīl* (Prattling over the Nile) and *Mīrāmār*. [14] The first is a story of a small group of Egyptians who meet regularly at night in an *ʿawwāma* — a houseboat — on the Nile, and the second is the story of a group of people who happen to stay at a pension in Alexandria during the winter.

Tharthara fawq al-nīl is written in an ironic mode, the heroes are "inferior in power or in intelligence to ourselves, so that we have the sense of looking down on a scene of bondage, frustration or absurdity." [15] But quite surprisingly, *Mīrāmār*, written so soon afterward, is a romance where "stylized figures expand into psychological archetypes," radiating a glow of subjective intensity.[16] *Tharthara* is iconclastic whereas *Mīrāmār* is a novel of worship. The difference is reflected in their forms: *Tharthara* is an author's story, told largely from the point of view of a narcotic outcast. *Mīrāmār* consists of the stories of four different persons as told by themselves, each one representing a particular experience. In spite of the difference, the basic story of both novels is the same and they should be put in a category of their own.

One of the stories takes place in an *ʿawwāma*, a symbolic ark floating on the water, the other in an inn, a symbolic cavern or grotto. In certain traditions cavern and ark are interchangeable [17] and we can therefore view both as representing a little world.[18] The geographical difference of location has little significance, considering that Alexandria, because of its proximity to the sea, evokes the same psychological reaction as the Nile. However, the difference between ark and grotto is significant. It suits fiction written in the ironic mode to depict the world as an ark tied to the shore by a string which can conceivably be cut off at any moment. Likewise, it is fitting for a story of worship to depict the world as a much more stable construction, erected on solid ground. Also, it may be assumed that the ready association of ark and the mythological mortuary voyage of ancient Egypt made the *ʿawwāma* more suitable for *Tharthara;* whereas the inn, closely associated with the grotto or cave, which is an essentially reverential symbol,[19] is more suitable for *Mīrāmār*.

The plots of both novels have a great deal in common. Samāra Bahjāt in *Tharthara* and Zahra Salāma in *Mīrāmār*, are both young, pretty and sincere. But Samāra is an intellectual, a reporter with literary ambitions who believes literally in the progressive ideals which have become so fashionable since the revolution of 1952. Zahra, on the other hand, is an illiterate peasant girl who fled her village to join the inn in order to escape the dead hand of the old, reactionary values which still dominate the countryside. Samāra joins the *ʿawwāna* for no such weighty reasons. She hears of those nightly gatherings of an interesting group of men and women, their *ḥashīsh* smoking and their flippant talk which is perhaps reactionary, but certainly non-conformist, and she asks to be invited.

Zahra with her seriousness of purpose, falls in love with Sirḥān al-Buḥayrī,[20] an active member of the Socialist Union and a fairly high-ranking official of a spinning company. Samāra falls in love with the good-looking cinema actor Rajab al-Qāḍī. Naturally Zahrā's disappointment is very deep at finding that Sirḥān has only wanted to use her, and has actually arranged to marry a middle class girl of a respectable family. Samāra's disappointment is different in nature. She never expected much from the group of the *ʿawwāna*, or from the good-looking actor. But she soon learns that personal attachment leads to social commitment. One night they all participate in the killing of an anonymous pedestrian, while riding in a car driven recklessly by Rajab. She compromises her principles and joins the others in shirking their moral obligations, preferring to escape rather than face the law.

The difference between Samāra and Zahra is fundamental. Zahra is unspoiled, and remains so throughout her ordeal. She never compromises The lesson seems to be fairly simple and straightforward: if, being ready to compromise you join the *ʿawwama* group you will soon become one of them. But if you join the inn out of necessity yet remain loyal to your principles, you may be hurt but you will not be degraded.

In both novels the events are being watched very closely by an inactive observer who sympathizes with the heroine of the story. In *Tharthara* the observer is Anīs Zakī,[21] a minor government official who runs the *ʿawwāma* as the meeting place for the group. Usually he is intoxicated by the narcotics he smokes and drinks and watches the events with a hazy and confused mind. Being well read in the history of Egypt his uncontrolled imagination sometimes confuses events and eras which place life in the *ʿawwama* in strange historical perspectives.

In *Mīrāmār* the observer is ʿĀmir Wajdī,[22] a very old man, extremely religious in spite of his colorful experience in younger days as a reporter of note. Whenever he can he reads the *Qur'ān*, and the passages he reads serve as a commentary on the events taking place in the inn.

The schemes of the two novels run fairly parallel and they both end by the devoted observer talking to the frustrated girl. Anīs talks to Samāra of man's endless road which he has trodden ever since he came down from the trees, holding a stick in one hand and a stone in the other — a vision of sinister monotony and pessimism. ʿĀmir, talking to Zahra, encourages her, telling her that she has learnt a great deal from her sad experience, "since he that knows who is unfit for him has learned in some mysterious way who is the one to be sought after." Then he turns to his *Qur'ān* and recites the Chapter of the Merciful, enumerating the great benefits God has bestowed on his creatures.[23] Thus, very much unlike *Tharthāra, Mīrāmār* ends on an encouraging note with a religious optimism which does not specifically promise happiness and success in this world but which at any rate stems from an unquestioning faith in God.

With the themes of the two novels thus outlined, it is possible to discuss their bearing on the realities reflected in these works. Sirḥān al-Buhayrī not only proves disloyal to the ideals he purports to serve, as is symbolized by his opportunistic approach to marriage, but he also turns out to be utterly corrupt in his work. Eventually, he is exposed and commits suicide to escape punishment. The other people at the inn are for one reason or another hostile to the revolutionary regime in Egypt. All except ʿĀmir Wajdī, that is, whose attitude is noncommital. They all however love Zahra, either for what she is -- a pretty young woman — or for what she symbolizes, Egypt's innocent search for redemption. She has recently been admitted to the inn as a servant, and her future depends on Sirhān. His duplicity is, therefore, doubly deplorable: he cheats Zahra as a woman and he betrays her as a symbol of the people on whose behalf the regime claims to be striving. Being the sole person in the novel who works in the service of the regime and who speaks for it, his dismal betrayal of all that the regime stands for acquires a symbolic significance far beyond that of mere criticism regarding the application of principles.[24] It is true that Sirḥān's suicide is an escape from justice which he knew would be meted out to him had he remained alive. Thus, indirectly the regime's presence and insistence on properly carrying out its task is admitted. However, the official judicial process could not possibly deal with Sirḥān's moral defection in his treatment of Zahra. He could be punished only for his corrupt actions as an official of a government firm. In fact the writer emphasizes that in committing suicide Sirḥān did not die because of a betrayal of ideals but only because of the damage to the firm. This is brought out by Manṣūr Bāhī, the sentimental and frustrated Communist, who attempts to murder Sirḥān for humiliating Zahra. But later a medical examination establishes that suicide was the cause of Sirḥān's death. Thus, Sirḥān's moral crimes are left unavenged, probably because Manṣūr was not fit for the task. Previously he had betrayed his closest friend who was kept in detention by the police. Therefore the hateful crime of *khiyāna* — treachery — which appears to be as rampant in Egypt as it has always been, still goes unavenged.[25] The worst aspect of it is the betrayal of ideals, a crime committed by Manṣūr as well as Sirḥān. The situation is basically the same as it was in *al-Liṣṣ wa al-kilāb*, only now there is no one to fight *khiyāna* as Saʿīd did.

A similar situation is to be found in *Tharthara*. The moral issue is again loyalty to principles. And just as in *Mīrāmār*, we find here, too that disregard for principles goes unpunished.

That nobody will fight society in these circumstances is a remarkable development in Najīb Maḥfūẓ's works. This change is so conspicuous that we would probably be justified in speaking of a new phase in his literary development. A work of Najīb Maḥfūẓ without a fighter, without a rebel, for whatever cause or purpose, is not to be found before *Tharthara*. But it must be pointed out that although we have no rebel, we still have all the rebel's arguments, all the criticisms levelled by the rebels of previous works against society. These criticisms are no less forceful and no less eloquent. The only visible change is that now they are not direct accusations issuing from the mouth of a rebel in a fit of madness, but are descriptions of unacceptable situations from the pen of Najīb Maḥfūẓ himself. The writer has himself become the rebel, he is the fighter now.

The change, though of the utmost significance, is very subtle. Criticism is not expressed in authorial comments nor by one of the characters. Nor is there any remarkable change in the typological array of the works. Sirḥān al-Buḥayrī is, at first sight, a fairly common Mahfuzian character. He is selfish, ambitious, contemptuous of inherited moral values, and consequently he dies. But it would be a mistake to consider him a replica of Ḥasanayn of *Bidāya was nihāya* for example. Ḥasanayn's predicament was that in coming from a socially low stratum he has tried very hard, by his own exertions, to break into a higher stratum. He has done this selfishly, and immorally; and eventually, realizing how morally untenable his situation has become, he comits suicide. Sirḥān on the other hand has risen in status on the wave of a social revolution, and from a peasant boy has become an important member of the new society. But then he abuses his newly gained privileges. He tries to attach himself to that very society against which the revolution was purported to have broken out. He goes one step beyond Ra'ūf ʿAlwān of *al-Liṣṣ wa al-kilāb*. He is not satisfied with the privileges that have accrued to him by virtue of being a supporter of the revolution. He actually wants to become one of the privileged of the old society. As one follows his story *khiyāna* — treachery — which so incensed Saʿīd, becomes that much more abominable.

Compared to Sirḥān, the other character in *Mīrāmār*, Ṭalba Marzūq, the blue-eyed aristocrat of a previous age, who now yearns for some moderately liberal regime in Egypt, looks like a reformed criminal. His hypocrisy is all too obvious. He talks of liberal moderation in politics thinking all the time of Kuwait, which is hardly the model of a moderately liberal political regime. But is there, morally speaking, any difference between him, the symbol of the defeated regime, and Sirḥān, the product of the new regime? Marzūq's hopes for the return of the past are depicted in one of the most forceful scenes of the novel in which he and the old Greek lady are hopelessly trying to make love to each other after a Christmas Eve party. It is a futile and a humiliating attempt. Sirḥān's behavior, on the other hand, is unpardonable because it deprives the people of their hopes. His suicide, therefore does not have the cleansing effect of Ḥasanayn's suicide. Ḥasanayn took his life when he admitted his moral defeat. No one was pursuing him, and he was not fleeing from any one. Sirḥān's suicide is nothing more than a flight from justice, a means of escaping well-deserved punishment.

The situation thus created by the writer speaks louder than all of Saʿīd's wild raving. In this way the writer emerges from behind his characters and launches the most penetrating criticism against *khiyāna*, against the betrayal of the people's hopes.

This change is not as abrupt as it may seem. Already in *al-Summān wa al-khārif*, published in 1962, only one year after *al-Liṣṣ wa al-kilāb*, we meet the man who benefits from the revolution in too materialistic a manner while caring little for its deeper meaning.

Ḥasan, who was a small clerk before the revolution, has become the director of a company, and marries Salwā, the girl who was previously engaged to marry ʿĪsā, his cousin. Salwā is an upper class girl, the daughter of a supreme court judge, who represents all the social and moral values of a society the revolution was supposed to reject. Realizing that circumstances have changed, the judge rescinds the engagement of his daughter to ʿĪsā, and gives her in marriage to Ḥasan, the promising rising young man.

As for Ḥasan, the creature of the revolution, he does what the less fortunate Sirḥān of *Mīrāmār* later unsuccessfully attempts. He gladly marries into a respectable family of property thus symbolizing the ready acceptance by workers of the revolution of the moral values of the old regime. Looked at from this point of view the so-called revolutionary change seems to have rather limited significance. Ḥasan, furthermore, in the best tradition, remains loyal to his family and works out a plan whereby ʿĪsā is to marry his sister and join his firm with a fairly high rank. ʿĪsā's mother, the old woman with the old-world mentality, is overjoyed with Ḥasan's plan, and she cannot, for the life of her, understand why ʿĪsā rejects it. After all, this is the traditional way of adapting oneself to the vicissitudes of life. But to ʿĪsā it seems false, too stale to be attractive. He prefers to marry a woman of means, attractive but barren, and resigns himself to an arid life of sullen aloofness.

ʿĪsā's life and that of Sirḥān of *Mīrāmār*, have a great deal more in common than either would care to admit. Soon after the revolution ʿĪsā is adjudged by a revolutionary tribunal unfit to continue in government service. He then goes to Alexandria and lives for a time in seclusion in the Greek quarter of the town, "a stranger among strangers." There, in the seaside city, he finds a street girl whom he makes his mistress. She is a poor girl who, together with a lover, fled her home town of Ṭanṭa, where the prevailing conservatism make life impossible for her, and came to Alexandria.[26] Thus we find ʿĪsā and Rīrī in the Greek quarter of Alexandria preceding by five years Sirḥān and Zahra at an inn in Alexandria owned by a Greek lady.

Rīrī is not as idealistic as Zahra, and has given herself to ʿĪsā hoping to gain no more than temporary shelter, It is a vain hope, for as soon as ʿĪsā discovers that she is pregnant he repudiates her and returns to Cairo. But we must remember that pregancy is a good omen in Najīb Maḥfuẓ's world of symbols. When ʿĪsā returns to Alexandria a few years later trying to escape his barren post-revolutionary life, he meets Rīrī and her daughter. She appears to be comfortable and satisfied. He tries to establish his fatherhood, which means that he now realizes his past mistakes. He notices that she is well-dressed and that she has a little shop of her own, and as he later finds out she is married to an old man, who has adopted the girl and has given both mother and daughter the securi they need. At the moment this good old man is in prison under a long term sentence for dealing in drugs, but he is nevertheless well respected by th people who knew him. Rīrī is loyal to him and contemptuously rejects the suggestion to divorce her imprisoned husband and return to ʿĪsā.

Who is this good old man who has proved to be Rīrī's savior? We are faced now with a new archetype of Najīb Maḥfūẓ's creation. In *Mīrāmār*, too, it was the good old man, ʿĀmir Wajdī, who backed Zahra and gave her moral support. The good old man figures also in *Tharthara*. There he is ʿAmm ʿAbduh, an ageless peasant, strong, tall, healthy and, like ʿĀmir, deeply religious. Although a servant he has a feeling of ownership towards the *ʿawwama*, for he knows that if he does not look after it and make sure that it is well kept and well tied to its pier, it will sink. He observes the activities on the *ʿawwama* but he is unaffected by them. He procures girls for Anīs Zākī, he buys the drugs for the group gathering and prepares the *ḥashīsh* smoked by the guests, but he never misses a prayer. Near the *ʿawwama*, on the shore to the east, he has built a place of prayer for himself and at times, when the insolent prattle of the guests subsides, the sound of his prayers can be heard. Like ʿĀmir Wajdī, he is deeply religious, and like Rīrī's husband he is dealing in drugs.

The three old men are one, in fact, symbolizing Egypt, the old, reliable, admirable land that is deeply religious, deeply moral, and good natured, even if not particularly discriminating when it comes to making a living. But this is the only reliable factor on which Egypt's hope, symbolized by a pretty, sincere but often quite lost girl, can depend. Although they all represent the same idea, there is a marked difference in the characterization of these old men. Rīrī's husband is a rather abstract idea. We never meet him, we are merely told about him. ʿAmm ʿAbduh is a living character, who in spite of his healthy attitude and his religiosity, can hardly affect the course of events.

ʿĀmir Wajdī is also very much alive as a character. Indeed he practically dominates the scene. Among the agitated, restless, unyielding medley of people he is the only collected, confident and optimistic person. He derives his composure from a long experience of life and from the *Qur'ān* the two most cherished properties of the Egyptian people. It is, therefore, with a note of great optimism that he sends Zahra off on her next voyage in life and returns to recite the praises of the Lord.

The apparently small point of Rīrī's remaining faithful to her imprisoned husband, should not be lost sight of. In this connection we remember, of course, the issue of the wife's *khiyāna* -- treachery -- which is so conspicuous in *al-Liṣṣ wa al-kilāb* and which so engages the thoughts of Mansūr Bāhī in *Mīrāmār*. But it is ʿĀmir Wajdi who understands what loyalty means, as do Rīrī and her imprisoned husband and ʿAmm ʿAbduh. Here, too, there is an interesting progression. ʿAmm

ʿAbduh's loyalty is practically wasted on the *ʿawwāma* people; it exists for its own sake. The loyalty of Rīrī's husband is rewarding; it enables Rīrī to recover, and to repay loyalty with loyalty. But the old man himself is away, in prison. ʿĀmir Wajdī's loyalty is already a factor of great importance, it is rewarded by Zahra's great love for him and it seems that eventually both the young woman and the old man will see their hopes fulfilled.[27] She walks away reassured and he turns to his *Qur'ān.* Of the three novels, this one ends the most happily with the victory of the two great values: age and religion. A victory which consists in supporting successfully a young, innocent hope.

There is no need to look for a logical sequence of development in the five novels, from *al-Liṣṣ wa al-kilāb* to *Mīrāmār*. But there can be no doubt that the conceptual world created by them is a world alternating between two poles: loyalty and treachery. Loyalty is symbolized by the good natured old men, deeply religious, with a rich and varied experience of life; in short, loyalty is symbolized by Egypt. Treachery is symbolized by insincere opportunists, unprincipled young men and women who get lost in the tangle of their own confused catch-phrases. The pole of loyalty is located in the east, close to the desert. The pole of treachery is located in the west, by the water.

It would probably be wrong to read this imagery of Najīb Maḥfūẓ as an indication of a tendency toward cultural isolationism. Nevertheless, he does display a marked distrust for slogans or catch-phrases used to cover up the same impulses which for generations on generation have denied Egypt its due in the world. And when it comes to this denial of Egypt's hopes it makes little difference whether it stems from impulses found in blue-eyed foreign conquerors or in brown-eyed local impostors.

NOTES

1 Bāb al-Naṣr means the gate of victory, commemorating Saladin's victory over the Crusaders.

2 It will be recalled that for Ibn Khaldūn the desert is the source of all the primordial qualities needed for the creation of the truly religious state. See *al-Muqaddima,* V. 1, Ch. 2. "Bedouins are closer to being good than sedentary people," *ibid.,* p. 255. This concept is very common in biblical stories.

3 Printed in *Khummārat al-qiṭṭ al-aswad* (1968).

4 A peculiar name, which sounds more like a popular nick-name than a regular proper name. It consists of two distinct elements: *sharr* meaning evil or mischief, and *shāra*, meaning sign or token. Therefore, Sharrshāra can be understood to mean "a mark of evil."

5 See M. L. von Franz. "The Process of Individuation," in *Man and his Symbols,* p. 235, where the Iranian fairy tale "The Secret of the Bath Badgerd" is reproduced. The delivery from the rising water takes the form of being miracuously placed in the desert.

6 Reprinted in the collection *Taḥt al-miẓalla* (1967).

7 Thus in *al-Sarāb* and *Bidāya wa nihāya.* Cf. also *al-Juʿ* (Hunger) in *Hams al-junūn.*

8 E.g. *al-Liṣṣ wa al-kilāb,* and *al-Tarīq.*

9 Gaston Bachelar, *L'Eau et les Rèves*, Paris, 1942, p. 138.

10 Bachelard says: L'eau mèlée de nuit est un remords ancien qui ne veut pas dormir..." *ibid.,* p. 139.

11 G. Durand, *Les Structures Anthropologiques de l'Imaginaire,* University of Grenoble Publication, n.d., p. 21.

12 Bachelard, *ibid.*

13 E.g., the nocturnal sail on the Nile in *al-Qāhira al-jadīda.*

14 Published respectively in 1966 and 1967.

15 Cf. Frye, *Anatomy of Criticism*, pp. 33-34.

16 *Ibid.*, p. 304.

17 Durand, *op. cit.*, p. 266.

18 That the inn of *Mīrāmār* should be taken as symbolizing the world is suggested by Fāṭima Mūsā, "*Mīrāmār, rubāʿiyyat al-iskandariyya,*" *al-Katīb*, No. 73, April 1967.

19 Neumann, *The Great Mother*, pp. 44 *seq.* The image of belly or womb is reflected also in the ark, which again shows that basically both *ʿawwāma* and inn symbolize similar concepts. But the differences enumerated are, nevertheless, significant.

20 The second name, al-Buḥayrī, is perhaps not without significance, It means that the person has come from the province of al-Buḥayra, which is the western province of Egypt lying between the Nile delta and the sea. As will be seen, Sirḥān al-Buḥayrī symbolizes treachery and corruption which are usually found in the west of Najīb Maḥfūẓ's conceptual world, and by the water. Buḥayra also means a lake.

21 Anīs means a close friend or an affable, kind person. Zakī means pure, chaste.

22 ʿAmir means cultivated, civilized. Wajdi is a relative adjective derived from *wajd*, emotion or ecstasy, or even existence.

23 *Qur'ān*, 55, 1-12.

24 *Mīrāmār* was produced as a film that seems to have been much admired by the public. A television version of Sirḥān al-Buḥayrī's story was shown for a while and then discontinued by the authorities.

25 Manṣūr, answering ʿĀmir Wajdī says:

- I am thinking of writing a feature on the history of treachery in Egypt.

ʿĀmir: - Treachery! what a rich and many-sided subject.
He laughed long and then added:
- You must come to me. I shall supply you with sources and memories."

26 All of the young women in Najīb Maḥfūẓ's works who run away from home to live immorally go west. In Cairo the movement is from the Old City to the modern city to the west. Otherwise the movement is to Alexandria or the sea. Zahra of *Mīrāmār* is no exception, and Rīrī of *al-Summān wa al-kharīf* is a typical case.

27 In *Walīd al-ʿanāʾ* (The Child of Agony) there is a scene of an unexpected love affair between a young woman who turns away from a man courting her, and a very old man of magic attraction. The flabbergasted young man cries derisively: " A romantic relation is being developed between the stone age and modern times!"

Bibliography

Works by Najīb Maḥfūẓ:

ʿAbath al-aqdār, Nazareth, n.d.

Rādūbīs, Cairo, 1963.

Kifāḥ ṭayba, Cairo, 1962

Hams al-junūn, Tel Aviv, n.d.

Al-Qāhira al-jadīda, Nazareth, n.d.

Khān al-khalīlī, Cairo, 1964.

Zuqāq al-midaqq, Cairo, 1961.

Al-Sarāb, Cairo, 1963.

Bidāya wa nihāya, Cairo, 1967.

Bayn al-qaṣrayn, Nazareth, n.d.

Qaṣr al-shawq, Nazareth, n.d.

Al-Sukkarīyya, Nazareth, n.d.

Awlād ḥāritnā, Beirut, 1967.

Al-Liṣṣ wa al-kilāb, Cairo, 1964.

Al-Summān wa al-kharīf, Nazareth, n.d.

Dunyā Allāh, Cairo, 1963.

Al-Ṭarīq, Nazareth, n.d.

Bayt Sayyiʾ al-sumʿa, Cairo, 1965.

Al-Shaḥḥādh, Cairo, 1965.

Tharthara fawq al-nil, Cairo, 1967

Mīrāmār, Cairo, 1967.

Khummārat al-qiṭṭ al-aswad, Cairo, 1968.

Taḥt al-miẓalla, Cairo, 1968

Other Works:

ʿAbd al-Hamīd Jawda al-Saḥḥār, *Jisr al-shayāṭān.*

ʿAbd al-Muhsīn Taha Badr, *Taṭawwur al-riwāya al-ʿarabiyya al-ḥadītha fī miṣr*, Cairo, 1963

Abū Bakr Ibn al-ʿArabī, *al-ʿAwāsim fī al-qawāsim*, Cairo, 1375.

Abū Bakr al-Shiblī, *Dīwān*, Baghdad, 1967.

Aḥmad Amīn, *al-Sharq wa al-gharb*, Cairo, 1955.

Aḥmad Ibn Ḥajar al-Haythami, *al-Sawāʿiq al-muḥriqa*, Cairo, 1965.

Anīs al-Khūrī al-Maqdisī, *al-Ittijahāt al-adabiyya fi al-ʿalam al-ʿarabī al-ḥadīth*, Beirut, 1960.

Ghālī Shukrī, *Azmat al-jins fi al-qiṣṣa al-ʿarabiyya*, Beirut, 1962.

------, *al-Muntamī*, Cairo, 1964.

Fathī Ghānim, *al-Rajul alladhī faqada ẓillahu*, Cairo, 1969.

Ḥusayn Fawzī, *Sindbād miṣrī*, Cairo, 1961.

Ibn al-Fāriḍ, *Dīwān*, Beirut, 1962.

------, *Taḥqiq al-burīni*, Marseille, 1853.

Iḥsān ʿAbd al-Qudūs, *al-Nazzāra al-sawdāʾ*.

Luīs ʿAwaḍ, *Dirāsāt fī al-naqd wa al-adab*, Beirut, 1963.

Maḥādir muḥādathāt al-waḥda, *al-Ahrām*, August 1963.

Al-Māwardī, *al-Aḥkam al-sulṭāniyya*, Cairo, al-Maktaba al-Maḥmudiyya, n.d.

Muḥammad Ḥasan ʿAbdallah, *al-Waqiʿiyya fi al-riwaya al-ʿarabiyya*, Cairo, 1971.

Muḥammad Kāmil Ḥusayn, *Qariya ẓālima*.

------, *al-Wādī al-muqaddas*.

Muḥammad Sayyid al-Kīlānī, *al-Adab al-miṣrī fī ẓill al-ḥukm al-ʿuthmānī* Cairo, 1965.

Muṣṭafā Luṭfī al-Manfalūṭī, *al-Naẓarāt*, Cairo, 1923.

M.S. Khaffaja and A. Badawi, *Herudut yataḥaddath ʿan misr*, Cairo, 1966.

Nabīl Rāghib, *Qaḍīyat al-shakl al-fannī ʿind Najīb Maḥfūẓ*, Cairo, n.d.

Rajāʾ al-Naqqāsh, *Udabāʾ muʿasirun*, Cairo, 1968.

Al-Risāla al-qushayriyya, *taḥqīq ʿAbd al-Ḥalīm Muḥammad and Maḥmūd Ibn al-Sharīf*, Cairo, 1969.

Taha Ḥusayn, *Adīb*, Cairo, 1961.

Ṭaha Wādī, *Madhkal ilā ta'rīkh al-riwāya al-miṣriyya,* Cairo, 1972.
Tawfīq al-Ḥakīm, *ʿUsfur min al-sharq,* Cairo, 5th edition.
Wajīh Fāris al-Kīlānī, *ʿUqalā' al-majānin (taḥqīq),* Cairo, 1924.
Yūsuf al-Sibāʿī, *Al-Saqqā māt.*

Articles:

ʿAbbās Khiḍr, "*Ṭufūlat al-udabā',*" *al-Risāla al-Jadīda,* No. 54, September 1958.

ʿAbd al-Tawwāb ʿAbd al-Ḥayy, *al-Muṣawwar,* January 31, 1969.

Aḥmad ʿAbbās Ṣāliḥ, *"Qirā'a jadida li Najīb Maḥfūẓ," al-Kātib,* No. 57, December 1965, No. 59, February 1966.

Fāṭima Mūsa, *"Najīb Maḥfūẓ wa tatawwur al-riwāya fī miṣr," al-Kātib,* No. 86, May 1968.

Fū'ād Dawwāra, *"Maʿa Najīb Maḥfūẓ," al-Kātib,* No. 22, 1963.

------, *"Al-Liṣṣ wa al-kilāb ʿamal thawrī," al-Kātib,* No. 22, January 1963.

Ghālī Shukrī, *al-Hiwār,* No. 3, March-April 1968.

Al-Hilāl, Special edition dedicated to Najīb Maḥfūẓ, February 1970.

Muḥammad Tabāraka, *Ākhir Saʿa,* December 12, 1962.

Najīb Maḥfūẓ, *"Ittijāhī al-jadīd wa mustaqbal al-riwāya," al-Kātib,* No. 60, March 1966.

------, *"Mulāḥaẓāt ʿalā mushkkila al-mītāfisīqīya," al-Kātib,* No. 60, March 1966.

Sāmī Khashba, *"Al-Waqiʿiyya wa al-Thawra al-Thaqafiyya fi al-riwaya al-ʿarabiyya al-hadītha," al-Adab,* May 1970.

A General List:

Abdel Malek, *Egypt: Military Society,* New York, 1968.

Abdel Aziz Abdel Maguid, *The Modern Arabic Short Story,* Cairo, n.d.

Ammer Ali, *The Spirit of Islam,* London, 1967.

Anawati and Gadet, *Mystique Musulman,* Paris, 1961.

E. Atiyah, *The Arabs,* Edinburgh, 1958.

E. Auerbach, *Mimesis,* Princeton, 1965.

G. Bacherlard, *L'Eau et les Rêves,* Paris, 1842.

J.M.S. Baljon, *Modern Muslim Koran Interpretation,* Leiden, 1960.

M. Berger, *Islam in Egypt Today,* Cambridge, 1970.

J. H. Breasted, *Development of Religion and Thought in Ancient Egypt,* London, 1912.

H. Butterfield, *The Historical Novel,* Cambrïdge,1963.

W. Budge, *The Gods of the Egyptians,* London, 1904.

------, *A Short History of the Egyptians,* London, 1914.

K. Burke, *The Philosophy of Literary Form,* New York, 1957.

M.R. Cox, *Cinderella,* London, 1893.

G. Durand, *Les Structures Anthropologiques de l'Imaginaire,* Grenoble, n.d.

A. Erman, *The Ancient Egyptians,* New York, 1966.

B. Fares, *L'Honeur chez les Arabes avan l'Islam,* Paris, 1932.

Fathi Ghanem, *The Man Who Lost His Shadow,* London, 1966.

G. Ferrand, *Relations de Voyages,* Paris, 1914.

L. Feuchwanger, *The House of Desdemona,* Detroit, 1963.

N. Frye, *Anatomy of Criticism,* New York, 1966.

L. Gardet, *La Citè Musulman,* Paris, 1954.

J.C. Garret, *Utopias in Literature,* Canterbury, 1968.

H.A.R. Gibb, *Modern Trends in Islam,* Chicago, 1945.

------, *Mohammedanism,* London, 1957.

------, *Studies in the Civilization of Islam,* London, 1962.

A. Gardiner, *Egypt of the Pharaohs,* Oxford, 1968.

R. Gerber, *Utopian Fantasies,* London, 1955.

S.G. Haim, *Arab Nationalism,* Los Angeles, 1964.

I. Hasan, *Radical Innocence,* Princeton, 1961.

A. Hourani, *Arabic Thought in the Liberal Age,* London, 1962.

M. K. Husain, *City of Wrong,* Amsterdam, 1959.
E. Heller, *The Disinherited Mind,* Cleveland, 1965.
S.E. Hyman, *The Armed Vision,* New York, 1955.
Ibn Batuta, *Travels in Asia and Africa,* London, 1953.
M. Iqbal, *The Construction of Religious Thought in Islam,* London, 1934.
------, *The Secrets of the Self,* tr. Nicholson, n.d., n.p.
C.G. Jung, *Psychological Types,* Pantheon, 1964.
------, *Two Essays on Analytical Psychology,* New York, 1970
------, *Man and His Symbols,* New York, 1970.
R. Loosen, *Die Weisen Narren des Nsaburi,* 1912.
E. Lane, *Manners and Customs of the Modern Egyptians,* Everyman, 1966.
R. Levy, *The Social Structure of Islam,* Cambridge, 1962.
G. Lukacs, *The Historical Novel,* London, 1962.
R. May, E. Angel, H.F. Ellenberger, *Existence,* New York, 1958.
R. Makarius, *Anthologie de la Litterature Arabe Contemporaine: le Roman et la Nouvelle,* Paris, 1964.
A.M.A. Mazyad, *Ahmad Amin,* Leiden, 1968.
A. Mez, *The Renaissance of Islam,* 1937.
A.F. Morgan, *Nowhere was Somewhere,* New York, 1947.
E. Muir, *The Structure of the Novel,* A Harbinger Book.
G. Murray, *Euripides and His Age,* Home University Library.
J.W. McPherson, *The Moulids of Egypt,* Cairo, 1941.
W. Nelson (ed.), *Twentieth Century Interpretations of Utopia,* Prentice Hall, 1968.
E. Neuman, *The Great Mother,* New York, 1955.
R. Nicholson, *Studies in Islamic Mysticism,* Cambridge, 1967.
R. Petrie, *Egyptian Tales,* London, 1926.
F.A. Polak, *The Image of the Future,* Leiden, 1961.
G. Rawlison, *The History of Herodotus,* New York, 1859.
T. Raik, *Myth and Guilt,* New York, 1970.

P. Roche, *The Songs of Sappho*, Mentor, 1966.
F. Rosenthal (tr.), *Al-Muqaddima of Ibn Khaldun*, London, 1958.
------, *Knowledge Triumphant*, Leiden, 1970.
E. I. J. Rosenthal, *Political Thought in Mideival Islam*, Cambridge, 1962.
A.H. Sayce, *The Ancient Empires of the East*, London, 1893.
S. Somekh, *The Changing Rhythm*, Leiden, 1973.
L. Strauss, *Persecution and the Art of Writing*, Glencoe, 1952.
J. Tebbel, *Facts and Fiction, Problems of the Historical Novelist*, Lansing, 1962.
L. Tolstoy, *War and Peace*, Norton Critical Edition, New York, 1966.
H. Vaihinger, *The Philosophy of "As if"*, New York, 1925.
G. Vaucher, *Gamal Abdel Nasser et Son Equipe*, Paris, 1959.
G. E. von Grunebaum, *Islam*, London, 1961.
------, *Medieval Islam*, Chicago, 1962.
------, *Modern Islam*, New York, 1964.
M. Watt, *Islamic Philosophy and Theology*, Edinburgh, 1962.
R. Wellek and A. Warren, *Theory of Literature*, New York, 1956.
K. Crag, *Counsels in Contemporary Islam*, Edinburgh, 1956.
J. R. Wilson, *Islam in Modern History*, Princeton, 1957.
N. Safran, *Egypt in Search of Political Community*, Cambridge, 1961.
Yakubi, *Les Pays*, Ed. G. Wiet, Cairo, 1937.

Articles:
A. Abadir and R. Allen, "Nagib Mahfuz, His World of Literature", *The Arab World*, September-October 1970.
L. Fiedler, "Archetype and Signature," *Sewanee Review*, V. 60, No. 2, April-June 1952.
P. Green, "Aspects of the Historical Novel," *Essays by Divers Hands*, London, 1962.

J. Jomier, "Trois Romans de M. Naguib Mahfuz," *MIDEO*, No. 4, 1957.

F. Meier, "The Transformation of Man in Mystical Islam," *Man and Transformation*, Eranos Year Books, Pantheon, 1964.

M. Milson, "Nagib Mahfuz and the Quest for Meaning," *Arabica*, T. XII, Fasc. 2, 1970.

S. Somekh, "Zaʿbalawi -- Author, Theme and Technique," *Journal of Arabic Literature*, V.I, 1970.

Index

Ali, Ameer: *The Spirit of Islam,* 123.
Allen, Roger: *Nagib Mahfuz, His World of Literature,* 52.
Arawati, 226, 229.
Ancient Egypt, 2.
Anīs al-Khūrī al-Maqdisī: *al-Ittijāhāt al-adabiyya fī al-ʿālam al-ʿarabī al-ḥadīth,* 38.
Arab World, The, 52.
Arabica, 222.
al-Ashʿarī, 158.
Atahaddath ilaykum, 6.
Atiyah, Edward, 115. *The Arabs,* 125.
Auerbach E.: *Mimesis,* 38.
Awlād Ḥāritnā, 97, 118, 170, 171, 172, 173-181, 184, 185, 186, 187, 188, 199, 204.

Bachelar, Gaston: *L'Eau et les rêves,* 245.
Badawi, A.: *Herūdūt yataḥaddath ʿan miṣr,* 51.
Baikie, James, 14.
Baljon J.M.S.: *Modern Muslim Koran Interpretation,* 17.
Barthold, W., 124.
Bayn al-qasrayn, 37, 99, 105, 122, 125, 162, 200.
Bayt Sayyiʾ al-sumaʿa, 118, 204, 229.
Berger, Morroe, 159, 226.
Berque, Jacques, 123, 165. *L'Egypt,* 194.
Bidāya wa nihāya, 117, 118, 141-145, 146, 151, 166, 191, 239, 245.
Bleuler, Manfred, 165.
Breasted J. H.: *Development of Religion and Thought in Ancient Egypt,* 40.
Budge, Wallis: *The Gods of the Egyptians,* 39, 52, 67, 91.
A Short History of the Egyptians, 40, 69.

Green, Peter: *Aspects of the Historical Novel*, 74, 75, 88.

Haim, Sylvia, 115. *Arab Nationalism*, 125.
ha-Mizraḥ he-Ḥadash, 224.
Hams al-junūn, 17, 48, 50, 52, 62, 117, 226, 245.
Ḥasan al-Baṣrī, 203, 223.
Hāshim al-Naḥḥās: *Dawr najīb maḥfūẓ fī al-sinamā al-miṣriyya; Najīb maḥfūẓ ʿalā al-shāsha*, 16.
Hassan, Ihab: *Radical Innocence*, 18, 19.
Ḥayāt li al-ghayr, 226.
Heller, Erich: *The Disinherited Mind*, 18.
Herodotus, 41. *The Ancient Empires of the East*, 51.
Al-Hilāl, 14, 15, 16, 18, 40, 119, 121, 164, 182, 224, 225.
Ḥiwār, 37, 92, 181.
Hordedef's Tale, 29.
Hourani, Albert: *Arabic Thought in the Liberal Age*, 162.
Ḥusayn, Fawzī: *Sindbād miṣrī*, 93.
Hyman, S.E.: *The Armed Vision*, 166.

Ibn al-ʿArabī, 167, 195.
Ibn Baṭṭūṭā, 114. *Travels in Asia and Africa*, 125.
Ibn Buṭlān, 113.
Ibn al-Fāriḍ, 216, 227.
Ibn Khaldūn, 83, 196. *al-Muqaddima*, 90, 245.
Ibn Ṭufayl: *Ḥayy ibn yaqẓān*, 92.
Ibrāhīm ʿAbd al-ʿAzīz, 164.
Ibrāhīm ʿĀmir: *Najīb Maḥfūẓ siyasiyan*, 50, 181.
Iḥsān ʿAbd al-Quddūs: *al-Naẓẓāra al-sawdāʾ; Sayyida fī ṣālūn*, 122.
Iqbal, Muhammad, 149, 150, 157. *The Reconstruction of Religious Thought in Islam*, 156, 168. *The Secrets of the Self*, 166.